CONTAINMENT IN THE MIDDLE EAST

CONTAINMENT in the MIDDLE EAST

EHUD EILAM

Potomac Books
An imprint of the University of Nebraska Press

All rights reserved. Potomac Books is an imprint of the
University of Nebraska Press.
Manufactured in the United States of America.

♾

Library of Congress Cataloging-in-Publication Data
Names: Eilam, Ehud, author.
Title: Containment in the Middle East / Ehud Eilam.
Description: [Lincoln, Nebraska]: Potomac Books, an
imprint of the University of Nebraska Press, 2019. | Includes
bibliographical references and index.
Identifiers: LCCN 2019005308
ISBN 9781640121881 (cloth: alk. paper)
ISBN 9781640122505 (epub)
ISBN 9781640122512 (mobi)
ISBN 9781640122529 (pdf)
Subjects: LCSH: Middle East—Foreign relations—21st
century. | Israel—Foreign relations—Middle East. | Middle
East—Foreign relations—Israel. | United States—Foreign
relations—Middle East. | Middle East—Foreign relations—
United States. | Russia (Federation)—Foreign relations—
Middle East. | Middle East—Foreign relations—Russia
(Federation)
Classification: LCC DS63.18.E45 2019 | DDC 327.56—dc23
LC record available at https://lccn.loc.gov/2019005308

Set in Arno Pro by E. Cuddy.

CONTENTS

Preface   vii

1. The Effort to Contain Iran   1
2. The Iranian-Israeli-Arab Triangle   31
3. The War in Syria   51
4. Russian Military Involvement in Syria   69
5. Israel, Hamas, and the Palestinian Authority   87
6. Egypt's Security and Stability Problems   125
7. IDF's Buildup and Preparations for War   147
    Conclusion   157

    Notes   169
    Index   203

PREFACE

For the United States, during the Cold War, containment meant blocking the expansion of Soviet influence, including in the Middle East.[1] The containment started with the Truman Doctrine in the late 1940s.[2] In 1980 the implementation of the Carter Doctrine required more than just containment, unlike the Truman Doctrine.[3] The Reagan administration managed to change the Soviet policy from increasing its influence worldwide to taking care of troubles at home.[4] President Reagan not only contained the Soviet Union but he also strove to defeat it.[5]

In recent years containment in the Middle East has been expressed in many ways. The United States and Israel have been wishing to contain Iran, including its nuclear project. However, between 2012 and 2016 there were disputes between the United States and Israel about how to do that, particularly with regard to the military option. In a way the United States sought to contain Israel so the latter would not bomb Iran. At the same time the United States also managed to contain Iran's nuclear project, following the agreement that was signed in July 2015. Iran too played a double game, since it basically exploited the United States to contain ISIS (Islamic State of Iraq and Syria) and used ISIS to contain the U.S. presence in Iraq.

In the Middle East there are Arab nonstate organizations that serve as Iran's protégés, such as Hezbollah in Lebanon. Israel has been containing Hezbollah's military buildup, mostly by bombing deliveries of advanced weapons before they reach that group.

Yet Hezbollah has contained Israel by forcing it to strike only in Syria and not in Lebanon.

Another kind of containment has been part of the effort by Arab states to control their territories. Egypt has been struggling to contain both its huge economic problems and ISIS, in the Sinai Peninsula, with Israeli assistance. In Syria Bashar al Assad and his allies, Russia, Iran, and Hezbollah, have managed to suppress various rebel groups after several years of tough fighting.

Israel has been containing the friction on its border with Syria, in the Golan Heights, following the battles between Assad and his rivals in Syria, which often led to firing into Israel. Israel has been much more focused on the West Bank, where it has been striving to contain the Palestinian Authority (PA) from becoming a state unless the PA accepts Israel's conditions. At the same time Israel has collaborated with the PA in containing Hamas in the West Bank. Israel also has been containing Hamas in the Gaza Strip.

The text includes hundreds of endnotes supporting my ideas. This book is based on sources published in books and articles. The information is always incorporated into the text itself, in a way that does not disrupt the flow of reading. The only purpose of the endnote is to reveal the details of the source. The links appearing in the endnotes were last accessed again before the book was published.

My master's and doctoral degrees examined Israel's national security. I have been studying this subject for more than twenty-five years. I worked for a few years for the Israeli Ministry of Defense. This book is a completely personal project, and it is not part of any research I did for the Ministry. The book expresses my personal views, and it does not necessarily represent the opinions of others. Of course all the errors here are mine alone. For readers with questions or comments about the book, please write to me at Ehudei2014@gmail.com.

ABBREVIATIONS

APC	armored personal carrier
AWACS	airborne warning and control system
CW	chemical weapons
CNFI	Congress of Nationalities for a Federal Iran
EU	European Union
EUCOM	U.S. European Command
GCC	Gulf Cooperation Council
GDP	gross domestic product
IAEA	International Atomic Energy Agency
IAF	Israeli Air Force
IDF	Israel Defense Forces
IED	improvised explosive device
IMF	International Monetary Fund
IRGC	Islamic Revolutionary Guard Corps
ISIS	Islamic State of Iraq and Syria
JCPOA	Joint Comprehensive Plan of Action (Iran nuclear deal)
MB	Muslim Brotherhood
MFO	multinational force and observers
MOP	massive ordnance penetrator
NATO	North Atlantic Treaty Organization
NCRI	National Council of Resistance of Iran
NPT	nonproliferation of nuclear weapons
OIC	Organization of Islamic Cooperation
PA	Palestinian Authority

PDKI	Democratic Party of Iranian Kurdistan
PLO	Palestine Liberation Organization
PMOI	People's Mojahedin Organization of Iran
THAAD	Terminal High Altitude Area Defense
UAE	United Arab Emirates
UAV	unmanned air vehicle
UNCTAD	United Nations Conference on Trade and Development
UNIFIL	U.S. Interim Force in Lebanon

1

The Effort to Contain Iran

On July 14, 2015, Iran and P5+1 (the United States, France, Britain, Russia, China, and Germany) reached an agreement (the JCPOA) about Iran's nuclear project. There was a possibility that Israel or the United States would have bombed Iran's nuclear sites as part of their goal to contain Iran. It seems the United States considered the military option, following references that were made by President Barack Obama and Defense Secretary Ashton Carter. Israel could have attacked Iran, but it was not clear whether Israel was capable of carrying out such an operation without U.S. assistance. This was a major issue not only with regard to Iran, Israel, and the United States but for other states as well.

Israel, the Obama Administration, and Iran before the JCPOA

Israel assimilated American arsenal, which helps to maintain Israel's qualitative defensive edge.[1] Secretary Carter said on October 28, 2015, that the United States "always stands with Israel and always will. It's a top priority for America, for its military, for President Obama, and for me personally." Israeli defense minister Moshe Ya'alon claimed then that Israel "has no greater friend than the United States of America" and that U.S. support "is a cornerstone of our national security."[2] The United States also assisted Israel in developing its antimissile and antirocket defense.[3] On April 25, 2016, eighty-three U.S. senators signed a letter urging Obama to give Israel more than the current $3 billion aid package.[4] Others claimed that Israel receives too much U.S. aid, which should be reduced.[5] There has been the possibility that the United States will withdraw from the Middle East. David Makovsky argued on April 19, 2016, that generally speaking if it happens it will make both the United States and Israel weaker.[6] It will also make it much more difficult to contain their enemies, like Iran and its protégés.

In the 1970s the United States relied on Iran as a major force in its region.[7] Israel, like the United States, had friendly relations with Iran until the 1979 revolution. Since then Iran has considered both Israel and the United States as its sworn enemies.[8] Iran also assumes that the power structure in the region "favors the United States, Israel, and Sunni Muslim regimes such as Egypt, Jordan, and the Gulf states."[9] Yet at least until 2014 the United States did not make "a systematic effort to isolate Iran in its immediate neighborhood."[10] Iran sees itself as a dominant player in the Middle East that could try to reach a bargain with a world power, the United States.

"Iranian leaders appear to constantly weigh the relative imperatives of their revolutionary and religious ideology against the demands of Iran's national interests." Iran's foreign policy is similar to its traditional strategy.[11] Iran has been spreading its influence across the Middle East and has been involved in wars in Syria, Lebanon, Iraq, and Yemen.[12] Iran also seeks to have nuclear weapons because of its fear of the United States, Pakistan, and Israel and "traumatic memories" from its war against Iraq (1980–88).[13] For many in Iran the nuclear program is "a symbol of national strength."[14] The United States used sanctions and cyber warfare in order to persuade Iran to discuss its nuclear program.[15] The United States sought "to sharply limit the enrichment program and thereby extend the time it would take Iran to "break out" and build a bomb."[16]

Charles Freilich, a former deputy national security adviser in Israel, mentioned that for Israel, "Iran's nuclear program continues to be perceived as an imminent existential threat."[17] Israel is thought to hold nuclear weapons, according to non-Israeli sources, but they have been reserved for emergencies, such as if the IDF were about to be defeated.[18] In that sense Israel has contained itself.

Israel fears that Iran might use its bomb against Israel and not as a last resort but as part of a first strike, since Iranian leaders repeatedly expressed their desire to destroy Israel. Iran might also use a nuclear arsenal as part of its effort to contain both Israel and the U.S. presence in the Middle East. On November 2013 an interim agreement about Iran's nuclear project was signed between Iran and the P5+1, yet it was by definition not final. Israel sought to prevent another accord like that and at least to use it to contain Iran's nuclear program as much as possible.

Brig. Gen. Michael Herzog (Ret.) argued in late November 2014 that the more likely scenario is an "Iranian 'sneak out' or 'creep out' toward a nuclear weapon." Some Arab states and Israel were worried in 2014 that the United States would not prevent such scenarios from happening.[19] Iranian foreign minister Javad Zarif claimed on January 6, 2015, that Saudi Arabia and Israel opposed the nuclear agreement.[20] It was about six months before the deal was signed. The Saudis might have preferred that the United States or Israel destroy Iran's nuclear project. They would not have openly supported such an attack, yet after allowing a massive foreign presence in 1990–91 in the kingdom, it could have unknowingly allowed Israeli and U.S. jets to cross its land on their way to attack Iran.

On March 5, 2015, Zarif argued that Iran did not wish to produce nuclear weapons.[21] On April 19 Iran's supreme leader, Ayatollah Ali Khamenei, claimed that Israel and the United States are "the biggest threats for the region and the world."[22] Israel and the United States should not have believed Zarif's statement while taking seriously what Khamenei said. Iran sees itself as an enemy of both Israel and the United States. The United States is considered to be the "great Satan" while Israel is only the "small Satan." Yet Iran was willing to talk directly with the United States but not to negotiate in any way with Israel. Such a situation gave the United States the opportunity to contain Iran using peaceful means, as long as Iran did not outmaneuver the superpower.

On April 3, 2015, the Pentagon revealed that its largest bunker-buster bomb had been upgraded so that it could penetrate Iran's highly protected nuclear sites, such as Fordow. This is the MOP (massive ordnance penetrator), which weighs 30,000 pounds.[23] Secretary Carter said several times in 2015 that his country might consider an attack in certain circumstances. However, the Obama administration wanted its legacy to be avoiding a war with Iran, not starting one. The main purpose of U.S. announcements about a military option was to urge Iran to accept an agreement and by that to contain Iran's nuclear ambitions by negotiations and without actually attacking Iran.

Demonstrating to Israel that the United States is the only one capable of destroying Iran's nuclear infrastructure was part of the American strategy. Israel has been well aware that the U.S. military has much more power than the IDF. In a way the United States strove to contain Israel so it would not disrupt the talks with Iran by bombing Iran's nuclear sites. The Obama administration struggled to persuade Israel to put its trust in its American patron. Therefore, the United States wanted to contain both Israel and Iran in this matter.

In April 2015 Russia announced it would provide Iran with the S-300, an advanced antiaircraft system. Russian foreign minister Sergei Lavrov said that "those who want to deliver a strike at Iran will have to think at least twice before doing it."[24] In regard to that, Obama claimed on April 21, 2015, that since the U.S. defense budget is more than thirty times bigger than the Iranian one, American planes could penetrate Iran if necessary.[25] Yet budget cuts in the U.S. military affected its readiness against weapon systems like the S-300.[26] Maj. Gen. Amir Eshel, commander of the Israeli air force, argued that "the S-300 is a very sophisticated system . . . with very impressive capabilities." But he added that the IAF has been preparing to face this challenge.[27] In 2016 Iran started to assimilate the S-300.[28]

There were major disputes between the Obama administration and Israeli prime minister Benjamin Netanyahu concerning Iran's nuclear project. Amos Yadlin, a former head of the IDF intelligence directorate, mentioned in March 2015 several fundamental differences between the two governments. The first one was that for Israel, Iran has been an existential threat, while the United States sees Iran only as a strategic threat like North Korea. Second, Israel and the United States have a different trauma. For the United States there is the bitter experience of the wars in Iraq and Afghanistan in the past decade while Israel still lives with the horrible memory of the Holocaust. Third, in contrast to the United States, Israel is "convinced that at some point Iran will burst ahead. And if it's too close to the threshold, it won't be possible to stop it." Fourth, the United States might attack "only when they see the Iranians break out to a bomb. For the Israelis, it's connected to the threshold, if [Iran] is too close." Fifth, "the U.S. can allow itself to wait more because its operational abilities are meaningfully greater than Israel's."[29] Therefore, in comparison with the United States, it was much more important for Israel to contain Iran and its nuclear program.

Yossi Kuperwasser, former director general of Israel's Ministry of Strategic Affairs, claimed in June 2015 that even if Israel receives weapons and security guarantees from the United States, it must not limit its actions, even if there is a deal, and it should continue to make sure that Iran does not produce the bomb.[30] A month later, on July 14, 2015, the agreement with Iran was signed. For Israel and other states as well, the JCPOA was far from a perfect solution, since Iran did not dismantle most of its nuclear program. Even the constraints on Iran's nuclear project were temporary. The JCPOA also made it much more difficult for Israel to attack Iran. Although Israel opposed the deal and was not part of it, it was unlikely that it would have bombed Iran. The political fallout for Israel, including to its relations with the United States, might have been quite negative. In that sense the JCPOA contained Israel. However, Israel's approach in this matter, even its threats, helped in pushing world powers and maybe also Iran to reach an agreement that contained Iran's nuclear program. Israel has been continuing to monitor Iran, waiting and maybe hoping that Iran will breach the deal, which will give Israel an opportunity to act against Iran, even militarily, before Iran actually produces a nuclear weapon.

There were periods when it seemed Israel was about to attack Iran, but that did not happen and possibly Israel never really intended to bomb Iran. In case Israel did consider that seriously, since the United States' goal was to prevent such a move, it looks like the Obama administration was more successful than Israel, left to tolerate Iran's nuclear program proceedings, albeit under some severe constraints. Although Israel lost this struggle, one should bear in mind that there was a limit to what it could have achieved. The United States obviously looks after its own interests first, not those of its allies, including Israel. Israel is a regional power in the Middle East, but its American patron showed it could ignore Israeli demands, particularly when the price and risks of accepting them seemed too high. Israel was forced to concede to this reality.

The United States and Israel have vast experience in dealing with mutual problems. Sometimes the United States has favored Israeli actions, but in other times Israeli steps were less desired and in some cases not at all. The stakes with Iran's nuclear project might be higher than any other former challenge the United States and Israel had to handle, including also the 1973 war. The tension that was created between Israel and the United States, regarding Iran's nuclear program, indicated how Iran profited from the ongoing negotiations about its nuclear project, even before an agreement was reached. In the future Iran will again benefit from any falling out, let alone a rift, between Israel and the United States. Both states are seen by Iran as enemies, obstructing its efforts to reach hegemony in the Middle East. Weakening the ties between the United States and Israel will enfeeble both nations' position in that region, thus paving the way for Iran to spread its influence in the region. This is often a zero-sum game, since a loss for Israel or the United States serves Iran's interests. Subsequently Iran has an ulterior motive lurking behind its other, more obvious goals, to destabilize the Israeli-American alliance. Iran wants to contain both the United States' presence in the Middle East and Israel so they can not contain Iran.

Israel, the Obama Administration, and Iran Following
the Signing of the JCPOA

On August 4, 2015, the Obama administration, as part of its effort to justify the JCPOA, warned that without it, if the United States had attacked Iran, Iran would have confronted Israel.[31] Israel has already absorbed rockets from the pro-Iranian groups Hezbollah and Hamas. A full-scale war against Iran and Hezbollah would have cost Israel much more. Yet Israel might have been willing to pay this price, assuming that in return Iran's nuclear program would be destroyed by U.S. forces.

President Obama emphasized on August 5, 2015, his willingness to provide Israel with military aid to help it handle Iran.[32] Israel asked to assimilate the MOP but was turned down.[33] That huge bomb might have been the only way to crack Iran's nuclear sites. If Israel had received the MOP, it could have deterred and contained Iran and its nuclear project. It might have been enough that Iran understands what Israel could do to convince Iran to accept severe restrictions on its nuclear program, out of fear Iran might lose this project if Israel drops the MOP on Iran's nuclear sites.

The JCPOA was endorsed by UN resolution 2231, which said that the JCPOA might build a "new relationship with Iran."[34] There was a chance that the agreement might "unleash forces beyond Khamenei's control."[35] Yet Ray Takeyh argued in August 2015 that the Iranian regime wanted to isolate its country from western ideas and that Iran will continue to oppose both Israel and the United States. To the Iranian elite, "Obama's promise of global integration is not an invitation but a threat."[36] On September 10, 2015, Khamenei made clear there would not be talks with the United States in other areas.[37] Iran did not want to be contained, but it also strongly opposed outside influence that might undermine the regime there.

On September 2, 2015, the U.S. State Department issued more sanctions "against individuals and companies linked with Iranian proliferation." A month later "the Commerce Department restricted trade with ten entities in China and South Korea because they illicitly procured sensitive U.S. items for end use in Iran." The sanctions targeted "firms supporting Iran's missile program, as well as entities tied to Iran's sponsorship of terrorism."[38] Those steps took place in spite and even because of the deal with Iran. The goal was to prove that the Obama administration could go on putting pressure on Iran. Nevertheless, from the Israeli perspective, sanctions could have been much more effective in forcing Iran to make bigger concessions with regard to its nuclear program.

During the talks, western powers concentrated on the nuclear issue solely without connecting it to Iran's subversion around the region. The idea was that the accord would eventually bring a change in Iran's foreign policy, which would contain Iran by slowing down its aid to its partners and protégés. This shift would have benefited Israel, western powers, and Arab Sunni states as well, yet it did not occur.

According to a CNN-ORC poll from mid-September 2015, most Americans assumed Iran would breach the agreement, and most thought that in such a situation there should be a U.S. military action.[39] On September 28, 2015, Obama claimed that he would protect U.S. allies, including by force.[40] Yet he also argued more than once that an attack on Iran was not the solution, since it would only delay Iran's nuclear project.

On September 22, 2015, Maj. Gen. Ataollah Salehi declared that Iran would destroy Israel.[41] On November 12, 2015, Iranian president Hassan Rouhani said that "Israel in its current form is not legitimate; this is why we don't have any relations with it."[42] Yossi Cohen said on January 6, 2016, as he was sworn in as the new head of Israel's Mossad intelligence agency, that Iran was a serious threat to Israel despite the JCPOA.[43] On February 9, 2016, James Clapper, director of U.S. national intelligence, said that Iran "presents an enduring threat to U.S. national interests." This assessment included Iran's hostile intention toward Israel, since Israel's security is a U.S. interest.[44] Therefore, the United States and particularly Israel, with all their disputes regarding Iran, had to work together to contain Iran.

Israel's submarines are supposed to carry missiles with nuclear warheads. On January 12, 2016, Israel's fifth submarine arrived in Haifa. Netanyahu said that Israel's submarine fleet "acts as a deterrent. . . . Israel can attack, with great might, anyone who tries to harm it."[45] The process of assimilating those submarines started in the early 1990s. It seems that even then, when the Iranian nuclear program was in its early stages, Israel assumed it should get submarines armed with nuclear weapons for first or second strike capability. Israel wants them in case it cannot contain Iran and mostly if Israel does not manage to stop Iran from producing nuclear weapons.

Matthew Kroenig argued in February 2016 that Iran must dismantle nuclear facilities "that can be used for the production of fuel for nuclear weapons."[46] Iran might breach the agreement, particularly since some in Iran don't like the JCPOA, to put it mildly. Yet Iran could restrain itself, fearing the ramifications of officially ignoring the agreement. Israel will do its best to prove that Iran violates the accord. Israel is particularly eager to find clear evidence that Iran tries to produce nuclear weapons because that might push the international community and at least the United States to contain Iran, including by taking military action aiming at destroying Iranian nuclear sites. If after that Iran starts to rebuild its nuclear program, then another round of air bombardments can be carried out. At least Israel will hope for a better agreement, one in which the terms and constraints are much stricter than the current one.

In early March 2016 Iran tested missiles that could carry nuclear warheads in defiance of UN Security Council resolution 2231.[47] Iran accepted constraints on its nuclear program, but developed missiles that could deliver nuclear cargo, which exposed Iran's future intentions, if and when it tries to build nuclear weapons. Israel was obviously worried about those missile tests. In the United States some concerns were expressed, but the Obama administration did not see that as breaching the JCPOA. So from this American perspective, Iran continued to be relatively contained in this issue.

The resolution by the U.S. Senate from May 22, 2013, urged that if "Israel is compelled to take military action in legitimate self-defense against Iran's nuclear weapons program," then Israel should receive "diplomatic, military, and economic support."[48] In early March 2016 the IDF and the U.S. military conducted their eighth "Juniper Cobra" exercise since the program was created in 2001. Some 3,200 soldiers from the IDF and the U.S. European Command (EUCOM) took part in the drill. It was the U.S. "premiere exercise in this region and EUCOM's highest priority exercise in 2016," according to Lt. Gen. Timothy Ray, head of the U.S. Third Air Force.[49] In March 2018 another "Juniper Cobra" exercise took place in Israel, involving 2,100 U.S. troops.[50] In February 2019 "Juniper Cobra" 19 took place. The purpose was, again, to defend Israel against missile attacks, which were expected to occur following an Israeli strike against Iran, maybe also bombing Iran's nuclear sites. However, if the United States opposes the Israeli strike, then its aid might be more limited. Either way it will take time for the U.S. military to deploy its forces in Israel. This step could not be done in advance, even if the United States approves the Israeli military action, since it could disrupt the element of surprise. Iran will suspect that the increased American military presence in Israel is a preparation for an Israeli bombardment in Iran. In response Iran could strike first, before Israel and its American patron are ready to shoot down Iranian missiles.

On September 23, 2016, Mohammad Zarif said with regard to Iran's approach to Israel that "we never threatened to use force against anybody. We say we will defend ourselves. If anybody is foolish enough to attack us, we will defend ourselves as it is our right."[51] On October 1, 2016, the head of the International Atomic Energy Agency (IAEA) claimed that Iran was obeying the terms of the JCPOA.[52] On April 18, 2017, the Trump administration, after agreeing that Iran was complying with the JCPOA, extended the sanctions relief given to Iran. However, the Trump administration had "undertaken a full review of the agreement to evaluate whether continued sanctions relief is in the national interest."[53]

The main Iranian opposition group claimed in late April 2017 that Iran breached the JCPOA when it conducted secret research on nuclear weapon components such as bomb triggers.[54] David

Albright and Olli Heinonen argued on May 30, 2017, that if Iran produced advanced centrifuges in large numbers, it "would greatly expand Iran's ability to sneak out or break out to nuclear weapons or surge the size of its centrifuge program if the deal fails or after key nuclear limitations end."[55]

The JCPOA during the Trump Administration

On June 15, 2017, the U.S. Senate voted to impose new sanctions on Iran. The bill requires the Trump administration "to freeze assets and refuse entry to anyone deemed to be helping Iran's missile program."[56] On August 2, 2017, the United States, Britain, France, and Germany submitted a report to the UN Security Council's Iran sanctions committee and to the UN secretary-general, Antonio Guterres. The four powers referred to the launch of an Iranian rocket to space on July 27. They claimed that "the technologies necessary for the conception, the fabrication, and the launch of space launch vehicles are closely related to those of ballistic missiles, in particular to those of an intercontinental ballistic missile. This launch therefore represents a threatening and provocative step by Iran. . . . Iran's long-standing program to develop ballistic missiles continues to be inconsistent with [the UN resolution] and has a destabilizing effect in the region."[57] Iran's missile program was clearly one important factor that was not contained.

On May 22, 2017, President Trump, in his visit to Israel, agreed with Netanyahu on the need to handle Iran and its partners by strengthening Israel's military capabilities.[58] On December 12, 2017, Israel and the United States "secretly signed a far-reaching joint memorandum of understanding providing for full cooperation to deal with Iran's nuclear drive, its missile programs, and its other threatening activities."[59] The United States and Israel had to resolve any major quarrel between them before that became a time bomb. In fact, they should have viewed Iran and its nuclear project not as an obstacle to their relations but as an opportunity to improve them. They could agree on several basic principles that will assist both in containing Iran and in building the U.S.-Israel bond. It does not mean Israel and the United States should sign an official defense treaty, a well-known dilemma for those two countries that goes back decades. It is enough to establish a clear understanding about the Iranian matter.

In August 2014 the new government of President Hassan Rouhani managed to return "a certain degree of calm and balance on the domestic front."[60] In spite of the sanctions in 2014, Iranians lived "much better than most of their neighbours."[61] Yet by 2018 Iran's economy was struggling.[62] In late March 2018 Iran's Rial fell to a record low, "breaking through the 50,000-to-the-dollar mark for the first time."[63] The lifting of some sanctions, following the JCPOA, gave the Iranian government a chance to help its population, based on the rich resources and huge potential of that country. However, large amounts of funds continued to be sent to support Iranian allies, mostly in Syria, and economic benefits of the agreement did not materialize, which caused frustration. This led to demonstrations in late December 2017 and early January 2018, although the regime was able to contain them, as it did on previous occasions, such as in 2009. The United States should "encourage domestic unrest in Iran to divert resources that might otherwise be spent on capabilities to engage in troublemaking abroad."[64]

Karim Sadjadpour claimed in December 2017 that "in his classic book *Strategies of Containment*, Yale historian John Lewis Gaddis argues that the United States' successful containment of the Soviet Union—conceived by George Kennan—consisted of three pillars: (1) restore the balance of power left unstable by the defeats of Germany and Japan and by the simultaneous expansion of Soviet influence in Europe and Asia, (2) fragment the international communist movement, and (3) convince Russian leaders that their interests could be better served by learning to live with a diverse world than by trying to remake it in their own image. While the Islamic Republic of Iran is a much less formidable adversary than the Soviet Union, a variation of this approach is a sound template for U.S. strategy toward Iran: (1) build global unity and regional capacity against malign Iranian actions, (2) fragment Iranian power projection, and (3) compel Iran's leadership to prioritize national interests before revolutionary ideology."[65]

On February 17, 2018, U.S. national security adviser H. R. McMaster said that Iran built proxy armies in Iraq, Syria, and Lebanon, aimed at weakening Arab governments. Furthermore, if the Arab governments do not obey Iran, then those Arab regimes will face Iran's protégés in their states.[66] For the United States it was mostly necessary to contain pro-Iranian groups in Iraq.

It was reported in early April 2018 that the head of Israel's Mossad intelligence agency, Yossi Cohen, argued that he was "100 percent certain" that Iran is determined to produce a nuclear weapon and that the international community must change or abolish its nuclear agreement with Iran.[67] He therefore did not believe that the JCPOA actually contained Iran's nuclear project.

In mid-April 2018 an analyst in the Saudi-owned site Al-Arabiya called upon the United States to corner Iran and "completely end Iran's destructive influence throughout the Middle East." This strategy had to include "meaningful sanctions targeting Tehran's financial network" and supporting regime change.[68] It was all part of the Saudi desire to contain Iran.

On May 8, 2018, Trump announced that the United States would withdraw from the JCPOA. One of the questions was if the United States could "eventually bring Iran into a new order rather than merely contain it?"[69] The next day White House spokeswoman Sarah Sanders claimed that the United States was "100 percent committed to making sure that Iran does not have nuclear weapons."[70] It demonstrated how the Trump administration has been striving to contain Iran at least in the nuclear issue.

Secretary of State Mike Pompeo gave a tough speech against Iran on May 21, 2018. He demanded that Iran makes serious changes in its policy in the Middle East and also with regard to its nuclear program or face powerful sanctions. Following that, journalist David Ignatius claimed that Russia would probably be needed to contain Iranian meddling in the Middle East.[71] Meanwhile, some believed that Iran could handle economic pressure.[72] On November 5, 2018, the Trump administration restored the U.S. sanctions that were lifted following the JCPOA. Those steps harmed Iran.

The Possible Outcome of an Israeli Raid in Iran

If Israel strikes, Iran could retaliate. Iran's long-range attack planes such as the *Su-24* might reach all the way to Israel, but they will probably be intercepted by Israeli fighters and antiaircraft batteries. Iran also has hundreds of long-range surface-to-surface missiles that could hit Israel. Israel could then return a favor with air bombardments.

Iran has upgraded its air defense beyond the s-300 by declaring it has assimilated the advanced Qaem radar system, which has a range of 1,000 km.[73] However, Iran has sometimes claimed to have produced new weapon systems that might not have been as sophisticated as Iran claimed they were. There were also entire projects that were a pure and not very reliable deception such as Iran's so-called stealth fighter.[74] The IAF might be able to crack Iran's air defense with pinpoint strikes and electronic and cyber warfare, aiming at neutralizing Iran's command and control centers, radars of antiaircraft batteries, and so forth.

On September 9, 2015, Israel's state comptroller and ombudsman published a harsh report that emphasized Israel's lack of readiness to absorb an attack on its rear if Iran retaliates following an Israeli attack.[75] It depends how much Israel and Iran want and are able to contain the fight. Either way Israel should add and upgrade shelters for its population. There are not enough shelters, and many of the existing ones are neglected and not prepared for a conventional war.

U.S. and Arab Gulf States

Iran opposes Israel for ideological reasons while "the Saudi-Iran rivalry is sectarian (Sunni vs. Shiite), ethnic (Arab vs. Persian), ideological (U.S. allied vs. U.S. opposed), and geopolitical."[76] The Gulf Cooperation Council (GCC) is composed of Sunni-led Arab states in the Persian Gulf, like Saudi Arabia. On May 14, 2015, the United States and the GCC members declared that they opposed and worked together against Iran's subversions.[77] For Saudi Arabia its top regional priority has been to contain Iran.[78] Yet Saudi

Arabia assumed that the Obama administration underestimated Iran as a threat to the region.[79] Kenneth M. Pollack mentioned on July 14, 2016, that "the GCC wants the United States to commit to its regional allies." If not, they might not be able to collaborate with each other.[80] Arabs had to be sure that the United States does not neglect them, let alone plan a fundamental shift by reaching over to Iran and less to U.S. Arab allies.

While the United States had been focused on ISIS, Saudi Arabia was worried more about Iran.[81] The Saudis and the United States fought ISIS in Iraq. Israel and Sunni-led Arab states did not want to see the United States collaborating with Iran more than necessary as part of the conflict with ISIS. The containment of ISIS in 2016–18 reduced the need for U.S.-Iranian cooperation, which makes it easier for the United States to contain Iran with Arab and Israeli support.

Arab Gulf states might create a "new regional order that embraces controlled economic liberalization, autocratic political order, apolitical Islamic conservatism, and an ambivalent relationship with the United States."[82] Zalmay Khalilzad is a former U.S. ambassador to Afghanistan, Iraq, and the United Nations. He claimed in late March 2016 that the United States should push for an agreement between Iran, Saudi Arabia, and Turkey on the region's ongoing conflicts.[83] Considering the hostility between Iran and Saudi Arabia and their suspicion toward the United States, then an accord between Iran and Saudi Arabia, in which the United States serves as a mediator, seems unlikely. Israel will definitely not be part of it. Israel rather joins an anti-Iranian alliance between it, the United States, Arab Gulf states, and maybe even Turkey.

If Iran produces nuclear weapons, Saudi Arabia might develop a "defensive weaponized nuclear program."[84] Saudi crown prince Mohammed bin Salman argued in mid-March 2018 that his country will get nuclear weapons if Iran produces the bomb.[85] Saudi Arabia might buy nuclear weapons from Pakistan.[86] Concerning a possible promise for an American nuclear shield, Saudi Arabia is aware of the difference between the Middle East and a similar situation that was in Europe during the Cold War between the United States and the Soviet Union. The United States will probably refuse to go into a nuclear war with Iran in order to protect Arab states, particularly if U.S. objectives, like bases near Iran, might be exposed to a massive Iranian retribution. Therefore, Saudi Arabia might understand it can only trust itself in this crucial matter that is to get its own nuclear weapons and match Iran's nuclear arsenal. The United States and Israel can prevent such a dangerous development by containing Iran and its nuclear program.

If Iran produces a nuclear weapon, then Israel might change its nuclear strategy by declaring it also has nuclear weapons, which could help to deter and contain Iran. However, it might present Israel, and not Iran, as the problem in the nuclear issue. Iran and Arab states strongly oppose Israel having a nuclear arsenal, and they have called over and over again to disarm its nuclear arsenal. If Israel officially admits it possesses nuclear weapons, then Iran and the Arabs could use this declaration against Israel, while leaving Iran alone, particularly if Iran does not announce it has nuclear weapons. Furthermore, the United States might continue to allow and even prefer that Israel keep its current nuclear policy, for lack of a better choice. There might not be American or international pressure on Israel to confess it has the bomb. The international community might actually try to convince Israel not to initiate any drastic step in order to contain and prevent a nuclear escalation in such an unstable region.

The Saudi-American Arms Deal, May 2017

Between May 2015 and March 2016 Arab Gulf states bought weapons in the amount of $33 billion, which included "ballistic missile defense capabilities, attack helicopters, advanced frigates, and anti-armor missiles."[87] Prof. Efraim Inbar claimed in mid-2016 that "Washington's attempt to compensate its Arab allies for the Iranian nuclear deal by providing them with the latest state-of-the-art weapons erodes Israel's qualitative edge."[88]

On May 17, 2017, the U.S. State Department announced a giant arms deal with Saudi Arabia worth $110 billion, which was meant to help the kingdom to "deter regional threats and enhance its ability to protect its borders and contribute to coalition counterterrorism operations."[89] Following that, two Israeli ministers from the Likud Party voiced concern about Israel's ability to keep its qualitative military edge.[90] Defense Minister Avigdor Lieberman said, "I'm not at peace with any arms race, and the huge Saudi purchase for sure doesn't add much to our peace of mind."[91] In the past Israel was very much concerned about arms deals between its American patron and Arab states, including the famous struggle in 1981 when Israel failed to persuade the Reagan administration not to sell AWACSs (airborne warning and control systems) to Saudi Arabia.[92]

The military buildup of Arab Gulf states is not aimed against Israel. Israel does not pose a threat to those Arab states and has never attacked them. Israel does not even have a border with them, which reduces the possibility of friction. Therefore, there is no dispute on land like the one that exists between Israel and the Palestinians. It means also that arsenal that was purchased by Arab Gulf states for land combat does not put Israel in danger because they can't confront each other in a ground war. Other Arab states that do not share a border with Israel sent a substantial force to confront Israel during the Arab-Israeli wars, yet Arab Gulf states stayed out or participated in a symbolic way. In wars like the one in 2006 between Israel and Hezbollah, Arab Gulf states actually wanted Israel to defeat Iran's Lebanese proxy.

Israel might even want Saudi Arabia to become stronger militarily so the kingdom can help to contain Iran. If Iran tries to produce a nuclear weapon, Israel might attack and might need permission from Saudi Arabia to fly through its skies on the way to Iran. Saudi Arabia could agree to that unofficially, but Iran might still retaliate against the kingdom. If the Saudis have military might, they will be less afraid of Iran's retribution. This is another reason for Israel to tolerate the Saudi-American arms deal.

If the United States does not sell weapons to the Saudis, then the Saudis might approach the European Union or Russia. As long as Saudi Arabia depends on the United States, it gives the superpower a certain leverage over the kingdom. This works for Israel, too, since it has much more influence in the United States than in the European Union, let alone in Russia.

The deal with Saudi Arabia includes tanks, artillery, armored personnel carriers, and helicopters that will assist in securing the kingdom's borders and in containing Iran's proxies, the Houthis, in nearby Yemen. Saudi Arabia will also get vessels that will assist in defending sea routes near the kingdom in the Gulf, like in the Strait of Hormuz, and in the Red Sea. Israel strongly opposes the Houthis in Yemen closing the Bab-el-Mandeb Strait, the southern gates to the Red Sea. The Red Sea is Israel's shortest sea route to Asia and a large part of Africa, which is very important for trade.

The U.S.-Saudi arms deal is supposed to modernize the Saudi air force. According to the U.S. State Department, the aim is to "maintain airborne surveillance, secure its airspace, and provide close air support with improved precision targeting capabilities and processes."[93] If there is some kind of an alliance between Israel and Saudi Arabia against Iran, then an upgraded Saudi air force could serve Israel's interests. On the other hand, here lies Israel's greatest concern. Saudi Arabia already has advanced aircraft such as F-15 that could reach any spot in Israel. Any improvement of the Saudi air force will increase the potential threat to Israel if the two states become enemies. This might happen if Saudi Arabia changes its current policy or the regime there is toppled.

If, like following a revolution, there is a new Saudi regime, it might not trust the loyalty of many of the Saudi troops who served the former regime. Those soldiers might refuse to accept their new leadership. If some ground and air crews will not be part of the Saudi military, then it will lose their expertise and will find it very difficult to operate its sophisticated U.S. weapon systems, mostly aircraft and missiles. Furthermore, if the new Saudi regime opposes the United States, the latter will stop the delivery of ammunition and spare parts as it did with Iran following the 1979 revolution. Saudi Arabia will then struggle to maintain its highly complicated aircraft. Nevertheless, Israel does not want to rely on this way of containing an Arab military capability, assuming that somehow advance weapons could be turned against Israel. The United States obviously also objects that its weapon systems are used against its allies and its own troops in the Middle East. Yet the superpower is willing to take a risk by selling weapons to its Arab partners.

The 2017 arms deal includes Patriot and THAAD systems to protect Saudi Arabia from Iranian missiles. There were reports that Saudi Arabia might have considered buying the Israeli system, the Iron Dome, which intercepts rockets.[94] Israel has an interest in assisting the kingdom in this matter, as part of an anti-Iranian pact. Even if Israel does not sell the Iron Dome to Saudi Arabia, Israel could agree that the Saudis will shoot down missiles and rockets, only with American systems and not Israeli ones.

The United States, as part of the 2017 arms deal, will improve Saudi's cybersecurity and communications. It is important for Saudi Arabia because Iran has been getting better in cyber warfare and Israel wants the Saudis to be ready to confront Iran. Israel could take a calculated risk that if the Saudis try to conduct cyber operations against Israel, Israel could handle this issue due to its advanced cyber capabilities.

U.S. Role in Iraq

In the 1990s the United States strove for dual containment of both Iran and Iraq. For the United States, Iran had been a pariah since 1979. Iraq became one, too, following its invasion of Kuwait in 1990. The United States enforced restrictions on Iraq such as a no-fly zone, which confined Iraq's air operations in Iraq itself. There was an attempt to slow down the development of Iran's ballistic missiles and to deny access to international finance. One of the goals of this dual containment was to stop Iraq and Iran as well from disrupting the peace process between Israel and the Palestinians, in which the United States served as a broker.[95] Yet Iran and Iraq had other priorities, and they could not have done much due to their distance from Israel and because they did not have powerful proxies near Israel at the time. Even without an Iraqi or an Iranian intervention, the Israeli-Palestinian conflict had enough hardships that eventually prevented a final agreement.

When the war in Afghanistan began in 2001, Iran helped the United States, but later on Iran assisted insurgents there. Iran also supported guerrilla and terrorist groups during the war in Iraq since 2003.[96] Iran wished to contain and eventually get rid of the American deployment in both Afghanistan and Iraq, two countries that have a border with Iran. Eventually the United States took all its forces out of Iraq by December 2011 and in the upcoming years the United States significantly reduced the number of its troops in Afghanistan.

In 2014 it was not clear if Iraq could survive as a state, following ISIS's success there.[97] The Obama administration saw Iran as a potential enemy but also as kind of an ally in confronting ISIS in Iraq. ISIS threatened the Shiite government in Bagdad. The United States wanted to contain and defeat ISIS to keep Iraq united as much as possible while maintaining relations with the Iraqi government, and this required collaborating with Iran.

On June 29, 2015, Israel's defense minister Ya'alon said that the United States "see Iran as a part of the solution; we see it as part of the problem."[98] For Israel to watch the United States strike ISIS in both Iraq and Syria was a grim reminder of the lack of American will to bomb Iran's nuclear sites. If it eventually gets nuclear weapons, Iran will be much more dangerous than ISIS. Nevertheless, the United States preferred to sign an agreement with Iran not only as a way to prevent Iran from producing nuclear weapons but also to make it possible to collaborate with Iran against ISIS. Without the accord there would have been tension between Iran and the United States, which could have prevented them from joining forces against ISIS.

The fight against ISIS had much more international consensus and fewer negative ramifications, compared with an attack on Iran. The Obama administration also sought to limit its military involvement in the Middle East. Yet an attack against Iran would have required air bombardment without dispatching U.S. ground forces, maybe only Special Forces. This offensive might have lasted several weeks; at most, assuming the Iranian regime would have been deterred from an escalation, fearing it would have jeopardized its survival. In contrast, the war against ISIS has been going on for several years now.

The Obama administration had a reason to be worried that if ISIS were not stopped, it would gather more men and support, and then the United States would have to invest more resources in the fight. For the Obama administration, ISIS was worse than Iran, since ISIS might have destabilized not only Iraq but Sunni-led Arab states as well, like those in the Persian Gulf, which would have shocked the global oil market. Yet Iran also seeks to take over Arab states in the Gulf, although unlike ISIS and most of the Arab world, Iran is not Sunni, which makes it harder for Iran to spread its influence in the region.

The United States lost about 4,500 lives in Iraq and spent more than $1 trillion.[99] It also trained and equipped the Iraqi military, which was quickly defeated by ISIS in northern Iraq in June 2014, not necessarily because of reasons that have to do with the United States. Iraq was lucky that ISIS was not able to capture most of Iraq. ISIS, like Iranian forces in the 1980s, seized only part of Iraq, unlike U.S. forces in 2003. It took about two years before the Iraqi armed forces had recovered and were more or less ready to retake northern Iraq, mostly Mosul, the major city there. Iraq did it with strong Iranian and U.S. support. Even then the campaign was tough and lasted almost a year. It showed the difficulty of defeating ISIS.

In 2014 Iraqi Shiites and their Iranian patron could have stood by if ISIS, following its success in Iraq, had focused on Saudi Arabia, but in order to do that, Iraqi Shiites and Iran had to allow ISIS to cross Iraq. Iraqi Shiites and Iran could not have permitted that, since ISIS would have exploited that to seize large parts if not all of Iraq. In that sense, by fighting to contain ISIS, Iraqi Shiites and Iran helped the United States to protect Saudi Arabia against their will.

In September 2015 Michael Eisenstadt said that "despite significant investments to expand its influence in Iraq, Iran's efforts have yielded only mixed results."[100] On July 23, 2017, Iran and Iraq signed an agreement "extending cooperation and exchanging experiences in fighting terrorism and extremism, border security, and educational, logistical, technical, and military support are among the provisions of this memorandum."[101] At the time "even the most senior Iraqi cabinet officials have been blessed, or bounced out, by Iran's leadership . . . politically, Iran has a large number of allies in Iraq's Parliament who can help secure its goals." Iran also has significant control over the interior minister and the federal police. "Perhaps most crucial, Parliament passed a law last year that effectively made the constellation of Shiite militias a permanent fixture of Iraq's security forces. This ensures Iraqi funding for the groups while effectively maintaining Iran's control over some of the most powerful units."[102] Therefore, in August 2017 Iran had "huge political, military, and economic influence in Iraq."[103] Iran's goal has been to prevent Iraq from endangering Iran again and to create a corridor from Iran to the Mediterranean across Iraq.[104] Yet Iraqi Sunnis and "Iraq's clerics in Najaf, including Grand Ayatollah Ali al-Sistani, the world's pre-eminent Shiite spiritual leader, oppose the Iranian system."[105] "The greatest bulwark against Iranian influence" in Arab countries like Iraq "is for national and/or Arab identity to supplant sectarian (Shia) identity."[106] This is one way in which the United States, with the help of Arab states, can help anti-Iranian Iraqis to contain Iran in Iraq. The United States should not tolerate that Iran has been increasing its foothold in Iraq at the expense of the United States. Iran basically exploited the United States to contain ISIS in Iraq and in the same time Iran used ISIS to gain influence in Iraq and by that to contain the U.S. presence in Iraq.

Iraqi Kurds have some kind of autonomy. The Iraqi Shiites tolerate that, but they strongly oppose a Kurdish state that will split Iraq. Iran is also against a Kurdish state, fearing that the next stage will be demanding that Iran give autonomy to the Kurds and other minorities in its country. Israel could help Iraqi Kurds to upgrade their autonomy. Israel already expressed its support of them in establishing a state in Iraq. Sunni-led Arab states could assist the Kurds who are Sunnis. The Iraqi Kurds could be an Israeli or

Arab ally. Iraqi Kurds can serve as a base close to Iran as part of the effort to contain Iran.

If Iran gains nuclear weapons, its leadership might feel more confident not only to suppress the Kurds but also to deter those who help them. This could encourage Kurds to assist in preventing Iran from producing the bomb. Under certain circumstances Iraqi Kurds might allow Israel, as part of an attack on Iran, to use an airfield in Kurdish areas or even a road long and fit enough to serve for Israeli planes for refueling and emergency landing.

The United States and Hezbollah

"Hezbollah had killed more Americans than any other terrorist group before 9/11."[107] In October 2017 the Trump administration was convinced that Hezbollah sought to conduct attacks against the United States. In that month, for the first time since 2007, the United States offered rewards in the amount of up to $7 million for two Hezbollah operatives.[108] Hezbollah could attack Americans, civilians and members of security forces, particularly if Iran orders the group to do that. Meanwhile Hezbollah has been supporting Assad and cooperating with Russia in Syria, while the United States opposed both Assad and the Russian intervention in Syria. Yet Hezbollah, who are Shiite extremists, confronted other radicals, Sunnis, which serves the interest of the United States, Israel, and Sunni Arab states. In Iraq Hezbollah has been involved, where it assisted in the campaign against ISIS, so Hezbollah, the United States, Israel, and Sunni states again had a common enemy. For the United States, Israel, and Sunni states, having Hezbollah in Syria and Iraq, as a force that confronts Sunni radicals, was like fighting fire with fire.

Ron Prosor said on May 29, 2017, that "for the Arab states, led by Saudi Arabia and Egypt, containing Hezbollah and Iran is a priority." He had suggested that "the U.S. should seek a UN Security Council resolution amending 1701 and providing UNIFIL with explicit powers to disarm Hezbollah and demilitarize South Lebanon under chapter 7 of the UN charter, the section that deals with peace enforcement. Currently UNIFIL derives its legal mandate from chapter 6, which deals with peacekeeping." The United States pays 43 percent of UNIFIL's $488 million annual budget.[109] On August 31, 2017, the UN Security Council agreed that UNIFIL will increase its oversight operations in southern Lebanon, including by entering villages where Hezbollah has a presence. The resolution highlighted that UNIFIL has the authority to "take all necessary actions" in areas where its forces are deployed and must ensure that its areas of operations are "not utilized for any kind of hostile steps."[110] Yet nothing really changes in regard to containing Hezbollah's buildup in Lebanon.

In South America, especially in the triborder area, where Argentina, Brazil, and Paraguay converge, Hezbollah earns tens of millions of dollars "while laundering money for local organized crime." Those operations sometimes "extend into the United States, posing a direct threat to the integrity of its financial system."[111] On January 11, 2018, the U.S. Justice Department announced it would create a team to investigate Hezbollah financing and narcoterrorism.[112] Latter on the United States took action against Hezbollah in this matter. It was another field in which the United States must contain Hezbollah's activities as much as possible.

"During the second Lebanon war in 2006, compliance with the American demand that it refrain from attacking Lebanon's civil infrastructure left the IDF without a viable military strategy and was one of the main causes of the severe difficulties Israel encountered in that conflict."[113] At the time the United States wished to assist the relatively moderate Lebanese government. In the next war in Lebanon, the United States might not try to contain Israel, particularly since the Lebanese government has been much more under Hezbollah's influence compared with 2006.

The Stability of Jordan

The unrest and the series of wars that occurred in the Middle East since 2011 happened for economic and political reasons.[114] This ongoing turmoil destabilized several Arab states, but Jordan managed to hold on, in spite of its many economic problems. The kingdom has a lot of experience in knowing how to survive, following many crises that took place in the past in and around Jordan.

In 2014 the 1994 peace treaty between Israel and Jordan was "solid." Jordan also had close ties with the United States. Yet Americans were not that popular in Jordan.[115] Still, U.S. assistance to Jordan continued. Total bilateral U.S. aid to Jordan until 2016 amounted to approximately $19.2 billion.[116] There has been vast and close security cooperation between the United States and Jordan.[117] The United States and Israel need the Hashemite Kingdom as both a buffer and an ally against many foes including ISIS and Iran.

In 2016 "slow pace of reform and a widespread perception of corruption" remained significant sources of popular frustration in Jordan.[118] If Jordan is destabilized, Iran could increase its influence there, using the nearby Iraq and Syria as a bridge to the kingdom. This kind of development worries two states that have a border with Jordan. Saudi Arabia and Israel should cooperate with other states, including the United States, in containing Iran so Iran will not subvert Jordan.

Jordanian security forces manage to contain jihadism inside Jordan by responding quickly when there is a threat. Yet Jordanian security forces have been avoiding a heavy-handed approach by allowing jihadists to express their views while they are monitored.[119] Palestinians, are another source of concern in Jordan. They are the majority in that kingdom, but they don't rule that state. This situation could be used by Iran for subversion inside Jordan. With assistance from the United States, Israel and Arab states, Jordan should contain those in Jordan, not only Palestinians, who might try to undermine the state with Iranian support.

Iran's leaders have called time and again for destroying Israel while hiding behind the distance between the two states, which prevented them from confronting Israel directly. Other states, mostly Iraq, were in the same spot. When it sent forces against Israel, Iraq had to request that Jordan serve as a bridge to Israel. Iran, following its grip in Iraq, could do the same. Yet Jordan, according to its peace treaty with Israel, can't allow any foreign military to enter its land in order to attack Israel. Furthermore, from the 1950s to the 1980s, when Jordan might have had to consider or actually permit Iraqi forces to move through its land, it suspected that Iraq could exploit this opportunity to increase its influence in the kingdom and maybe even to take over. Jordan fears the same and even more about Iran. Jordan is aware that it might not be able to contain the Iranian presence in the kingdom.

On February 10, 2018, Iran launched an unmanned air vehicle (UAV) from Syria. The UAV was shot down by the IAF after it penetrated Israel.[120] The UAV actually reached Israel from Jordan. In spite of the relations between Jordan and Iran, it did not prevent Iran from violating Jordan's air space. Jordan did not intercept UAV, maybe because it passed inside the kingdom only for a short time. Israel, which monitored the UAV during its flight, could have told Jordan to shoot it down, but this did not happen. It was a clear Iranian provocation toward both Israel and Jordan.

The War in Yemen

Saudi Arabia has been struggling to contain its Shiite minority, following the tension between the Shiites and the Sunnis.[121] Saudi Arabia has also been facing a front in Yemen.

Since March 2015 Saudi Arabia, with some help from Sunni-led Arab states, has been running a campaign against the Houthis in Yemen. Iran, which supports the Houthis, spends only a few million dollars a year on this war, while for the Saudis the cost is at least $5 to $6 billion a month.[122] Furthermore, Saudi Arabia fears that Iran might establish a base in Yemen strong enough to pose a threat to the south of the kingdom. The latter already has to watch its northern border with the pro-Iranian Iraq. Saudi Arabia does not want to split its forces between those two fronts, as each stretches over hundreds of kilometers. The border with Yemen is in the far south of the kingdom and the border with Iraq is on the other side of the country, which means it will take time to send reinforcements from one border to another. Those constraints make it harder for Saudi Arabia to protect its territory against Iranian allies. Saudi Arabia has better chances to stop Iran in Yemen than in Iraq, since compared with the Iraqi Shiites, the Houthis are less close to Iran, both geographically and as far as their ties with their Iranian patron. In Yemen the United States assists Saudi Arabia against Iran, while in Iraq the United States had to work with Iran against ISIS.

Marc Lynch mentioned that the war in Yemen was supposed to be a new model, in which Gulf Arab states act alone against Iran without relying on the United States.[123] However, the Obama administration backed the Saudis by providing them with munitions and technology for air strikes. The United States also accepts the Saudi blockade of Yemeni territory that is held by Houthis, which caused a huge humanitarian catastrophe.[124] It has been the result of the Saudi attempt to contain the Houthis in Yemen in order to make it harder for them to receive help from their Iranian patron.

Could There Be a Regime Change in Iran?

In Iran there has been an ongoing political struggle between moderates and extremists. The international community hopes that the moderates in Iran can contain the extremists there. Yet later on hardliners could tip the scales in their favor. It happened in 2005 when the relatively moderate president Mohammad Khatami left office and Mahmoud Ahmadinejad came in his place.

Iranian moderates, if they become more powerful, might focus on internal Iranian issues and not on foreign adventures such as supporting guerrilla and terrorist groups across the Middle East. However, Iran's nuclear program might stay active. For Israel and Sunni-led Arab states, as much as they wish to weaken Iranian protégés like the Hezbollah, allowing Iran to keep its nuclear program is much riskier. As long as there is no fundamental shift in the current Iranian regime, Israel and Sunni-led Arab states will find it difficult to trust the Iranian leadership, including a moderate one.

In early June 2017 James F. Jeffrey claimed that "the United States must set clear final goals. Does it merely want to push back on Tehran's regional aggression, as it did with Slobodan Milosevic in the 1990s? Or does it seek a long-term containment policy to effect fundamental policy changes in Iran."[125] The United States, with the help of Israel and Sunni-led Arab states, could try to contain Iran as much as possible while striving for regime change.

Roy Takeyh claimed in early July 2017 that in case there is another outbreak of protests in Iran, the United States plans to "weaken the regime's already unsteady security services" and to strengthen "domestic critics."[126] It followed the unrest that occurred in Iran from June 2009 to early 2010. When another round of protests started across Iran in December 2017, the United States expressed its support for the demonstrators but without doing much more, perhaps waiting to see if the crisis intensified. The protests melted away in about two weeks. It showed, however, that there is a certain probability for a major change and maybe even a revolution in Iran in the future. It might occur due to corruption, suppression, and the shaky condition of Iran's economy.

Following the agreement from July 2015, Iran's economy might eventually recover, but it may not be that easy considering the low price of oil, Iran's main source of income, and major structural problems in Iran's economy. If Iran's economy deteriorates, it might undermine the regime there. In such a situation, Iran's regime might be so frantic that it might change its policy in order to concentrate its efforts and resources on saving the crumbling economy. As a result Iran's proxies might receive less aid. Israel and Sunni-led Arab states will benefit from that, yet the best outcome for Iran's foes is a collapse of the Iranian regime if an economic and political crisis in Iran leads to a revolution. Another possibility is that Iran breaches the JCPOA or provokes the international community in such a way that might lead to crippling sanctions, which cause an economic low point and as a result an uprising. For Israel, western countries including the United States, Sunni-led Arab states, and many in Iran, a new Iranian regime will be welcomed with all the risks that come with such a transition. A new Iranian leadership might be more moderate. It might not be very friendly to Israel and Sunni-led Arab states, but Iran could stop or at least reduce actions that cause concern and high tension.

Minorities in Iran

There was once an independent Kurdish state in Iran that lasted eleven months in 1946. Since then another Kurdish state has not been established due to the lack of a popular Iranian Kurdish leader and the ability of Iran to curb Kurdish political activism such as making it difficult for Kurdish parties to operate from exile like in Iraq. It is also important to mention that more than three-quarters of Iranian Kurds are Sunnis who support the reformist movement in Iran. Those Kurds expect the regime to improve their economic conditions. The rest of the Iranian Kurds are Shiites, who are less of a concern to the Iranian regime.[127]

The Democratic Party of Iranian Kurdistan (PDKI) enjoys support of the 10 million Kurds in Iran.[128] There is also Hadaka, "a left-wing group that wants Kurdish self-determination in Iran." This outfit ran guerilla warfare against Iran from bases in northern Iraq from 1979 to 1996. Hadaka resumed its armed fight in 2016. It is tough for Hadaka to bring volunteers from Iran across the border into northern Iraq. The party's leader, Secretary-General Mustafa Hijri, said its group is willing to cooperate "with any political force that wants to help us achieve our goals against the Islamic Republic of Iran.... Our aim is to form a federal democratic Iranian government in which all ethnicities in Iran will have autonomy." Hadaka did not receive assistance from any state.[129]

The Congress of Nationalities for a Federal Iran (CNFI) is the biggest coalition in Iran, composed of sixteen parties and groups. "This organization calls to replace the regime with a federal Iran, a system in which Kurds, Arabs, Balouchs, Azari, and Turkmens all have their local democracies and enjoy some checks and balances through which political participation and democracy in the whole of Iran are guaranteed."[130]

The National Council of Resistance of Iran had a gathering outside Paris in early July 2017. It claims to represent Iranians who were killed by the regime there and those who had to flee Iran because they feared for their lives and also those who stayed there but support the People's Mojahedin Organization of Iran (PMOI or MEK), the largest constituent group in the NCRI. The PMOI wants regime change and opposes both appeasement of the Iranian regime and foreign military intervention.[131]

"The containment of Iran is not possible unless it is accompanied by a reliable movement inside of the country that has the ability to challenge Iran both militarily and socially. This movement can contain Iran's accessibility to its resources, challenge its legitimacy and accordingly, cripple its ability to act abroad."[132] The United States, Israel and Arab Sunni states could therefore assist organizations and groups inside Iran that could join the effort to undermine the Iranian regime or contain Iran. It is a way to show Iran that it too could suffer from subversion and incursion, following Iranian activities across the Middle East. The goal will be to convince Iran to hold and at least to minimize its support of its proxies in the region. Iran should also be encouraged to take better care of its minorities.

2

The Iranian-Israeli-Arab Triangle

The Arab-Israeli conflict continues, yet Iran poses a threat to both Israel and Sunni-led Arab states, mostly those in the Persian Gulf. So there are growing signs of cooperation between Arab Gulf states and Israel in an effort to contain Iran and its proxies like Hezbollah.

The Certain Decline of the Arab-Israeli Conflict

Israel's national security concerns since 1948 have had to do with Arabs, mostly Arab states near it.[1] Since the 1980s the conflict has been mostly about the cold war between Israel and Syria and the struggle between Israel and Palestinians, especially Hamas and the PA.

Egypt, Jordan, Syria, and Iraq carried the main burden of the conflict with Israel, certainly in the military dimension. Other Arab states gave political and financial support. In recent decades major changes occurred in Iraq and in the relations between Israel and Jordan and Egypt. Iraq has sent expeditionary forces to fight Israel in each war since 1948. The last time it happened was in 1973. Since 2003 Iraq has been coping with a fierce civil war and ongoing instability, which kept it out of the Arab-Israeli conflict. In that sense, from the Israeli perspective, Iraq is contained. Since 1979 there has been peace, yet a cold one, between Israel and Egypt. In recent years the two states have been collaborating against ISIS in Sinai. With Jordan Israel has both a cold peace, since 1994, and effective security cooperation.

There were peace talks between Israel and the Palestinians, Syria, and Lebanon and also various open and secret talks between Israel and Arab states. Most Arab states don't recognize Israel, but they do support the 2002 Arab peace initiative to end the Arab-Israeli conflict, which could also mean stopping the Arab attempt to contain Israel. Israel wants peace but does not agree with the terms and the demands of this Arab initiative. The Arabs have not abandoned their plan. They have been more concerned about internal affairs and Iran. All in all, the Arab-Israeli conflict continues, mostly between Israel and Palestinians, but other conflicts have become important, too.

On December 13, 2017, leaders of the member states of the Organization of Islamic Cooperation (OIC), which includes Iran, agreed to "reaffirm our attachment to the just and comprehensive peace based on the two-state solution with east Jerusalem as the capital of the State of Palestine and consistent with internationally recognized terms of reference and the 2002 Arab Peace Initiative adopted by the Extraordinary Islamic Summit Conference in Makkah Al-Mukarramah in 2005 as a strategic choice; and call on the international community to act in an effective and serious manner to achieve this solution."[2] Although Iran signed that declaration it still intends to destroy Israel. Iran also signed the NPT (nonproliferation of nuclear weapons), but it violated this treaty because Iran has been seeking to produce a nuclear bomb. So Israel seriously doubts that Iran is willing to accept a two-state solution and recognize Israel.

Israel and Arabs Against Iran

The Arab peace initiative from 2002 was formed because Arab states like Saudi Arabia realized that Iran is their real foe, not Israel. Therefore Saudi Arabia required "peace and quiet in their backyard in order" to focus on Iran.[3] Israel and those Arab states could "quietly share intelligence" and have "indirect secret cooperation vis-a-vis Iran."[4] They could avoid establishing formal relations while keeping their ties.[5] Actually Arab states like Saudi Arabia and the United Arab Emirates (UAE) have had secret ties with Israel for many years.[6] They could even collaborate with Israel against Iran without solving the Arab-Israeli conflict, particularly considering all the obstacles it involves. In the past Israel and Arabs had all kinds of cooperation with each other against other Arabs without signing an official agreement, let alone a peace treaty. They could do the same against Iran. However, officially ending the conflict between Israel and the Arabs will help them to contain Iran.

On August 13, 2015, the IDF released to the public "IDF Strategy." According to it Israel has to realize "cooperative potential with moderate regional elements."[7] On July 30, 2015, "the director general of Israel's Foreign Ministry, Dore Gold, called the Middle East's Sunni Arab nations "Israel's allies."[8] In 2016 there was a media campaign in Saudi Arabia against anti-Semitism, maybe as an effort to prepare public opinion in the kingdom to be ready to accept better relations with Israel.[9] In mid-2016 "the iron wall separating Israel from its Arab neighbors is indeed showing cracks, but the prospects for a turn from confrontation to cooperation is still hampered by real differences of interests and priorities.[10]"The same could have been said on the upcoming years.

An anti-Iranian alliance, even an unofficial one, could be quite formidable between Israel and Saudi Arabia and Egypt, without including any other Arab state. The size of Iran is 1,648,195 km2 and it has about 75 million people. The size of Israel is 22,072 km2, and it has about 8.5 million people. Iran also has much more natural resources than Israel. Yet Egypt has more than 90 million people, and Saudi Arabia, which has the second largest amount of oil reserves in the world, spreads over 2,149,690 km2. Therefore the combined strength of Israel, Saudi Arabia, and Egypt more than matches Iran's strategic power. Obviously Israel, Egypt, and Saudi Arabia should have more Arab states on their side such as Jordan and UAE, which are known to have quite an effective military. Iran has allies across the Middle East, but they are relatively weak, so they could not significantly change the balance of power, particularly those in Lebanon (Hezbollah) and Yemen (Houthis). As for Assad, he has regained control of most of his country, but he is still vulnerable, and the same goes for Iraq, where Iran has quite an influence.

Sunni-led Arab states in the Gulf oppose Iran's Arab partners. Some of the latter are Israel's foes too, such as Assad and Hezbollah. Iran runs its proxy wars in Arab countries and territories where there is a border with Iran's enemies, such as in Syria, Iraq, Lebanon, Yemen, the West Bank, and the Gaza Strip. The spreading of Iranian influence across the region demonstrates to Israel and Arab states both the need and the challenge of containing Iran.

Saudi Arabia, due to internal problems, might find itself in a turmoil, which will impact the region, including the Arab-Israeli conflict. The Arab peace initiative started as a Saudi move. If the Saudi kingdom is destabilized, the initiative might go down with it. Egypt is heavily dependent on Saudi Arabia for economic aid. Without this help Egypt might become a failed state and the peace between it and Israel might be in danger. There will also be a strong effect on the world oil market if Saudi Arabia is in deep trouble. The price of oil might go up. Iran will benefit from all that, and it will be much more difficult to contain it.

In late 2016 there was an ongoing arms race in the Gulf that Arabs were "decisively winning." Yet Iran could have disrupted naval traffic and hit its Arab neighbors with missiles. There was a "high level of mutual deterrence" between Iran and Arab Gulf states, yet a war might have started because of miscalculations.[11] If such a war happens in the future, Israel will hope that such a war will distract Iran from other areas, those near Israel. Israel might even assist Arab states, indirectly, to defeat Iran, which will help to contain the latter. Israel certainly does not want Arab Gulf states to lose, since then the Arab regimes there might be destabilized and be replaced by those that might decide to improve ties with Iran at the expense of their relations with Israel. In addition, a war in the Gulf will test the militaries of both sides, an experience that could upgrade their capabilities, which is not an Israeli interest, assuming that Arab Gulf states and especially Iran might use this knowledge if they ever turn against Israel.

On October 27, 2016, a letter signed by UN ambassadors of Egypt, Jordan, Morocco, Saudi Arabia, UAE, and Yemen was given to UN Secretary General Ban Ki-moon. The letter said that Iran "continues to play a negative role in causing tension and instability" in the Middle East by intervening in internal affairs of Arab states.[12] The UN is known to be quite hostile toward Israel, mostly because of the approach of Arab states, including those that were behind that letter. Yet Israel could have joined this letter because it agrees with its message.

Saudi Arabia sees its oil "as a weapon to limit Iran's economic gains."[13] The Saudis seek to exploit this measure to make Iran weaker, which will help in containing Iran. In the past Saudis used the oil weapon against Israel too, as part of the effort to contain it. This kind of soft power has been a preferred way for Saudi Arabia to run a cold war without risking an actual confrontation. Israel could have retaliated by attacking Saudi Arabia from the air, but it did not do that. If it assumes that Saudi Arabia provokes them too much with its oil weapon, Iran might retaliate.

In 2017 Saudi Arabia could have tried to encircle Iran by implementing "a variety of soft and hard power networks that are in Pakistan (Baluchistan), Tajikistan, Turkmenistan, Afghanistan, and Azerbaijan." As part of that effort Saudi Arabia could also tighten its ties with Iraq and African allies.[14] All of that could contribute in containing Iran.

Hezbollah

In the 1970s Israel clashed with the Palestine Liberation Organization (PLO), which was based in Lebanon. Israel strove to contain the PLO, but in 1982 this policy changed when Israel launched a massive offensive and succeeded in defeating the organization and kicking it out of Lebanon. Yet Israel was entangled in a long low-intensity war in Lebanon that lasted eighteen years, mostly against Hezbollah. Along this period Israel tried to prevent Hezbollah from harming the population in northern Israel. Israeli citizens were relatively safe. It was not necessarily because of Israeli actions, since at the time Hezbollah fired fewer rockets, as compared with the 2006 war, when the group bombed heavily inside Israel. In the 1980s and 1990s Hezbollah focused on the Israeli troops who were deployed in southern Lebanon. The Israeli Defense Forces' mission was to defend Israel, but its biggest challenge was to shield its soldiers in Lebanon. Ironically the Israeli presence in southern Lebanon was not the solution but the problem, since it put at risk both the Israeli soldiers there and the population in northern Israel. Following the Israeli retreat from Lebanon in 2000, the conflict between Israel and Hezbollah continued, but the number of Israeli casualties went down significantly. For Israel, the best way to contain Hezbollah at a minimum price was to stay away from Lebanon.

Hezbollah confronted Israel in 2006 in a tough fight that went on for more than a month.[15] It ended in a tie.[16] IDF's concept of relying on airpower to contain the firing of rockets at Israel failed to a large extent. Eventually Israel launched a major land offensive, but it was ineffective due to a lack of readiness. If in the future the Hezbollah hits Israel with barrages of rockets, the response will be a full-scale Israeli offensive.

"Iran's material support for Hezbollah has varied—when it was under heavy UN sanctions, it dropped to about $200 million a year, and after the JCPOA it has risen back to roughly $800 million."[17] Hezbollah has been relying on its Iranian patron for training, money, and weapons. Iran wants to decide when Hezbollah confronts Israel, not to be surprised by an escalation like the one that led to the 2006 war due to miscalculations. Iran has been using Hezbollah to confront its enemies, mostly in Syria. Yet Iran seeks to contain Hezbollah and to prevent the group from provoking Israel, when it does not serve Iran. If Israel attacks Iran's nuclear infrastructure, Iran will probably unleash Hezbollah against Israel.

Iran needs Hezbollah because it is an Arab group, so a war between Israel and Hezbollah will allow Iran to present itself as assisting Arabs against Israel and by that to increase its influence among the Arabs. However, Iran has much less capability to hit Israel with, whereas Hezbollah has about 150,000 rockets.[18] Furthermore, Iran does not want to be involved directly, in order not to be exposed to an Israeli retribution. Iran could assist Hezbollah with weapons, funds, and political support, but it prefers that Hezbollah carry the burden of combat. Iran at most might risk sending into battle several hundred of its Islamic Revolutionary Guard Corps (IRGC). So Iran will strive to contain the war to Lebanon and Israel. Israel might accept that, although it will be eager to make Iran pay for arming Hezbollah. Both states have a problem striking each other due to the distance between them (which is more than 1,000 km). The Israeli Air Force (IAF) is stronger than its Iranian counterpart, but Israel will be busy attacking Lebanon. Israel is also aware that expanding the war to Iran, even without striking Iranian oil sites, might cause turmoil in the oil market. Israel will wish to avoid that outcome, particularly if Israel is blamed for it. Another possible ramification of an Israeli offensive against Iran is an escalation in which Iran attacks Arab Gulf states, accusing them of supporting Israel. This could bring the United States into the war against its will. Israel does not want to be responsible for that. This is another reason for Israel to limit the war to Lebanon.

"IDF Strategy" explains, in general, how the IDF plans to deal with Arab nonstate organization such as Hezbollah. Israel could carry out a preemptive attack against Hezbollah, aiming at containing the fire from Lebanon by hitting various targets there and by destroying many of Hezbollah's rockets before they can be launched at Israel. The IDF has plans to conduct a massive air and ground offensive for this purpose. Yet Israel has been waiting to see the results of Hezbollah's involvement in the war in Syria. As long as Hezbollah has been pinned down and in a way contained to Syria, it reduces the chances that Hezbollah will try to go after Israel. Hezbollah must be aware that confronting Israel will be much more destructive to Lebanon than its war against the Syrian groups. Hezbollah will also need time to recover from the heavy losses it absorbed in Syria. Iran will also take this into consideration before asking Hezbollah to provoke Israel, assuming it might end in a war before Hezbollah is ready for that. Those constraints will help Israel to contain Hezbollah in Lebanon even if that group will be much less involved in Syria.

Tamara Cofman Wittes said on April 19, 2016, that by fighting in Syria, Hezbollah showed that it "is not so focused, as it claims, on defending Lebanon, but rather on increasing its own power and influence and securing Shia and Iranian influence in the Arab world."[19] Hezbollah has been an Iranian tool, and both should be contained. In regard to Lebanon as long as the IDF was deployed there from 1982 to 2000, Hezbollah could have claimed that the group fights to liberate its country. Yet in 2000 Israel not only left Lebanon but accepted the line that was set by the UN to be the border, even when it meant that some Israeli civilians found themselves residing very close to the border, with all the risk it involves in case of a penetration from Lebanon. In spite of that, Hezbollah claims there are areas inside Israel that belong to Lebanon. Hezbollah also argues that it has to keep its arsenal like its rockets if Israel invades Lebanon again. Yet ironically if the IDF goes into Lebanon, it will be because of Hezbollah's rockets. Israelis have no desire to return to Lebanon.

If Hezbollah has only light arms, not missiles and rockets that can hit Israel, then there will be less chance of a war, and if Hezbollah continues not to send details into Israel, then the probability of a war will be even lower. If Hezbollah focuses on its Arab foes, then Israel might ignore the group, as it did with other Arab rivals. In certain situations Israel might even assist Hezbollah indirectly, for example, in case the group confronts those who will seek to strike Israel from Lebanon.

Hezbollah strives to prove that even if Israel mounts "a successful preemptive attack on Hezbollah, the party would still retain a capacity to inflict unacceptable pain on Israel."[20] In 2017 Hezbollah had hundreds of drones,[21] which add strength to the group that already possesses massive firepower. Hezbollah might also consider launching a preemptive attack, particularly if the group or Iran assumes that Israel is about to attack one of them. If the threat is only to Iran and it orders Hezbollah to attack Israel, then the group might hesitate, but still it will obey its patron, knowing that such a war will cost the Hezbollah dearly. Hezbollah, a Shiite group, is well aware that it has no alternative to Iran, in contrast with other pro-Iranian groups like Hamas that as a Sunni outfit could be a protégé of Sunni states, including non-Arab ones like Turkey.

In 2016, following its losses in Syria, Hezbollah had to expand recruitment, "diminishing the quality of its personnel."[22] Hezbollah did gain "immeasurable battlefield experience from fighting in Syria."[23] However, its men got used to confronting rebels who have no armor, heavy artillery, or air force while the IDF has hundreds of aircraft and thousands of armored vehicles and artillery pieces. The IDF also has many more troops than Hezbollah and better training, weapons, and equipment. Confronting the IDF will be a very different challenge for Hezbollah than containing Syrian groups.

Israel's main goal with regard to Hezbollah, which probably could be achieved only in a war, is to drastically reduce Hezbollah's arsenal of rockets and missiles. Yet those weapons are used by Hezbollah to deter Israel from starting a war. In spite of its overwhelming superiority and desire to crush Hezbollah, Israel recognizes that a war in Lebanon might be costly. Meanwhile Israel strives to contain Hezbollah's military buildup by conducting strikes inside Syria, aiming to destroy deliveries of weapons to Hezbollah.

Dmitry Adamsky explained, "Another war could break out for a number of reasons: a misperception on the part of Hezbollah or Israel produces an unintended escalation; if one of the two decides to exploit a perceived moment of weakness on the part of the other to attack; or if the behavior of either side crosses the redlines of the other."[24] Hezbollah and Israel don't seek war, and they have managed to avoid one since 2006. Yet they are sworn enemies, and Hezbollah's effort to acquire better weapons while Israel tries to prevent that causes ongoing tension. One major incident between them, one that will get out of control, might lead to a confrontation. Until then Israel will continue to contain Hezbollah.

In February 2017 Nasrallah repeated previous threats to strike Israel's nuclear reactor in Dimona and the Haifa ammonia storage tank. The tank is supposed to be closed soon, partly because of that danger.[25] Hezbollah has missiles that cover all of Israel, so every sensitive site there is within range.

In mid-2017 Iran and Hezbollah planned to construct missile factories in Lebanon, deep below the ground. This would have protected the sites from air bombardments, allowing the production of "highly sophisticated rockets with ranges of more than 300 miles and equipped with advanced guidance systems." Israel considered a preemptive strike, which might have started a war.[26] Israel waited but might strike in the future, according to its policy of containing Hezbollah's military buildup.

In September 2017 the IDF carried out its largest exercise in almost two decades, aimed at defeating Hezbollah.[27] In the same month Giora Eiland, former head of Israel's National Security Council, said, "It will be very hard for Israel to defeat Hezbollah in a short period of time and at a reasonable price." Eiland added that Israel should threaten to destroy Lebanon if Hezbollah fires from there. The Israeli goal will be to turn public opinion in Lebanon against Hezbollah and to urge the international community to create a cease-fire that will benefit Israel.[28] In that sense Israel will seek not to actually win but to improve its containment of Hezbollah.

Hezbollah, besides or as an alternative to attacking Israel from Lebanon, could target Israeli and Jewish objectives around the world such as diplomats and tourists as it already did in Bulgaria on July 18, 2012.[29] This is another option for Iran to retaliate against Israel, with or without starting another front in the Middle East from Lebanon, Syria, the Gaza Strip, or Iran itself.

On December 2016 Hezbollah, which is about 30,000 men strong, had 8,000 fighters inside Syria. Hezbollah has lost 1,700 troops there since 2011.[30] At the time Daniel L. Byman claimed that there was tension inside Hezbollah among those who did not go to risk their lives in Syria and stayed in south Lebanon, and there was "also potential for greater friction between the leadership in Beirut and the soldiers on the frontlines fighting a seemingly endless war."[31] Indeed following the substantial price that was paid by Hezbollah in Syria, there was criticism inside the Shiite community in Lebanon about the ongoing involvement in Syria. The victories of Assad and his allies like Hezbollah helped to contain their rivals, which could allow Hezbollah to reduce its presence in Syria and to lower the certain unrest among the Shiites in Lebanon.

In the municipal elections that took place in the summer of 2017, "only 55 percent of the votes in Baalbeck—the biggest Shiite city in the Bekaa Valley—went to both Hizbollah and Amal combined. Much of this discontent among the Shiites and other Lebanese communities stems from the fact that people are beginning to realize that the enemy may be within."[32] A massive shift among the Lebanese Shiites against Hezbollah might be Israel's best hope to contain this group without starting a war. Yet such a process does not seem to have many chances due to Hezbollah's strong position in Lebanon and its willingness to use force to keep it.

In mid-2017 "almost all financial and economic indicators point[ed] to Lebanon's dramatic freefall into the abyss with public debt rising to $118 billion."[33] Hezbollah provides the Shiite community there with food and medical aid in return for total loyalty to Hezbollah and therefore to Iran. Hezbollah can afford that by creating dummy corporations and making contacts with businessmen.[34] A substantial and long-term effort to weaken Hezbollah requires containing its Iranian patron so that it will be harder for Iran to support Hezbollah. At the same time Hezbollah itself has to be contained, and there must be a reliable alternative for this group in Lebanon inside the Shiite community, one that will be more moderate than Hezbollah. This other outfit must have enough funds to provide the Shiites with their basic needs if the Lebanese government fails to do that. This process should be done without forcing the Shiites to be educated or to obey and fight for radical and destructive concepts like those of Hezbollah and Iran.

Saudi Arabia ended its military assistance to the Lebanese military in early 2016, following the cooperation between Hezbollah and the Lebanese military. Saudi Arabia acknowledged indirectly that they had failed in gaining influence in Lebanon through their allies there.[35] The Saudi aid was part of the effort to contain Iran and its protégés. In Lebanon the goal was to encourage the regime there to contain Hezbollah by strengthening the Lebanese military. It was a tall order, since Hezbollah not only is Iran's most powerful ally but it has managed to establish itself as the dominant force in Lebanon, including inside its government. The Lebanese military has been too weak compared with Hezbollah. The Lebanese military also have Shiite troops who might oppose fighting Hezbollah. Therefore Saudi Arabia has tried to cut its losses in Lebanon while trying to contain Iran and its protégés in other countries like Yemen, which is the Saudis' backyard, so it is obviously much more important for the kingdom. For Israel it is the opposite, that is, taking care of Lebanon and not of Yemen for the same reason, the proximity of Iran's proxy to its border. Israel could have used Saudi help in Lebanon, yet to begin with it has been a challenge to influence the government there to restrain Hezbollah.

Israel, the Palestinians, and Iran

"Iran cites its support for secular and Sunni Palestinian groups as evidence that it works with non-Islamist groups to promote the rights of the Palestinians."[36] Yet Iran's most powerful Palestinian ally has been Hamas, a radical Islamic movement. Hamas was created in 1988, when Israel and Iran were already foes, so Hamas and Iran had a common rival. Hamas is Sunni and Arab, in sharp contrast to the mostly Shiite and mostly Persian Iran, but they ignored that due to their hatred toward Israel. Since 2007 Hamas became more vital to Iran after Hamas seized the Gaza Strip. Iran considers that area as a fire base, as the one the Hezbollah created in Lebanon, to strike Israel with rockets. It is part of the Iranian plan to contain Israel.

The weapons Hamas acquired over the years, by smuggling or producing them, were based to a large extent on Iran's aid. Without Iranian backing and assistance, Hamas might have been forced to change its strategy to a less violent one. In previous confrontations between Israel and Hamas, mostly in 2008–9 and 2014, the population in the Gaza Strip paid a heavy price. Yet Iran, which had been willing to put Shiite Arabs in Lebanon at risk, had fewer doubts about doing the same with Sunni Arabs in the Gaza Strip.

Israel tries to contain Hamas in the Gaza Strip while the United States, Israel, and Arab Gulf states strive to contain Iran. Hamas and Iran therefore had to adjust to isolation, particularly Hamas, which has been under a siege in the Gaza Strip, yet Israel continued to provide that area with basic needs like food. Iran is much bigger and stronger than Hamas, but Iran suffered from heavy sanctions, which severely harmed its economy. Hamas and Iran are to be blamed for their economic troubles because their aggressive approach led to the steps that were taken against them.

Iran, following the civil war in Syria, had a conflict with Hamas. Israel, of course, sees Hamas as a sworn enemy. Israel would rather have someone else control the Gaza Strip, a party that will be more friendly to Israel, while Iran seeks to make Hamas more subordinate and loyal. Meanwhile Hamas has been trying to contain its internal rivals in the Gaza Strip, groups more radical than Hamas, including those that are associated with Al-Qaida and ISIS. Those are the enemies of Iran and Israel, too, so those two states want Hamas to succeed here. Yet sometimes non-Hamas groups serve the interest of Iran solely, like when they fire at Israel, which pleases Iran, particularly if it might cause a growing friction between Israel and Hamas, one that pushes Hamas to depend more on Iran. Iran and even Israel can also accept that Hamas will be contained and strong enough to run the Gaza Strip without becoming too independent. The difference is that Iran strives to turn the Gaza Strip, under Hamas, into a fire base against Israel, while Israel is clearly opposed to Hamas having weapons such as rockets that could strike Israel.

Hamas in the Gaza Strip has only two neighbors, Israel and Egypt. Those two states have been seeing Hamas as a threat, an

Iranian bridgehead in their region. Israel and Egypt seek to contain Hamas until the PA is back in charge of the Gaza Strip. There is also security cooperation between Israel and the PA that contains Hamas in the West Bank, a policy that is against Iran, too. Yet the PA has not been capable and willing to assist Israel, at least not openly, in retaking the Gaza Strip. As long as Hamas calls the shots in the Gaza Strip, it encourages Iran to support it, which helps Hamas stay in power.

Iran's supreme leader, Ali Khamenei, called twice in July and November 2014 to arm the Palestinians in the West Bank so they could fight Israel.[37] Iran, like Hamas, prefers a conflict with Israel. Iran opposes talks let alone an agreement between Israel and the PA. Such an accord could somehow include Hamas as well, which could substantially weaken the Iranian grip in the Gaza Strip. Meanwhile Hamas at most tolerates a temporary cease-fire with Israel that might break anytime.

The divide among the Palestinians makes it hard to reach and keep an agreement not only between them and Israel but also inside the Palestinian camp. If Hamas is not part of the solution, it will be a problem, and there are already enough severe obstacles in reaching an agreement. Hamas will have to be contained, but it will not be easy since the group, with strong Iranian support, could sabotage talks between Israel and the PA by conducting attacks.

In July 2016 Gregory Gause, an expert on Arab Gulf states, argued that "as long as the Palestinian question is unsolved, it remains highly unlikely for the Gulf states to formalize their ties with Israel." He added that Arab states can gain what they need from Israel "through secret channels and therefore see no reason to make the relationship public."[38] On April 6, 2017, King Abdullah of Jordan said that solving the Israeli-Palestinian conflict could bring Israel and Arabs together and start "a new era of stability in our area, where Israelis are truly a part of the neighborhood."[39] The Israeli-Palestinian conflict makes it harder to improve the relations between Israel and Arab states, including as part of the effort to contain Iran.

Israel, Egypt, and Iran

Egypt has consistently called for disarming, supervision, and containment of Israel's nuclear program. Following the July 2015 agreement with Iran, Arab states like Egypt could claim that since Iran ceased to be a nuclear threat to Israel, then Israel should waive its right to have nuclear weapons. Yet Iran's nuclear capability was only contained and not by much. Iran keeps its nuclear infrastructure and might breach the agreement any time. Arab states opposed to Israel holding the bomb, but they are even more afraid that Iran will have it.

There is another way to look at the relations between Israel and Egypt with regard to the nuclear issue. In the 1980s, during its war with Iran and because of its strategic position and strength, Iraq was the front guard in the struggle between Iran and most of the Arab world, which included Egypt. In recent years Iraq ceased to be an obstacle for Iran and became its ally. Jordan might be next to fall, and then Israel would be the only state that blocks Iran from getting closer to Egypt.

In the 1980s Egypt, with all its support of Iraq, objected that Iraq would have gotten too strong, which would have changed the balance of power inside the Arab world on the expanse of Egypt, since Egypt saw itself as the leading state among the Arabs. At that time Egypt was isolated in the Arab world because of its peace treaty with Israel. Egypt did not seek to give Iraq an opportunity to exploit those circumstances in order to reach hegemony in the region. In recent years Egypt has been in decline. Israel, as a Jewish state, could not be dominant in the Middle East, as Iraq could have been in the 1980s. However, Egypt still fears that Israel would gain substantial influence in the region. From Egypt's perspective, Israel should be just powerful enough to help in containing Iran but not more than that. Egypt could consider Israel to be a kind of a barrier against Iran.

Egypt, at least officially, does not endorse an Israeli raid on Iran's nuclear sites because it wishes to avoid Iranian retribution. Yet an Israeli strike in Iran will serve Egypt's interests. The same was when Israel contained Arab nuclear programs by destroying Arab nuclear reactors in 1981 in Iraq and in 2007 in Syria. Then Egypt did not want Iraq or Syria to have nuclear weapons, just as it opposes Iran holding this arsenal. Egypt likes this model in which Israel does the dirty work and takes all the risks, and Egypt benefits from the results.

On July 31, 2015, Egypt and Saudi Arabia signed an agreement to boost military and economic ties between them.[40] From 2013 through 2015, Saudi Arabia and the UAE "provided over $20 billion in grants, oil shipments, and support for the deteriorating reserve of Egypt's foreign currencies."[41] "Low oil prices and donor fatigue" may reduce this aid.[42] However, Saudi Arabia and UAE will not want to lose their investment. If Egypt turns into a failed state, it will not be able to assist those Arab Gulf states in containing Iran. In spite of its severe weakness, Egypt has the largest Sunni population in the Arab world, much more than in Saudi Arabia and the UAE combined. It means Egypt could be the main source of manpower in an anti-Iranian coalition. Egypt also has a strong and modern military. In 1990, following the crisis in Kuwait, two Egyptian divisions were deployed in Saudi Arabia as part of the anti-Iraqi alliance. In the future Egyptian forces can cross the Red Sea and land on the west coast of Saudi Arabia. From there they can be sent to deter Iran by defending the kingdom and other Arab Gulf states.

The Egyptian president, Abdel Fattah el-Sisi, had approved in late September 2017 an agreement with Saudi Arabia on cooperation in peaceful uses of nuclear energy. Egypt plans to complete the building of its first nuclear power plant in 2022 and have it operational by 2024.[43] It could be the first stage of producing a Saudi-Egyptian nuclear weapon if Iran's nuclear program is not contained or if Iran gets nuclear weapons.

In mid-September 2017 Egypt and Saudi Arabia conducted in Egypt a joint military drill, Faisal 11, the latest of joint exercises between the two states.[44] There were also talks about establishing a united Arab force. Sunni-led Arab states even fought together in 2015 in Yemen against the Houthis, an Iranian proxy, as part of the effort to contain Iran. However, Egyptian involvement in the Saudi-led coalition in Yemen was quite minor. In contrast with the mid-1960s, when Egypt's military presence in Yemen was massive. About 70,000 of its soldiers were entangled in what was a bitter experience for Egypt, one it does not seek to repeat. In Syria, Saudi Arabia has been eager to topple Assad, while Egypt does not seek to bring him down, which in a way puts Egypt at the side of Assad, that is, with Iran, which strongly supports him.

In the war of 2014 in the Gaza Strip, Egypt opposed assisting the pro-Iranian Hamas but did not want to seem indifferent to the suffering of Palestinians by closing the border between the Gaza Strip and Egypt, in Sinai. Egypt also served as a mediator between Israel and Hamas. Although Hamas is an Iranian ally, the group is independent enough to reach an understanding with Israel, regardless of the Iranian position. It points to a possible opportunity for Israel and other Arab states, and mostly Egypt, due to its proximity and influence on Hamas. The goal is to convince Hamas to break ties with its Iranian patron as part of the effort to contain Iran.

Israel's "Campaign between the Wars"

In the last decade Israel has been running what has been called in Israel "the campaign between the wars," a limited campaign that has been taking place between major confrontations. Israel's goals have been to postpone the next war, to slow down the buildup of nonstate organizations such as Hamas and Hezbollah, and to prevent the disrupting of the daily routine in Israel.[45] According to "IDF Strategy," a paper that was published by the IDF in 2015, the goal has also been to "establish optimal conditions for victory in a future war. Enhance legitimacy for Israel's actions, and negate the basis for legitimacy of the enemy's actions."[46]

Israel has been basing its operations on "a multi-disciplinary concept (military, economic, legal, media, and political), incorporating a unified strategic logic." For the IDF the guiding principles were "initiated on-going operational activity, in which forces operate in covert and clandestine manners during short periods of time. Inter-organizational, operational, and intelligence cooperation" was vital as well. International cooperation was needed "to maintain the legitimacy of the IDF's actions and reduce the legitimacy of the enemy's actions.... The methods of action in this campaign require employing the expertise of various elements within and without the IDF, to ensure flow of information and synergy between them. These methods include intelligence, cognitive, and psychological warfare, diplomatic and state channels, and legal processes."[47] It involves ground, air, and sea units that conduct various missions including raids and intelligence gathering. This approach was meant to weaken and contain Iran's proxies, which helps to contain Iran itself.

The IDF runs this campaign in several fronts, mostly in Syria, where Israel has been focused on preventing and at least reducing the delivery of advanced weapons from both Iran and Syria to Hezbollah. Israel wants to stop the Hezbollah from receiving sophisticated weapons such as antiship, antiaircraft, and surface-to-surface missiles. In other occasions the IDF captured a large number of weapons that were on their way by sea to Iran's allies in Lebanon and the Gaza Strip. One famous case was the seizing of the ship *Klos-C* in the Red Sea in early March 2014. After checking the cargo and the ship, the UN confirmed it came from Iran but claimed that its destination was Sudan, not the Gaza Strip.[48] However, weapons were smuggled from Sudan to the Gaza Strip.

As part of "the campaign between the wars," when rockets were fired from the Gaza Strip, Israel returned a favor, officially admitted hitting the Hamas, because there was no way to deny that. In other cases Israel's rivals were harmed in explosions. Israel kept silent or claimed it was not responsible in order to avoid retribution. Often a violent attack occurred because of internal disputes among Israel's foes. For example, the involvement of Hezbollah in Syria brought its Sunni enemies to initiate assaults against Hezbollah and Iran inside Lebanon. Sometimes it was also a result of an accident such as when a terror group prepared a car bomb and something went wrong during this dangerous process.

Another aspect of Israel's "campaign between the wars" was intelligence gathering across the Middle East by submarines. For example, in 2013 Israel's submarines allocated 58 percent of their hours at sea for operations while the rest were used for training. In 2012 only 36 percent of the submarines' hours at sea were allocated for operations, and it was more or less the same number in previous years.[49]

3

The War in Syria

Israel and Syria have confronted each other in several high-intensity wars like in 1967, when Israel took the Golan Heights. There were other confrontations like an attrition war following the 1973 war. Since 1974 there was only one war between them, in Lebanon, in 1982. There were also attempts to reach peace between the two sides, mostly in the 1990s and in 2008 but they failed.[1] A civil war in Syria has been raging since 2011. Israel has not intervened, striving to contain the battles there by monitoring and upgrading its deployment on the border, in the Golan Heights, in order to prevent attacks. Israel did carry out more than a hundred air strikes inside Syria, aimed at reducing the delivery of advanced weapons from Syria to Hezbollah, as part of the attempt to contain the latter's military buildup in Lebanon.

The Syrian Civil War

Hafez al-Assad ruled Syria from 1970 to 2000. He was a skilled politician who relied on the sect he came from, the Alawites, but he also promoted Christians, Druze, and even some Sunnis. His security services suppressed the opposition. The peak was in 1982 when Assad killed up to 10,000 people, following a mutiny in Hama.[2] When Hafez al-Assad died of a heart attack in 2000, his son, Bashar al-Assad, succeeded him after he was trained to be president in a hasty process, so there were doubts about whether he was fit to rule. In 2005 he had to take his forces out of Lebanon, a country that was part of the Syrian vision of "Greater

Syria." During the Syrian civil war, Bashar al-Assad lost most of Syria itself, although eventually he managed to gain back a large part of it. Assad did that after he contained the rebels, by isolating them and actually casting a siege on their strongholds such as in Aleppo. Assad did it while starving and bombing them and the population that was with them, without mercy.

In May 2017 there were over a hundred pro-Assad militias that constituted "around half of the available troop strength available to the regime. These militias are not mere servants of Assad. Rather, they are centers of power and resources for the men that control them. Some are small local groups, numbering just a few dozen fighters. Others are countrywide and make use of heavy weapons including armor and artillery."[3] Those units together with Assad's military and his allies, Russia, Iran and Hezbollah, made it possible for him to hold his ground, to seize more land and to contain the rebels.

By May 2018 there were 5.6 million Syrian refuges. About 3.5 million went to Turkey while the rest fled to Arab states, mostly Jordan and Lebanon.[4] Probably more than half a million people were killed in that war.[5] It was the price the Syrian people paid for Assad's determination to contain the rebels and stay in power.

Since the start of the Syrian civil war in 2011, Israel was not sure if it wanted to get rid of Assad or not, assuming his successor might be worse. Either way Israel stayed out of that war and tried to contain it because Israel wanted to prevent the war from spilling over into Israeli territory in the Golan Heights. Israel also did not seek to see the war spreading into Syria's neighbors, which would have destabilized them. One of them is Turkey. In spite of the disputes between Israel and Turkey, the former prefers a stable Turkey, among others because of economic reasons like the mutual trade between the two states, which amounts to several billion dollars a year. Israel was particularly worried about Syria's southern neighbor, Jordan, where Israel has not only its longest border but one that is closer to its population centers than any other border.

The Golan Heights

The Golan Heights is relatively far away from the most vital areas in Israel like Haifa and Tel Aviv. It has no access to the sea or a major airfield. It became officially part of Israel after it was annexed in 1981, yet only 21,000 Israeli Jews live there, together with 25,000 non-Jews, mostly Druze. (Israel has more than 6 million Jews.) Therefore only a tiny part of the Jewish population resides there. Still the Golan Heights is essential to Israel in monitoring Syria from Mount Hermon, where the IDF has a highly valuable intelligence base. The Golan Heights could also serve for an Israeli offensive toward Damascus, which is 65 km away from the border or as a forward defense area, although it is not that big, about 1,200 km2. Its industry is based on tourism and producing wines and milk. It could be said that Israel wishes to contain the Syrian civil war in order to defend not so much the heart of Israel but its periphery, which serves above all for security purposes.

Between 1974 and 2011, the border between Israel and Syria, in the Golan Heights, was quiet. Since then hundreds of violent incidents have occurred there, like mortar fire. Most of those assaults were clashes between Assad's forces and his rivals, which sometimes led to firing from the Syrian side that reached Israel. Israel shot back but in a very minor way, such as destroying a tank, aiming at containing the event. This method worked. Israel fired at Assad's positions because Israel always saw Assad as responsible for whatever happens in Syria. Yet often it was not clear which party inside Syria had conducted the assault against Israel and if it was done deliberately.

In other cases it was obvious the goal was harming Israelis, like when an explosive device was placed along the border where Israeli troops patrol. After such an attack wounded four Israeli paratroops on March 18, 2014, Israeli aircraft bombed several targets inside Syria. It was not the first time the IAF attacked Syrian objectives during the civil war. Yet the other sorties were part of a different struggle: Israel's effort to stop the delivery of advanced weapons from Syria to Hezbollah in Lebanon. On March 18, 2014, Israel took responsibility, for the first time during the Syrian civil war, for its air strike inside Syria. This time Israel probably assumed it could not deny its actions because of the scale and the location of its attack near the border. In previous Israeli strikes inside Syria, there were fewer targets, and they were far from the Golan Heights, some in the area of Damascus. Nevertheless, even the strikes on March 18 were limited.

Prime Minister Benjamin Netanyahu warned on October 1, 2015, that "Israel will continue to respond forcefully to any attacks against it from Syria."[6] Yet Israel remained careful, striving not to increase the tension on the border. Until 2018 only one Israeli was killed there, a teenager, which also helped Israel to restrain itself. Meanwhile the IDF prepared for an escalation by building a new fence in the Golan Heights, fifteen feet high, with double obstacles. Intelligence and observation systems were added as well. The IDF also replaced in the Golan Heights its veteran 36th division with the new 210th division. Its mission is to secure the border in case of a low-intensity war. The last time such a confrontation happened there was in the late 1960s. It was all part of the Israeli effort to prevent the war in Syria from spilling over into Israel.

Following the Syrian civil war ISIS gained presence on the border with Israel. The group was focused on the east and north of Syria and on other Arab states, mostly Iraq, but Israel was aware that if ISIS had grown and become more powerful, then sooner or later ISIS would turn against Israel. ISIS has more motivation than Assad to confront Israel, due to the group's harsh ideology. ISIS also has less to lose because, unlike Assad, it does not have vulnerable objectives that the IDF could attack. Assad and Israel also have a history of understandings, official or not, while Israel and ISIS don't have such a background. So preventing a clash or reaching a cease-fire might have been difficult. Eventually ISIS was defeated and contained in both Syria and Iraq.

Other anti-Assad groups captured parts of the border in the Golan Heights from the Syrian side. Israel has been regularly supplying Syrians on the border with food and fuel. Israel aimed at creating a buffer zone, where pro-Israeli forces would be present to oppose Assad and Iran's proxies in Syria.[7] Israel also gave medical treatment to about 5,000 Syrians who were wounded in their country, not because of Israel. Although they were educated to hate Israel, they understood that their best chance to get proper help was to go to Israel. All that assisted Israel in making contact with relatively moderate Syrian groups, as part of containing security problems on the border. Yet Israel could not have relied too much on any Syrian group. In the 1982 war Israel made a similar attempt with Christians in Lebanon, a gamble that ended in failure and cost Israel dearly. Israel should have not repeated that policy in Syria.

Israel avoided hitting Syrian groups who were against Israel, leaving that to Assad, who confronted and contained those groups. For Israel it was very comfortable to stay out of a war. Israel's foes were kept busy fighting each other. Assad gradually took back the border between Israel and Syria, pushing aside armed groups who controlled that area for several years. Although Israel developed its ties with some groups and in spite of the hostility between Israel and Assad, it might be better for Israel to have Assad's troops on the border. It depends on whether Assad goes back to the previous status quo, which kept the border quiet from 1974 until 2011.

Israeli Air Strikes inside Syria

In the 1973 war Israel had conduced strategic bombardments in major parts of Syria, including in Damascus. Since then Israel has bombed inside Syria only in a few cases. The most famous strike was the destruction of the nuclear reactor in 2007, when Israel suspected that Assad planned to build a nuclear weapon.

Since the 1990s Israel has restrained itself when Assad sent missiles and rockets to Hezbollah, which put Israel at risk. Israel accepted that for lack of a better choice even after the war of 2006, when Hezbollah received many more rockets and missiles. Hezbollah had about 30,000 rockets in 2006, 70,000 in 2013, and 150,000 in 2016.[8] Yet only since 2012 has Israel declared that sending weapons to Hezbollah is a "red line," particularly if Hezbollah receives advanced arsenal such as antiaircraft, antiship, and surface-to-surface missiles that are very accurate or have a long range. Israel used force when it assumed that this "red line" was about to be crossed. Israel launched air strikes inside Syria, aimed at stopping Assad from supplying Hezbollah with sophisticated weapons. The change in the Israeli strategy was due to the Syrian civil war, which occupied and significantly crippled Assad's military. Therefore Israel rightly assumed that Assad would tolerate the Israeli strikes. Without the Syrian civil war, Israel would have had to continue to tolerate Hezbollah's buildup, as it did in the years before that war. Assad's troubles gave Israel an opportunity to contain Hezbollah's buildup.

The Israeli air strikes inside Syria in 2013 "attempted to contain the crisis to the Syrian territory."[9] The Israeli defense minister, Avigdor Lieberman, said on December 7, 2016, that Israel tries "to prevent the smuggling of advanced weapons, military equipment, and weapons of mass destruction from Syria to Hezbollah."[10] On March 20, 2017, the IDF chief of staff, Lt. Gen. Gadi Eisenkot, mentioned that the IDF "will continue to prevent the transfer of advanced weapons to Hezbollah."[11] On April 27, 2017, Israel's intelligence minister, Israel Katz, said "the incident in Syria corresponds completely with Israel's policy to act to prevent Iran's smuggling of advanced weapons via Syria to Hezbollah."[12] Between 2012 and 2017, the IAF bombed weapon deliveries at least 100 times that were on their way from Syria to Lebanon.[13]

When Israel attacked inside Syria, Hezbollah had to be careful not to respond in a way that would have embarrassed Assad.[14] It was enough for Assad that he, a leader of a state that used to have quite a powerful military and dominated Lebanon, required the assistance of a Lebanese group in order to survive. In addition Hezbollah had to be careful not to ignite a war with Israel in Syria, since it might have spread into Lebanon, and this did not serve the group's interest. Hezbollah was well aware that in Syria its main goal is to defeat and at least to contain the rebels, not Israel. This is why Hezbollah had a relatively vast deployment in Syria, although it did not have much of a presence near the Syrian border with Israel, so Hezbollah could not have done much against Israel. Furthermore, its main firepower, the rockets, is in Lebanon, not in Syria.

Another reason why Hezbollah did not attack Israel from Syria was that Syria was considered by Hezbollah to be a battlefield whereas Lebanon is home, and the group had sworn to protect it. Hezbollah restrained itself, following the Israeli bombardments inside Syria. But when Israel bombed inside Lebanon on February 24, 2014, Hezbollah retaliated by laying down an IED that almost injured Israeli troops along the border between Israel and Lebanon. Hezbollah did that, although it risked an escalation that could have led to a war with Israel, and the group did not want it at the time. Israel also strove to avoid such a war. Therefore, because of Hezbollah, Israel attacked only in Syria, not in Lebanon. In that sense Israel, unofficially of course, accepted that its attacks on weapon deliveries, which were sent from Syria to Hezbollah in Lebanon, were contained by Hezbollah to Syria solely. The IDF continued to watch and monitor Hezbollah in Lebanon by gathering intelligence, including with aircraft that flew over Lebanon, but they did not bomb there.

Assad, during the Israeli strikes, did not dispatch his fighters to intercept Israeli aircraft, knowing the IAF has a huge edge in air combat. Assad's air defense did launch an antiaircraft missiles. Assad, with Iranian aid, could have hit back without admitting it, by conducting a terror attack against a Jewish /Israeli objective around the world. Assad could have also retaliated directly with his long-range surface-to-surface missiles and rockets. Some of them would have probably missed their targets. Others might have been intercepted by the Arrow and Iron Dome systems. If the fire from Syria had continued, the IAF would have bombed launchers of missiles and rockets, although hunting them inside Syria would not have been easy because there are many places to hide them. Yet Assad did not want an escalation let alone a war, since in a matter of days Assad would have lost his air force. This would have opened the way for his foes inside Syria to annihilate his regime. In the end, Assad's military low point forced him to contain his actions against Israel.

Israel attacked the deliveries, not the Assad regime itself, hoping to deter Assad from sending more weapons to Hezbollah without getting entangled in a war against Assad. Assad did not retaliate, but he also did not stop providing Hezbollah with weapons. Neither Israel nor Assad had any interest in a war. Even after his victories in 2016–18, Assad was still too occupied with the rebels, and even without fighting them, he was well aware that he was too weak to open another front against Israel.

By launching its raids, Israel contained Hezbollah's buildup, which reduced its ability to harm Israel in a time of war, but each time Israel attacked, it increased the probability of an escalation that might have led to a war. Assad, Iran, and Hezbollah also did not seek war, yet by continuing with the deliveries they provoked Israel and raised the chances of a confrontation. Both sides were playing with fire.

Each time Israel bombed inside Syria, the Israeli population was not put on any alert. Israeli civilians knew about the air raid only after it happened. Israel did not warn its people, assuming correctly that Assad would not retaliate. It was a calculated risk. The Israeli government exposed its people to Syrian retribution in order to gain tactical surprise during the air attack and as part of denying Israel's bombardments. Israel wished to avoid a possible escalation. If it had called its people to run for shelters, not only Syria but Iran and Hezbollah might have assumed that Israel was about to start a war against one of them and they might have opened fire at Israel. Since Israel could not have known for sure if and where Assad might have retaliated, then it was difficult to decide which part of Israel would be in danger. Assad has long-range missiles that could hit every spot in Israel, including its population centers. The risk Israel took was part of its ongoing effort to contain Hezbollah's buildup.

In 2017 Israel's air strikes in Syria seemed "to underline to Hezbollah and its Iranian and Syrian allies the extent of Israeli intelligence penetration of their activities. This, too, may further Israeli deterrence, since an enemy that considers itself too exposed may be reluctant to risk entering into a larger conflict."[15] On September 5, 2017, the IAF bombed a research and production center in Syria. That strike was different from the previous ones. Amos Yadlin claimed that Israel strove to prevent Assad and Hezbollah from producing advanced weapons.[16] It was a new stage in containing Hezbollah's military buildup.

On February 10, 2018, an Iranian unmanned air vehicle (UAV) was shot down by an Israeli gunship, soon after the UAV penetrated northeastern Israel. Israel retaliated immediately by attacking the command and control center of that Iranian UAV, which was located deep inside Syria. In response, a barrage of antiaircraft was launched from Syria. As a result, one Israeli F-16I crashed inside Israel, so Israelis conducted a vast attack on several Syrian antiaircraft batteries and airfields.[17] It was the most severe event since Israel bombed the Syrian reactor in 2007. Yet all sides avoided another move, since all of them wanted to contain this major incident and to prevent further escalation.

On May 9, 2018, the Islamic Revolutionary Guard Corps (IRGC) fired twenty rockets into the Golan Heights.[18] In response, twenty-eight Israeli F-16s and F-15s bombed fifty positions into Syria, belonging to the IRGC. Assad's SA-2, SA-17, SA-22, and SA-5 air defense batteries fired dozens of missiles, but they missed. Five of the Syrian antiaircraft batteries were destroyed by the IAF.[19] The Israeli bombardments were considered to be one of the largest in recent years "and the biggest against Iranian targets."[20] It was a major escalation, yet it was still part of the Israeli effort to contain the Iranian presence in Syria without going to war. Iran and Syria also did not seek a war. Syria was too weak and Iran had to concentrate on responding to the withdrawal of the United States from the JCPOA on May 8.

In late May 2018 the U.S. House of Representatives shelved a Republican lawmaker's proposal for the United States to recognize Israeli sovereignty in the Golan Heights."[21] In spite of its support for Israel, the United States still avoided officially accepting the Israeli annexation of the Golan Heights. It could complicate Israel's steps in protecting the Golan Heights, since its foes could claim that they fight to liberate this territory, as the Palestinians have been arguing in regard to the West Bank.

The Iranian Presence in Syria

Since 1979 Iran and Syria have been allies.[22] Syria and Israel had peace talks in the 1990s and in 2008 as well. Yet Joseph Olmert claimed that Syria "was never ready to renounce its strategic alliance with Iran in order to achieve peace with Israel, even if the reward were the return of the entire Golan."[23] It had to do with Israel's hope that a peace treaty with Syria would reduce and maybe end the ties between Syria and Iran, which would help Israel to contain Iran. Sunni-led Arab states, even when they did not support peace talks with Israel, also wanted to cause a split between Iran and Syria as part of containing Iran. Among Arab states Syria has been the most pro-Iranian over the years, such as during the Iran-Iraq war in the 1980s.

In 1982 Hafez al Assad managed to crush a rebellion without getting Iranian aid, while in the civil war that started in 2011 Bashar al Assad became dependent on Iranian support. Iran has been invested heavily in Assad, although Iran was involved in other confrontations, in Iraq and Yemen. Iran needs Syria to contain Israel. Iran was also aware that Assad's downfall would have shown that Iran failed to save its closest ally among Arab rulers, with all the ramifications this would have had on Iran's prestige in the Middle East.

Iran claimed it fights in Syria in order to protect Shiite holy shrines, but there were claims that almost all those sites are actually "burial places of ancient Jewish prophets or Sunni Muslim theologians and scholars." Syria also "has always had a black image in Iranian religious folklore as the base of Ummayads whose caliphate was destroyed by an Iranian revolt led by Abu-Muslim Khorasani. Seen by Iranian mullahs, Damascus is regarded as "Gateway to Hell" because it was there that, according to folklore, the head of Hussein bin Ali, the third Shiite Imam, was presented to the Umayyad Caliph Yazid." Iran tries to present Syrian Alawites as "almost Shiites," who deserve protection like those in Lebanon.

Yet "not a single Ayatollah has agreed to cancel the countless historic fatwas that castigate Alawites as 'heretics' or even crypto-Zoroastrians." It could affect the willingness of Syrian Alawites to support Iran, although they could do that even without being recognized as Shiites.[24] Others did the same, including Sunnis like Hamas, for the same reason: to receive Iranian aid.

By 2015 it seems that Saudi Arabia managed to contain Iran in Syria.[25] Saudi Arabia was eager to bring down Assad. However, a collapse of Assad's regime, a major Iranian ally in the Levant, may have convinced Iran to loosen its hold there and focus on the area near Iran in the Persian Gulf. Israel would have benefited from that shift while Saudi Arabia and other Arab Gulf states might have gotten more negative attention from Iran.

By 2018 Assad and his allies had the upper hand in Syria. Iran tried to exploit that to run Syria or at least part of it. Israel strongly opposes that idea. Israel does not want Iran to do to Syria what Iran did with the Gaza Strip and mostly with Lebanon: to turn countries and territories around Israel into an Iranian fire base against Israel. Hamas sometimes had severe disputes with Iran, which led to a rift between them following the Syrian civil war. Hezbollah in Lebanon has been much more obedient to Iran. However, the threat to Israel from the Gaza Strip became more serious as Hamas managed, with Iranian aid, to increase the range of its rockets so they could hit deeper inside Israel. The same happened with Hezbollah in Lebanon on a much bigger scale than in the Gaza Strip.

By early 2018 Iran had lost 2,100 troops in Syria.[26] Iran had 82,000 fighters in Syria under its direct control: 3,000 troops of the IRGC, 9,000 fighters from Hezbollah, 10,000 gunmen from Shiite militias, based on recruits from Iraq, Afghanistan, etc., and 60,000 gunmen from Syria itself.[27] In November 2017 Prime Minister Netanyahu and Defense Minister Lieberman expressed their rejection to the establishing of an Iranian stronghold inside Syria. Israel was concerned that Iran would have air, naval, and land bases inside Syria, which could serve to strike Israel. Israel should not underestimate this threat but also not overestimate it either.

Since 1948 Syria has been an enemy of Israel. Prior to the Syrian civil war there were periods when up to six Syrian divisions were deployed near the Golan Heights, with thousands of tanks, artillery pieces, and so forth. They could have launched a massive surprise offensive, storming the Golan Heights while firing hundreds of thousands of shells and rockets. Compared with that, the Iranian order of battle in Syria is far weaker with fewer troops and weapon systems like tanks and artillery.

In containing Iran inside Syria, Israel has a kind of an ally in Assad. Like Israel, Assad is not an Iranian, Persian, or a religious extremist. Unlike Israel, he is a Syrian nationalist. It is also important to remember that there were always conflicts of interests between the Assad regime and Iran, long before the Syrian civil war, including with regard to Israel. Assad also proved he will do anything to stay in power, including gassing and massacring his own people. He did not do all those horrible actions while taking huge risks and investing so much to beat a tough internal foe just to let Iran take over his country. As in Iraq in Syria, the local Arab government collaborates with Iran against their common enemy. Assad had required Iranian assistance to contain the rebels, but after his victory Assad had to contain Iranian influence inside Syria. Israel was not sure if it wanted Assad to survive, but it sought to contain the Iranian presence in Syria.

During the Syrian civil war, there were clashes between Assad and his rivals on the border of the Golan Heights. During the exchange of fire, some of it landed in the Golan Heights. Even when Assad's forces were not the ones to blame for that, Israel retaliated by striking Assad's positions. Israel could do the same if attacked from Syria by one of Iran's proxies there. Israel could undermine Assad's rule such as by attacking his air force. After investing so much in helping Assad, Iran will not want to see all of that go to waste. Iran therefore might hesitate in provoking Israel from Syria. Iran might contain its own actions in this matter.

Israel might hesitate to confront Iran officially by accusing Iran of starting a war from Syria. However, it might be a way to prove to Iran that it could not run a proxy war against Israel without paying a price; Iran will be attacked directly if an Iranian protégée confronts Israel from Syria. In the past, when Israel fought against Hamas and Hezbollah, Iran was safe, but that does not mean it will be like that in the future.

Is There an Iranian Threat to Israel from Syria?

Iran needs to protect itself not only against possible Israeli bombardments but also against the United States and Arab Gulf states, mostly Saudi Arabia and the UAE. Allocating crack Iranian units to Syria could help Iran against Israel but not against the United States or Arab Gulf states. While Syria is a kind of buffer between Iran and Israel, it is not the case with regard to the U.S. military, Gulf states, and Iran.

There are more reasons why Iran might contain its deployment in Syria. Iran assimilated since 2016 the S-300, an advanced anti-aircraft system, one that Iran can deploy in Syria. From there Iranian air defense can monitor and intercept Israeli aircraft while they are still inside Israel. However, sending Iran's best systems such as the S-300 to Syria will leave dozens of key sites in Iran exposed, such as those that have to do with nuclear, oil, and gas infrastructure. Camps and headquarters of Iran's regime and Revolutionary Guard will be at risk, too. All those places require Iran to deploy near them its most modern air defense. The same goes with Iran's aircraft, armor, and so forth. Iran can send units to Syria and then recall them when required, but it can take time, and until they return, Iran will be vulnerable.

Iran uses proxies in order not to take responsibility. Yet it will be more difficult to do that if Iran deploys weapon systems in Syria that are clearly Iranian, such as the S-300. Iran also avoided giving its proxies chemical weapons. Iran might therefore avoid sending the S-300 to its proxies in Syria.

Iran's air force is quite frail.[28] Its old fighters such as F-4, F-5, F-14 and MiG-29 are no match to Israel's F-15I and F-16I. Even if Iranian aircraft challenge their Israeli counterparts over Syria, the IAF will have the upper hand, which will humiliate Iran. When Iran's proxies absorbed a hit, Iran could have blamed them for that, even when they were trained and armed by Iran. But it could not do that if its aircraft, with their Iranian crews, will be beaten by the IDF.

If Iran attacks Israel from Syria, then Israel can justify its actions as self-defense, since the frontline will be in the Golan Heights. In contrast, there are those in Iran who oppose the enormous investments in the war in Syria. For Iran the war in Iraq against ISIS made sense because it was close to home, while the war in Syria ran far from Iran. If after the long and costly war in Syria Iran is entangled again in a fight there and against a stronger rival, Israel, which means paying a higher price, it could cause resentment inside Iran against the regime.

Iran and its protégés might not be able to gather all their forces in the Golan Heights if they continue to face other challenges in Syria. Furthermore, Iran does not possess a formidable conventional military, one that has a significant and capable armor corps, since Iran relies on a symmetric warfare. Even if Iran concentrates its units and partners in the Golan Heights, they will still be too weak to seize any territory in the Golan Heights, considering the might of the IDF. The main danger to Israel will be from guerrilla and terrorist raids, which is a problem but not as severe as a massive conventional offensive like the one the Syrian military carried out in the Golan Heights in 1973.

Israel will enjoy short supply lines if it confronts Iran in the Golan Heights. In contrast, for Iran transferring large amounts of supply and manpower, during a long period of time, by relying on a communication line that stretches more than 1,000 km, might not be that easy. Iran will have to invest a lot of efforts in securing this "Tehran express" from possible attacks in Iraq and Syria by Sunnis who are hostile to Iran like the Kurds, who might confront Iran with or without collaborating with Israel. The IDF, mostly with its aircraft and special forces, will attack this Iranian route.

It will be a challenge for Iran to protect long convoys. Even if they are smaller, the IAF can still find them. As for attacks from the ground, the smaller convoys will be less defended by armed units because Iran could not attach a major force to defend any convoy. Furthermore, Iranian armored vehicles, including tanks, will be at risk all over Syria. Syria is quite big, 185,000 km2, so Iranian vehicles can hide and maneuver there, but the frontline in the Golan Heights is a much more limited sector. There Iranian vehicles will be in danger because of Israeli aircraft, artillery, and tanks.

Iran might mix civilian and military supplies together in the same convoy to make it harder for aircraft to strike the military cargo solely. Yet sending civilian products such as food and gas could be regarded as part of a military effort, which will make it a legitimate target. For Syrian anti-Iranian groups that will storm the convoys, whatever they capture there, including civilian goods, will be the spoils of war, which will encourage those groups to conduct those raids.

Other Iranian units in Syria will also have to protect themselves, particularly aircraft that have to return to their airfields so the IDF knows where to find them. Some Iranian aircraft can be deployed outside the base, mostly gunships, but there they will not be provided with the same services and protection that a military airfield gives.

Iran uses the Mezzeh air base near Damascus to send supplies to Hezbollah in Lebanon. Israel's intelligence often managed to find out about those deliveries, which enabled the IAF to bomb them. This task will be more difficult if Iran establishes an airport deeper inside Syria.[29] However, from there it will take longer to send the cargo to Lebanon by land, which will give the IDF an opportunity to strike it. A remote air base might need heavy protection by Syrian aircraft and air defense.

Iran therefore might have a harder fight than it had in the Syrian civil war or in Iraq and Yemen for that matter. Israel is much more powerful than all the enemies Iran has been clashing with around the Middle East in recent years. In its war with Iraq in the 1980s, Iraq had a huge conventional military that suffered defeats but also managed to inflict major blows to Iran, and the IDF is better than the Iraqi military was in the 1980s. In the bottom line in a war in Syria against Israel, Iran might absorb heavy losses, leaving it weaker, which will damage its image in the region.

Iran exploited the wars in Iraq and Syria to create what was called a bridge from Iran to the Mediterranean Sea. It also seeks to possess a harbor on the shores of Syria in the Mediterranean Sea, but this goal causes friction between Iran and Russia, since Russia wants the same. It might be easier for Iran to get access to the Mediterranean Sea by using Lebanon. The Lebanese government is fragile and could not control Hezbollah, which is part of the government. Lebanon has been contained by Hezbollah, which can do whatever it wants. So Lebanon might not be able to resist much if Iran seizes one of the Lebanese ports. Iran does not have to do it officially to reduce the criticism against it, but everyone will know who runs that harbor.

Even if Iran gets access to a Syrian-Lebanese port, each time an Iranian ship arrives or departs, it will have to bypass all of Africa. Egypt, which strongly opposes Iran's regional ambitions, might not permit Iranian vessels to cross the Suez Canal. Such a constraint will make it much more complicated for Iran to use its Syrian-Lebanese naval base. In contrast, Israel's ports are several dozens of kilometers from Syria and Lebanon, which will make it easier for Israel to concentrate its naval forces there, using it to overcome and to sink an Iranian vessel. It will be an opportunity for Israel to humiliate Iran.

If Iran tries to produce a nuclear weapon, then Israel might strike Iran's nuclear sites. The Israeli raid might be considered an aggressive step by many in the world. However, if Iran attacks Israel from Syria, then Israel could bomb Iran itself, including its nuclear facilities.

Israel should emphasize the problems Iran creates in Syria not only to Israel but to others as well. Yet some issues are relevant only to Israel. Furthermore Israel is risking making too much noise about a matter that is not crucial. After all, as long as Iran does not hold nuclear weapons, then Iran cannot threaten Israel's existence. Israel should not underestimate Iran but also not exaggerate either in this matter. Israel should not make Iran look stronger than it really is, because by that Israel plays into its enemy's hands. Iran wants to be seen as a regional power and as a rising and dominant state in the Middle East. Israel also does not want to be seen as scared of the Iranian presence in Syria. Israel's former rivals who signed peace with it, Egypt and Jordan or other Arab states that are willing to cooperate with Israel, like Saudi Arabia, might think that Israel is a paper tiger. The United States also might assume that Israel loses its nerve, so it might not be such an effective and reliable ally.

Unlike in the past, mostly between 1948 and 1982, Israel does not face an Arab coalition. Actually there could be an alliance between Israel and Arab states against Iran. Iran has allies, but even with them it will not have the same military might that Israel confronted in the past. Israel therefore should have reduced its rhetoric in regard to Iran's presence in Syria and saved its warning to Iran's nuclear project, the main danger Iran imposes not only for Israel and Arab states but to other states as well, including in Europe. Iran, as a nuclear power, will also put at risk those that are currently its allies like Russia.

Israel does not wish to attract too much attention to the Golan Heights, since no other state besides the United States recognizes that it is an official part of Israel. (The Golan Heights were annexed in 1981.) If Israel emphasizes too much how the Iranian grip in Syria is a danger to Israel and the Golan Heights in particular, it might backfire because the international discussion could focus on the Golan Heights. After all, Assad accepted the deployment of Iranian militias in his country while mentioning in public that he still intends to reclaim the Golan Heights. Israel does not wish to be in a situation where the debate is how Israel should return the Golan Heights and not if and how much influence Iran should have in Syria.

Hezbollah in Syria

An Iranian domination of Syria could bring a war between Syria and Israel, "which would really mean an Iran-Israel war, one that would not be limited to Syria."[30] Both Iran and Israel have an interest in containing such a war to Syria. Iran and Israel might also oppose that the battles will spill over into Lebanon. Israel would rather not face Hezbollah's rockets. Iran might not want to involve Hezbollah, in order to preserve the group in case Israel attacks Iran and its nuclear sites.

Hezbollah's involvement in Syria dragged Lebanon into that war, yet not on a major scale. There were clashes along the border between the two states and some attacks deeper inside Lebanon, mostly in Beirut. Israel seeks to weaken Hezbollah, as part of containing it. If battles between Hezbollah and Syrian armed groups had spread much more into Lebanon, it could have forced Hezbollah to throw into combat all its forces, not only part of them, as it did in Syria. Even if Hezbollah had won the war, it might have cost the group more than it did in Syria. In addition, some of its infrastructure in Lebanon, which was built to confront Israel, might have been damaged, which did not happen when Hezbollah fought in Syria. Therefore a war inside Lebanon could have served Israel's interests. On the other hand, the fight inside Lebanon might have gotten close to Israel. Israel preferred to contain the war to Syria, as part of pushing the battles as far as possible from Israel. It also does not want Lebanon, following a major war there, to turn into a fail state, which could be a feeding ground for extremists.

On January 19, 2015, an air strike near the Golan Heights killed a high-ranking commander of Hezbollah and an Iranian general, Mohammad Ali Allahdadi.[31] Israel denied it bombed them. Unofficially senior Israeli figures claimed they did not know that the Iranian general was there. Israel conducted that strike, but maybe it was not aware of the presence of the Iranian general. Israel did not seek an escalation by killing a top Iranian officer. On the other hand, it could have been a message to Iran how far Israel is willing to go in preventing both Hezbollah and Iran from establishing a base near the Golan Heights.

Hezbollah does not need Syria in order to strike all over Israel with rockets and missiles, since the group already can do that from Lebanon. It could help Hezbollah to deploy some of its rockets and missiles in Syria as well, in order to increase the area the IDF will have to scan in search of them. It has to do mostly with the mobile rockets and missiles. Yet then Hezbollah will have to split its forces between Lebanon and Syria, not a minor challenge for that group, which has at most 30,000 men. In this sense Hezbollah rather contains the war to Lebanon.

4

Russian Military Involvement in Syria

The Russian military intervention in the Syrian civil war had a major impact on the war. It also affected Russian-U.S. relations as part of their new cold war. Israel had to take that into consideration during its air strikes inside Syria. Russia also maneuvered in regard to Iran, which is both an ally and a rival.

Russian Intervention

Russia has had a long relationship with Syria. Since the 1950s the Soviet Union has given Syria military, diplomatic, and economic support. In 2005 Russia agreed to write off most of Syria's $13 billion debt, which had been accumulated during the Soviet era.[1] This has not stopped Russia from investing heavily again in Syria since 2015, including by sending Russian troops there to fight.

In 2015, in spite of its nuclear arsenal, the Russian military was considered to be "a paper tiger."[2] Russia is not as strong as the Soviet Union was, but it is still a world power.

Since October 2015 Russia, which supports Assad, has inflicted blows to Syrian rebel groups. But it has never dispatched into Syria the same number of troops that were sent to Afghanistan during the war there in the 1980s. Around 100,000 Soviets troops were deployed in Afghanistan, whereas Russia has sent only a few thousand to Syria. Most of its presence there has been based on air power. Russia also dispatched ground units, mostly to secure its camps in Syria and special forces who participated in battles. The war in Afghanistan is a bitter memory for Russia. Syria did not become a "mini Afghanistan." Russia actually managed to handle the Syrian quagmire by defeating and containing its hybrid foes there.

In late September 2017 Russia announced that its troops had eliminated "approximately 45,000 militants, including over 210 field commanders, about 800 training camps, 550 munition factories, and 3,000 units of military equipment." Russia added that its military operation disrupted the rebels' "revenues, severely undermining their capabilities in recruiting new adherents, buying weaponry, and disseminating jihadist ideology. The Russian Air Force group in Syria destroyed 300 terrorist-controlled oil fields, pipelines, and refineries." Russia also claimed that "since February 2016, it had carried out about 1,000 independent humanitarian actions, delivering over 2,000 tons of food, medical supplies, and essentials to the civilians. Damascus, Aleppo, Afrin, and Deir ez-Zor, as well as settlements in Homs and Idlib provinces, are only a few of the places where Russian servicemen, at the risk of their lives, distributed humanitarian aid." Russia also argued in September 2017 that "during the past year they provided medical treatment to 34,000 patients. In Aleppo alone the total number of their patients amounts to 12,500 people." Russian field engineers defused explosive objects in territories such as in Aleppo. They neutralized "35,412 high explosives and 20,174 improvised explosive devices (IEDs)" planted by the rebels.[3] Russia therefore argued that it gained several achievements, but others have serious doubts about all of that. Russia was accused of committing war crimes, like when Britain claimed that "bunker-busting and incendiary bombs" were in widespread use by Russian aircraft when they attacked 275,000 civilians living in Aleppo.[4] The Russian contribution in containing the rebels in Syria cost the population there dearly.

Russia and Israel

The Soviet Union supported the establishment of Israel in 1948 and even provided the new Jewish state with weapons through Czechoslovakia. Yet in the 1950s the Soviet Union became the patron of Arab states, delivering them weapons on a grand scale. The crisis that led to the 1967 war started after the Soviet Union told Egypt that Israel was about to attack the Golan Heights. It was not true, although eventually Israel did so. Following the Israeli conquests in that war, the Soviet Union cut diplomatic ties with Israel.[5]

Henry Kissinger claimed during the 1973 war that like the United States the Soviet Union did not assume, prior to the war, that the Arabs could defeat the IDF.[6] Syria did manage to gain some ground in the Golan Heights, but then its forces were pushed back, and Israel launched an offensive inside Syria. The IDF conquered about 500 km2 and gradually approached Damascus. The Soviet Union sent Syria thousands of weapon systems such as aircraft, armored vehicles, and artillery pieces. This massive aid, which reached Syria before the war, made it possible for Syria to attack. During the war itself the Soviet Union poured supplies into Syria. There were a few cases in which the IDF hit Soviet transport aircraft and ships that delivered this arsenal in order to contain Soviet aid to Syria.

Following the 1973 war and during the 1980s, the Soviet Union continued to support Syria, including by providing weapons.[7] There was also a possibility that the Soviet Union would have dispatched troops if the IDF had advanced again toward the Syrian capital city. It could have happened if Syria had made another attempt to retake the Golan Heights and then Israel would have retaliated or if Israel had launched a preemptive strike, aiming to stop a Syrian offensive. There was a confrontation between Israel and Syria in 1982, but it was contained both in its scale and in the size of the battlefield, since it took place only in Lebanon. The collapse of the Soviet Union in 1991 was a major blow to Syria.

In the first years of the civil war Assad managed to hold on by relying on his own troops. Yet during 2015 Assad found himself at a low point due to the ongoing decline of his military and the successes of his foes in the battlefield. In the 1967 and 1973 wars there was a possibility that Soviet troops would have been deployed in order to protect Syria against Israel. In October 2015 Russian forces were sent to Syria to save the Assad regime from its internal enemies. This support, together with massive aid from Iran and Hezbollah, enabled Assad not only to hold key areas such as Damascus, Homos, and Hamas but also to gain the initiative in Aleppo.

Israel knows that Russia has quite a military might, and it also has an increasing political presence in the region, especially in Syria. Russia has been well aware of the tight relations between Israel and the United States, yet Russia could improve its relations with Israel. After all, many of the Jews who established Israel came from Russia or Eastern European countries where there was a strong Russian influence. Since the early 1990s about a million people have immigrated to Israel from the Soviet Union, which is a lot in a small state like Israel, which had fewer than 9 million inhabitants in 2018. There also have been ties in tourism and trade between the two states, and Russia considers Israel to be a powerful regional player due to its military might.

Russia assumes that Israel will be very careful not to provoke Russia. However, Israel did prove in the past that it was willing to challenge the Soviet Union. In the war of attrition (1967–70) the Soviet Union sent huge military aid and troops to Egypt. They have participated in the fight against Israeli aircraft across the Suez Canal. In one famous battle the IAF shot down five Soviet fighter jets. Israel does not want to repeat such a collision with Russia. It is much better to cooperate than to go back to the days of the Cold War.

King Abdullah II of Jordan claimed in January 2016 that "Jordanian and Israeli F-16s confronted Russian fighter aircraft as they approached the southern Syrian border. . . . 'The Russians were shocked and understood they could not mess with us.'"[8] However, this was a unique case. Israel, which stayed outside the Syrian civil war, did not seek to change that, let alone fight against Russia. Russia was not the USSR, and its military presence in Syria was quite limited, based on several dozen aircraft. Therefore, theoretically the IDF alone, with no American support, could have overcome them, but it was clear that Israel had no interest in confronting Russia.

Israel could have considered joining Russia as part of an international effort to end the war in Syria. Israel was not sure if it wanted to have Assad in power or not, but after the Russian intervention, particularly when it seemed that Russia, Iran, and Assad had gained the upper hand, then Israel could have tried to benefit from that by collaborating with the winning side. However, Israel was very reluctant to support Assad in containing the rebels because of all the horrible crimes he has committed. Iran would have also strongly opposed any cooperation with Israel.

Israel had hoped once that a peace treaty with Assad might cause him to abandon his alliance with Iran, in return for massive U.S. aid as part of a peace accord. But peace negotiations were not on the table during the civil war. Even when Assad came out as the winner, it was clear that neither Israel nor Assad thought about renewing the peace talks. The last round was in 2008. Although Israel did not try to use the war in Syria to topple Assad, he accused Israel of helping the rebels for propaganda reasons.

Since Israel and Syria have had peace talks in the past, in spite of the wars that occurred between them, they could do it after a war in which Israel was not involved. Russia might approve that, particularly if Russia could be the broker and by that to gain the credit, if there were an agreement, hoping to use it to increase Russian influence in the Middle East. Yet Iran will oppose it, exploiting its grip over Assad. Israel too might not be eager to sign a peace treaty with Assad due to his war crimes and since it will require Israel to return the Golan Heights. This might be too much of a cost to pay for peace with Assad, who could be considered to be too weak. He might not survive for long if Russia or Iran do not continue to support him. If Assad falls, his regime might go with him. Those who replace him will keep the Golan Heights, but they might ignore the peace with Israel. Furthermore Assad poses much less of a threat to Israel, compared with the last time they had peace talks. From the Israeli perspective, Assad's military potential is quite contained after losing so much during the war. Therefore it might not be worth it for Israel to make major concessions to Assad, let alone give him the Golan Heights.

Russia assisted Assad to regain territory he lost but did not pressure Israel to return the Golan Heights to Assad. Russia sought to help Assad to contain the rebels by capturing areas that are more important to Assad than the Golan Heights due to their size and location, like those in northwestern Syria. Furthermore Russia's main interest in Syria has been to secure its bases in northwestern Syria, while the Golan Heights is in southwestern Syria. Russia needs Assad to hold areas near Russian bases, including in Idlib, where there are radical Islamists who concern Russia because they have partners; some of them are in Russia. Those areas are also held by those who are much weaker than Israel, so it is much easier to defeat them. Russia did not want Assad to get into a major dispute with Israel.

On March 17, 2016, Maj. Gen. Yair Golan, IDF deputy chief of staff, said that with regard to the Russian presence in Syria, bilateral deconfliction mechanisms, aimed at preventing possible collisions, "were tested daily" over the skies of Syria. "We immediately dealt with and resolved problems" he claimed.[9] Yet the Russians did not always transmit notices to Israel before they "embark[ed] on aerial activity in regions tangential to Israeli borders or Israeli air force activity."[10] Israel continued its strikes inside Syria by launching missiles from outside Syria and doing that at night in order to avoid running into Russian planes that usually fly during the day.[11]

Russia deployed in Syria S-300 and S-400, advanced anti-aircraft systems that cover almost all of Israel, allowing it to monitor Israeli aircraft.[12] On May 9, 2018, the IAF launched a major attack in Syria, aimed mostly against Iranian targets. Israel informed Russia ahead of the strikes but did not disclose the targets.[13] Dennis Ross mentioned in late May 2018 that Israel tried to persuade Russia to contain Iranian deployment in Syria.[14] Israel therefore tried to maneuver, with both military and diplomatic measures, to urge Russia not only to avoid containing Israel's air strikes but also to help Israel in containing Iran's presence in Syria.

According to Eran Etzion, who was head of policy planning

at Israel's Ministry of Foreign Affairs, in July 2016 "contrary to media reports, the degree to which Israel and Russia's interests in Syria actually coincide is highly questionable."[15] Rachel Brandenburg, director of the Atlantic Council's Middle East Security Initiative, said on May 4, 2018, that "Russia may have the right channels of communication to be able to de-escalate a confrontation between Israel and Iran and Syria. To do so effectively, however, also requires leverage. I'm more skeptical Russia has sufficient leverage to successfully play such a role."[16] Israel was not sure what Russia would do if there were a war between Israel and Hezbollah in Lebanon.[17] Russia could try to contain Israeli operations in such a war. The IDF might be permitted by Russia, officially or not, to bomb in Lebanon and even in Syria as long as it did not hit Russian troops, camps, or planes. Since Hezbollah is concentrated in Lebanon, where Russia does not have a military presence, and since Lebanon is much less important to Russia than Syria, then the Russian factor might not be a major constraint for Israel during a war with Hezbollah.

Russia is familiar with Syria, which helps Russia in gathering intelligence. However, Russia has to allocate resources to take care of other priorities such as the war in Ukraine while Israel concentrates on countries near it, such as Syria. It gives Israel an edge in collecting data. Israel could help Russia by sharing information about Syrian outfits that might attack Russian troops and camps. In return Russia could use its influence in Syria to contain the Iranian presence there. Russia might help in preventing or at least reducing the ability of Iran and Hezbollah to turn Syria into a springboard to launching attacks against Israel.

Russia might try to restart the peace talks between Israel and the Palestinians. Russia could be a mediator, since it has ties with both the PA and Israel. Russia strives to present itself as a world power, one that the international community and particularly the United States could not ignore. After proving its military might in Syria, Russia could show its skills in diplomacy in the Middle East. Russia would be very pleased to help in reaching an accord between Israel and the Palestinians, especially after so many have tried and failed. Such an achievement will boost Russia's position. This status could help Russia to change its image as an aggressive power that relies on force to one that promotes peace.

The United States and Syria

In Syria, during the civil war, the Obama administration backed some of the rebels, but they did not receive much American aid because of the difficulty of both identifying them as moderate and trusting their capabilities. This made it harder to create a powerful pro-American force that could have overthrown Assad and secured the torn country. The United States, in contrast to its approach in Iraq during the war there, did not endorse Assad, although he was against ISIS. From a U.S. perspective there were several reasons for this policy. First, the Syrian and the Iraqi regimes had similar flaws, including discriminating against Sunnis in their country, yet in Iraq there was not an ongoing mass killing of Sunni civilians, certainly not on the same level as it was in Syria. Second, Iraq has much more oil than Syria, with all its implications on the global oil market. Third, Syria has strategic importance due to its location, yet Iraq might be more vital for the United States, since it has a presence, albeit a limited one, in the Gulf near Iran and Arab states, where there are U.S. bases. Fourth, the Iraqi Shiite government represented the majority in that country whereas Assad relied on a small minority, so Iraq has better chances to survive as a state. Furthermore, with or without Assad, the various groups in Syria would have continued to clash with each other. In Iraq there might be a higher probability of uniting the country, maybe as a federation, in spite of all the deep disputes inside the Shiite community and between the Shiites and Kurds and Sunnis. Fifth, after investing so much blood and treasure in Iraq, the United States was not willing to lose that country. In Syria there was not much U.S. involvement to begin with.

Although the United States was against Assad, the superpower focused on containing ISIS, not Assad, which reduced the friction between the United States and both its global rival, Russia, and its regional adversary, Iran. This U.S. approach created tension between it and Turkey and Arab states, mostly those in the Gulf that wanted to bring down Assad.

Russia and the United States

Following the 1991 war Saddam Hussein was at a low point not only because of his crushing defeat but also because he faced a rebellion. However, the United States did not use its forces to help topple him, which allowed Hussein to contain and eventually crush the mutiny. In 2003 the United States brought him down, although there was not then any uprising in Iraq, which could have served as a reason for American intervention. In 2011, during the Libyan civil war, the United States assisted but did not lead the effort to oust Muammar al-Gaddafi. Later, the Obama administration wanted to contain the Syrian civil war so that it would not destabilize the region, without sinking into another quagmire such as the one in Iraq. The United States, like Russia, strives to keep Syria from falling apart, but the United States does not want Syria to fall into the hands of Russia. Unlike Russia, the United States did not have much influence in Syria. However, the United States opposed that Russia would strengthen its position in Syria, which could help Russia in spreading its influence in the Middle East. The United States seeks to contain the Russian grip in that region.

The Obama administration did not carry out a limited strike in September 2013, following the use of chemical weapons (cw) by Assad, which was considered to be an American Red Line. Instead of attacking, the United States was part of an agreement that forced Assad to give up most of his cw. In late April 2017 an Israeli official claimed that Assad had up to 3 tons of cw, out of 1,200 tons he had had in the past.[18] The Obama administration absorbed a lot of criticism and lost credibility for not attacking in 2013, but such a strike might not have produced the results the agreement brought. Maybe a U.S. strike would have forced Assad to stop using cw, and in the beginning there were low expectations regarding the agreement that was achieved. Although Assad continued to use CW, the agreement had eventually significantly contained Assad's CW capabilities.

Israel had to adjust to the Russian military involvement in Syria. The United States, which bombed ISIS targets inside Syria, had to do that, too. Defense Secretary Ash Carter said on September 30, 2015, that there is a need "to insure we could avoid any unintended incidents over Syrian airspace" between American and Russian planes.[19] Israel and the United States sought to contain the Russian presence in Syria and vice versa, but all of them had to set up and follow procedures in order to avoid any clash between them.

On September 28, 2015, President Obama insisted on "transition away from Assad and to a new leader."[20] In 2014, when the United States started striking ISIS inside Syria, Assad stayed out of the way. Assad benefited from U.S. bombardments in both the military and the political level, since his argument was that he is part of the fight against ISIS. The Russian intervention strengthened Assad's case, yet the United States refused to see Russia or Assad as true allies in the war against ISIS. Israel, the United States, and Russia all agreed to contain ISIS and also that Assad should not be replaced by radical Islamic groups. This common ground gave them a base for certain cooperation, which was essential in avoiding friction between their militaries.

Russia wishes to protect its naval and air bases in northwestern Syria. Russia also wants to secure and expand Assad's grip in western Syria. The United States goes after ISIS, which is located mostly in eastern Syria, while Israel is focused on its border with Syria in the southwest. Therefore there are different priorities for Russia, the United States, and Israel with regard to sectors in Syria. However, sometimes there is an overlap between the sectors, which could lead to confusion, particularly if there is poor coordination. This issue has to do mostly with Russia and the United States, since the latter conducts more sorties in Syria than Israel does, which increases the probability of a collision between U.S. and Russian forces. Israel still has to be worried if it decides to strike deep inside Syria, like near the coast, where the Russian stronghold is. Israel bombed there on July 5, 2013, and might have to do that again in the future.

On November 24, 2015, a Russian plane was shot down by Turkey. It was an isolated incident, but it might have escalated. Turkey is part of NATO, so all the members of this powerful alliance, including the United States, are obligated to defend Turkey if Russia attacks Turkey. A showdown between Russia and NATO, not necessarily because of Turkey, is the worst case scenario and must be prevented, whatever the cost. It is the duty of both sides to show restraint by ignoring provocations and mistakes the other side commits. There has to be no skirmish between Russia and NATO, even at the expense of striking their enemies on the ground.

The United States launches sorties in Syria from bases in the region, such as in Turkey. Israel can't serve as a springboard for that purpose, and the same was true in other cases when the United States bombed Arab targets. This is because of the sensitivity in the region for the use of Israel as a base for American strikes inside Arab territory. Although U.S. planes bomb ISIS, the enemy of almost everyone in the Middle East, U.S. aircraft still have to stay out of Israeli airfields. Israel, for its own attacks, can send its planes from its own bases solely. Aircraft of both Israel and the United States, when they are on the ground, are in a safe place because they are deployed outside Syria. In contrast, Russia's jets and helicopters that are stationed inside Syria are vulnerable when they are on the ground, especially if they don't have hardened aircraft shelters. During the Syrian civil war, armed groups took several airfields from Assad. Those groups might not be able to seize a Russian airbase, but they could hit it with artillery and raids, aiming to disrupt its operations, inflict casualties, and undermine morale. This threat became a reality on December 31, 2017, when an attack on a Russian airfield in Syria destroyed seven aircraft. Western forces absorbed similar attacks in Afghanistan, like in a raid on a western airbase that occurred on September 14, 2012. As a result, eight planes were severely damaged or destroyed.

The United States seeks to see Russian forces leave Syria. Yet unlike the war in Afghanistan in the 1980s, the United States did not deliver antiaircraft missiles to anti-Russians groups in Syria, since those missiles could be turned against American planes as well. Maybe the United States could give moderate Syrian groups weapons like short-range rockets and antitank missiles. This arsenal, which will not threaten bases that the United States uses outside Syria, will make it easier for Syrian outfits to attack Russian camps inside Syria. On the other hand, such American military aid will raise the tension between the United States and Russia, and such friction should be avoided.

Militarily Israel, Russia, and the United States did not have to be worried about radical Islamic groups that have neither aircraft nor advanced air defense. So they were not supposed to fear that their planes would be intercepted by those outfits, particularly if the aircraft flies at high altitudes where they are safe from rebel fire. As for Assad, his air force and air defense failed in intercepting the Israeli aircraft that bombed inside Syria until the incident on February 10, 2018, when the IDF lost one plane to a Syrian missile. Still the Russians are more capable in this department, which worried and contained Israeli air activity over Syria. Russia might also give Assad advanced fighters and sophisticated antiaircraft missiles such as the S-300.

There are contacts between Israel and Sunni-led Arab states, aimed against their common foes, mostly Iran. Such an alliance will stay unofficial, due to the hardships of making it public, particularly as long as the Israeli-Palestinian conflict goes on. Yet if Sunni-led Arab states and Israel manage to overcome that and develop their ties, it will increase Russia's suspicion that Israel and those Arab states will create a bloc, together with the United States. Russia obviously prefers that such an Arab-Israeli alliance would be with Russia and not with the United States. Since the odds of that are quite low, Russia could try to contain as much as possible any partnership between Israel and Arabs, one that seems to favor the United States. If Russia cannot benefit and assumes that an Arab-Israeli-American pact is a threat, then Russia will act against it.

By helping Assad, Russia antagonized Arab Gulf states. Those Sunni-led Arab states gave aid to Syrian armed groups that oppose Assad. It was not enough, since Assad and therefore Russia won, but it did not bring Sunni-led Arab states like Saudi Arabia to boycott Russia. In late 2017 Saudi Arabia even signed on several arms deals with Russia. It was a missed opportunity for the United States that did not manage to exploit its influence on Arab Gulf states to turn them against Russia, as part of the American effort to contain the Russian grip in the Middle East.

In May 22, 2017, President Trump met Israeli prime minister Benjamin Netanyahu. They agreed that Syria needs "a political solution that will allow the Syrian people to return to secure environments and rebuild their lives."[21] Yet Israel and even the United States did not carry much weight in Syria, compared with Russia and Iran.

The U.S. decision in July 2017 to end the CIA's aid to rebels "was widely seen as an abandonment of any serious effort to stand up to the consolidation of Russian and Iranian hegemony in Syria."[22] In early June 2017 James Jeffrey claimed that if the United States does not block Iran in Syria, then Iran will emerge as "the dominant force in the region."[23] Preventing both Russia and Iran from using Syria was part of containing their influence in the region.

The United States and Russia agreed in 2017 that the Euphrates River would be a "deconfliction" line. Russia and its allies were supposed to stay west of the river while the east side had been under U.S. influence and its partners there. Russia and the United States therefore were each contained to part of Syria. The United States received areas where there are natural gas fields while Russia, Iran, and Assad gained control of areas where most of Syria's population is, together with access to the Mediterranean Sea and to the border with Israel. Israel would rather have pro-American forces as its neighbors.

Steven Cook called in March 2018 to give "the Israelis a green light to do what they believe is necessary to protect themselves from Iran and Hezbollah in Syria and Lebanon, obviating the need for Israeli leaders to constantly seek Moscow's assistance and reassurances."[24] Then and also during 2018 and early 2019 it was not clear if the United States is going to stay in Syria. Without the U.S. presence, Israel would have to rely much more on Russia in containing Iran in Syria.

Russia, Iran, and Hezbollah

Iran and Russia are allies as part of their fight in Syria, but Iran and Russia have all kinds of disputes, not only with regard to Syria but in the Caucasus and Central Asia as well. Furthermore, Russia helped Iran's nuclear program. Russia also provided Iran with advanced antiaircraft systems, the s-300 that protect Iranian nuclear sites. Yet Russia does not want Iran to produce a nuclear weapon, since it will make Iran stronger and encourage it to challenge Russia. Russia might oppose an Israeli strike against Iran's nuclear sites but might be pleased if Israel damaged Iran's nuclear capabilities.

There is an internal struggle inside the Assad regime between a pro-Russian faction, which has officers who were trained in Russia, and a pro-Iran faction.[25] Since Russia wants to strengthen its relations with Assad, it needs to weaken Assad's ties with Iran and reduce Iran's hold in Syria, a process that includes acting against Hezbollah. Israel prefers to have Assad, who answers to Russia but not to Iran.

Russia does not want Iran or Hezbollah to strike Israel from Syria without asking Assad or Russia, since it will undermine "the heart of the system Putin has so effectively constructed" in Syria.[26] From the Russian perspective, Israel, like Russia, seeks to avoid friction and an escalation with Syria, while Iran might try to provoke Israel from Syria. Israel therefore can assist Russia to get rid of or at least contain the Iranian presence in Syria.

Iran accepted the Russian involvement in Syria, although Iran objects to the intervention of world powers in the Middle East. Iran remembers that in the past Russia occupied part of Iran itself. Iran and Russia needed each other in order to save Assad, but Russia opposes the growing Iranian influence in Syria. Russia also wants to obtain U.S. concessions, such as in regard to sanctions on Russia, which could cause a conflict of interests between Iran and Russia about Syria. The relations between Russia and Hezbollah, an Iranian protégé, are part of the partnership between Iran and Russia. The tension between Iran and Russia reflects on the Russian approach toward Hezbollah. In Syria Russia therefore seeks to contain both Iran and Hezbollah.

On June 9, 2017, Russia's ambassador to Israel, Alexander Shein, said that Hamas and Hezbollah are both "radical organizations, which sometimes adhere to extremist political views." Yet according to him Russian law defines terrorist organizations as those that "intentionally conduct acts of terror in Russian territory or against Russian interests abroad—installations, embassies, offices, or citizens."[27] Therefore as long as Hezbollah did not attack Russians or their interests, then the group was not considered a terror organization by Russia. Russia did not care that Hezbollah has posed a threat to Israel and Jews around the world since the early 1980s, including Jews who came from Russia. At least Russia did not assist Hezbollah over the years as it did with the PLO when Palestinians conducted terrorist assaults against Israel.

For Russia, Hezbollah and Iran are not natural allies. It was just a necessity to join forces with radical Shiites, Iran and Hezbollah, against Sunnis, moderate and radical ones. Russia, until October 2015, preferred to stay out of the Syrian civil war and let Iran and Hezbollah carry the burden alone. When Russia assumed that Assad might lose, then it had to get more involved. Israel was not sure if it wanted Russia to save Assad. Israel certainly did not wish to see radical Islamists take over Syria. Israel had to tolerate that Russia intervened and cooperated with Iran. Israel has been watching Russia, Iran, and Hezbollah pay with blood and treasure for their Syrian adventure. Israel sought to see its enemies there clash and contain each other. Israel did not see Russia as a foe, but Israel might have hoped that Russia would decide in a certain stage to withdraw due to the cost of the war in Syria.

There might be a war between Israel and Hezbollah in Lebanon. In such a war Hezbollah will have to take its units out of Syria to face Israel in Lebanon. Hezbollah will need every man it can get. If Hezbollah loses the war while absorbing heavy casualties, it might not be able to resume its current deployment in Syria. Such a development will also impact Iran's position in Syria. This outcome will serve Russia and Israel, too, although Israel does not want to go to war and certainly not for that reason alone.

If a war between Israel and Hezbollah is against Russia's interests, then the latter could try "to restrict the freedom of action of both sides and to help settle the conflict."[28] Russia could even try to prevent such a war by putting pressure on Iran to stop the deliveries to Hezbollah. The group already poses quite a threat to Israel, but Iran wants to make its Lebanese protégé even more dangerous, in order to deter Israel from attacking Iran's nuclear sites. Meanwhile Iran does not seek war, but increasing Hezbollah's arsenal might cause a war. For Iran the survival of Assad is a top priority, and Iran has invested heavily in this matter. A war with Israel could bring down Assad, so Iran has to choose which is more important: upgrading Hezbollah's arsenal or securing Iran's ally in Damascus?

In Syria, Hezbollah fought rebels who had no aircraft. Hezbollah, on the other hand, following the Russian assistance, got used to enjoying air superiority. It meant that Hezbollah could have maneuvered to send supply and units from one place to another without fearing air attacks. Hezbollah also received air support from Russian aircraft, which was important, such as in storming an objective. In a war against Israel, the boot will be on the other foot. Hezbollah, which has no air force of its own, will have no air superiority and no air support while facing the powerful Israeli air force. Hezbollah, like the rebels in Syria, will be exposed to massive air bombardments that will inflict casualties, disrupt operations, and undermine motivation. It might be very difficult for Hezbollah to quickly adjust to such a drastic change, and meanwhile it will suffer.

During the Syrian war, Hezbollah acquired new skill sets, ones that the group could employ against Israel.[29] The war also encouraged Hezbollah to invest in its conventional capabilities. This ironically could serve Israel. One of the main military problems Israel had in confronting Hezbollah, as in the 2006 war, was to find its elusive enemy. It will be easier for the IDF to strike Hezbollah if the latter continues to become more like a military and less like a guerrilla or terrorist group. In this sense Israel could benefit if Russia encouraged Hezbollah's military buildup. Although Israel tries to contain this process, by attacking deliveries of missiles that are sent from Syria to Lebanon, if Hezbollah grows and maneuvers openly, it will help the IDF to defeat Hezbollah.

5

Israel, Hamas, and the Palestinian Authority

Since the 1990s relations between Israel, Hamas, and the PA have been complicated. The Hamas is a sworn enemy of both Israel and the Fatah movement that runs the PA. Hamas, which has controlled the Gaza Strip since 2007, seeks to take over the West Bank as well. Therefore Israel has contained Hamas both in the Gaza Strip and inside the West Bank. Israel has also contained the PA.

Background

In 1947 the Palestinians were not willing to share with the Jews the territory that was known as Palestine.[1] It led to a war in which the Palestinians lost and 600,000–760,000 of them became refugees.[2] Following that showdown, there were Palestinian incursions into Israel from nearby Arab states, mostly for economic reasons, but some were also aimed at harming Israelis.

During the 1960s the Palestine Liberation Organization (PLO) launched attacks against Israel such as laying mines and explosive charges along the border between Arab states and Israel.[3] In the 1967 war Israel seized the West Bank and the Gaza Strip, where there were some clashes between Israel and the PLO until 1971. Since then those areas were more or less quiet until the uprising in 1987. It was the start of an era of low-intensity wars in the West Bank and the Gaza Strip from 1987 to 1993 and 2000 to 2005.[4] The following decade saw the wars between Israel and Hamas in the Gaza Strip in 2008–9, 2012, and 2014.[5]

Robert M. Danin claimed in November 2014 that as far as the peace process goes, "we are at a stalemate."[6] In June 2015 Israel and Hamas had an "interest in preserving an uneasy calm . . . a stalemate that is largely the result of a lack of options on either side."[7] However, in the same month, French foreign minister Laurent Fabius warned that a stalemate could set the Israeli-Palestinian conflict "ablaze."[8] Anthony Cordesman claimed in November 2015 that neither side believes that "real progress is possible in moving to a two-state solution or any solution to the Israeli-Palestinian crisis."[9] Tamara Cofman Wittes said on April 19, 2016, that "the stalemate in the Israeli-Palestinian conflict carries a continuing cost for both societies, and that cost may be increasing over time."[10] On July 10, 2016, Egypt's foreign minister, Sameh Shoukry, visited Israel and claimed, as part of the effort to renew the talks between Israel and Palestinians, that "the current state of affairs . . . is neither stable nor sustainable."[11] On July 21 that year, Egypt's president, Abdel Fattah el-Sisi, said that "Egypt's recent serious effort aims to break the deadlock that has hung over peace efforts."[12] Hence there was a deadlock between Israel and both Hamas and the PA.

In 2016 "the West Bank and Gaza Strip are two separate entities. Despite their inhabitants' shared aspirations for a unified Palestinian state, these two territories grow more separate by the day. With distinct governments, economies, bureaucracies, and financial patrons, it is increasingly difficult to envision a reconciliation."[13]

The COGAT is Israel's military-run civil administration in regard to the West Bank and the Gaza Strip. Col. Uri Mendes, COGAT's deputy director, claimed on March 26, 2018, that the Palestinian population in the West Bank was between 2.5 and 2.7 million. There are also 2 million Palestinians in the Gaza Strip and almost 2 million Arabs inside Israel itself. Therefore there are about 6.5 million Arabs in Israel, the West Bank, and the Gaza Strip, where there are almost the same number of Jews.[14] This reality shows the need but also the hardships of reaching a reasonable solution.

The Israeli Position

During the confrontation of 2000–2005, terror attacks such as suicide bombers struck all over Israel, killing 789 civilians.[15] Max Abrahms claimed, "The Israeli response to it underscores that (1) the limited use of Palestinian terrorism had high correspondence, and (2) Israeli inferences of Palestinian objectives undermined support for making concessions."[16] Israel inflicted serious blows to the PA but did not bring it down due to the severe ramifications of such an approach. By containing what was left of the PA and not destroying it, Israel left the PA as a possible partner for the future. Since then both sides have had talks, like in 2014, but they have not managed to reach an agreement. Israel has gone on in containing the PA, not allowing it to expand or to be upgraded to a state, one that will be recognized by Israel unless the PA accepts Israel's terms. The PA, of course, opposed that policy. However, the PA and Israel avoided another clash in the West Bank and maintained security cooperation, aiming at containing their joint enemy, Hamas, in the West Bank. At the same time Israel has continued to contain Hamas in the Gaza Strip. It is part of the overall Israeli strategy of running the conflict until it can be resolved.

Some assume that "a combination of a strong performing economy, military superiority, a divided region, and an inept international community led the Israeli government to believe that it could pursue cost-free obstructive policies, policies which prevent an independent Palestinian state from ever becoming a reality."[17] Israel might accept a Palestinian state, according to Israeli terms. Meanwhile, Israel assumes that its position is strong enough to allow it to stick to its guns. Yet Israel is not that powerful. Its economy depends on its various commercial and diplomatic ties with other countries. Israel's military buildup also relies on its relations with other states, mostly the United States. Those constraints make Israel vulnerable to steps that the international community could take if it decides to pressure Israel's leadership to talk with the PA. Israel fears such a move, since Israel does not want to be contained.

There were about 350,000 Israeli settlers in the West Bank in 2012, almost twice the number in 2000.[18] In early 2017 there were about 420,000.[19] The UN Security Council approved on December 23, 2016, resolution 2334 "endorsed by its resolution 1515 (2003), for a freeze by Israel of all settlement activity, including 'natural growth,' and the dismantlement of all settlement outposts erected since March 2001."[20] Although the resolution was not expected to have any practical impact, it was seen as a major blow to Israel.[21] It was part of a long struggle that has been going on for decades now. For political and ideological reasons, building continues in the West Bank and in east Jerusalem, in spite of constant international pressure on Israel to stop. Even if Israel stops adding and expanding settlements, this issue may hinder any government in Israel from reaching an agreement with the PA. It is clear that such an accord involves giving up areas in the West Bank, resulting in the evacuation of tens if not hundreds of thousands of Israelis. Such a move would require the use of force, as in the withdrawal from the Gaza Strip in 2005. Israel will then have to confront its own people who strongly object to such a process. The Israeli government will find it difficult to contain such a big opposition.

The Israeli security forces try to prevent the more radical elements among the Jewish settlers in the West Bank from creating provocations and harming Palestinians, which might ignite an outburst. This is an ongoing and complicated challenge, since Israelis have to monitor their own people. However, as far as containing security problems in the West Bank, Israel invests mostly in containing Palestinians, usually from Hamas, who seek to attack Israelis, and sometimes they have managed to do so.

In mid-October 2014, Israel's defense minister Moshe Ya'alon said about the PA: "I'm not seeking a solution. I am looking for a way to manage the conflict and the relations."[22] Ya'alon's successor since June 2016, Avigdor Lieberman, thought that the circumstances were right to overthrow Hamas, since some of the clans and tribes in the Gaza Strip seek an alternative. Egypt, which strongly opposes Hamas, can assist in this matter by opening the Rafah border crossing and providing aid, if there is a new rule in the Gaza Strip. As for the PA, Lieberman wanted to topple Abu Mazen (also known as Mahmoud Abbas), although Lieberman did not know what would happen when Abu Mazen is gone.[23] On October 23, 2016, Lieberman threatened to destroy Hamas "completely" if there were another war.[24] In mid-February 2017 Lieberman suggested a deal in which Hamas would give up its attack tunnels and rockets in return for Israeli investments in the economy of the Gaza Strip.[25] On June 10, 2017, he said that the IDF will not seize the Gaza Strip but "we go in and destroy all their terror infrastructure" and then "we will come out."[26] Lieberman was a hard-liner, but he was also pragmatic. He was willing to continue containing Hamas by reaching a deal in which Hamas gives up its military option in return for economic benefits. Lieberman probably assumed Hamas would reject this idea, but raising this concept allows Lieberman to claim that since Hamas turned down a peaceful solution, Israel has no choice but to use force. Yet even then Lieberman did not call to retake the Gaza Strip but just to inflict a major blow to Hamas and then to leave.

On September 19, 2017, Israel's prime minister, Benjamin Netanyahu, said, "Israel is committed to achieving peace with all our Arab neighbors, including the Palestinians."[27] Many, in and outside Israel, did not believe him, and even if he meant that, they were not sure what kind of peace he referred to. It seems that Netanyahu would rather continue to contain the Palestinians, with all the risks of such a concept, instead of facing the many severe obstacles, uncertainty, and possible dangers of trying to establish a Palestinian state in the West Bank.

Simon Peres, one of Israel's most famous leaders, died September 28, 2016. Peres, at least since the early 1990s, strongly supported negotiations with the Palestinians. He was a peace icon. Following his death, those in Israel who sought to end the conflict with the Palestinians looked for a known figure, one who could persuade its people to vote for him so he could reach an agreement with the Palestinians. There are some who think that Ehud Barak could play this role. He has a long public career behind him. He was not only prime minister and minister of defense, like Peres, but also the chief of staff of the IDF, which is very important because security arrangements will be a key issue in any negotiations with the Palestinians. Many Israelis feel comfortable trusting a leader with a rich military background like the one Barak has. As prime minister, Barak tried to reach peace with Syria and the PA, but those efforts came to a dead end. It seems that at the time, Barak was willing to make quite a compromise. He also took the IDF out of south Lebanon in 2000. Barak has a respectable reputation worldwide, yet Peres had a much better image as a peacemaker among Israelis and certainly in the international community. In September 2016 there was a brief public attempt to call on Barak to run for office, but nothing came of it.[28] Barak is now a private businessman, but he also acts as an elder statesman by giving interviews and speeches and by publishing announcements regarding Israel's national security. This suggests that he seeks to come back to political life. Yet he might not do that, and even if he does, he might not be able to regain his former position as the head of a major political party and then to win the general elections and become prime minister.

In 2015 Prime Minister Netanyahu had a government with "just a one-seat majority" in the Knesset (the Israeli parliament), which made it very hard for him to negotiate with the PA. Any concession by him to the PA might have caused his government to collapse.[29] Furthermore, it was a right-wing government that was suspicious, and many of its members were even unwilling to negotiate on establishing a Palestinian state in the West Bank. In May 2016 Avigdor Lieberman entered the government, which gave the government a little bigger majority in the parliament. Yet it did not increase the odds of a change in the policy; the government continued containing the Palestinians. That government, as stated, is also based on right-wing parties. There were talks between Netanyahu and the main opposition party, the Zionist camp, which is center-left, that might have led to an agreement between them. The international community sought that, too. If the Zionist camp had joined the government, the latter would have been based on a vast coalition, strong enough to do whatever is necessary to restart the peace talks. Although such an attempt in 2014 had failed, Israel should not lose hope. Israel should be encouraged to have a government that could take decisive actions with regard to the Palestinians.

On October 1, 2016, a survey by the Project HaMidgam Institute showed that 64 percent of Israelis (Jewish and non-Jewish) believed that there will never be peace.[30] In late November and early December 2017, a poll that was run by the Palestinian Center for Policy and Survey Research and the Tami Steinmetz Center for Peace Research found that 46 percent of Israeli Jews backed a two-state solution.[31] It meant that most Israeli Jews preferred instead the policy of containment of the PA, if only for lack of a better option.

There is perhaps an option, one that has been known for decades now: to divide the West Bank, unofficially or not, into cantons that are ruled by local groups. Those who support a Palestinian state are strongly against this concept, even if cantons might later join together to form a state. For those who oppose a Palestinian state, it will be a way to divide the Palestinians who are already split between the West Bank and the Gaza Strip, which could help in containing them.

There was an initiative in Israel in 2016 calling for a referendum on the West Bank fifty years after the 1967 war, when those areas were seized by Israel. The plan was to call the Israelis to finally decide whether to annex the West Bank or choose a two-state solution. This idea did not gain much momentum, since Israelis tend to avoid this major issue to begin with, particularly as long as the containment of both the PA and Hamas prevents another confrontation. This approach stayed the same in the upcoming years.

The Palestinian Position

The Palestinians want to replace Israel with their own state. By signing the Oslo Accords in the 1990s, it seemed that the PLO was officially willing to resolve the conflict in a peaceful way after recognizing that it could not destroy Israel by force, at least for now. The Oslo treaties, with all their blunders, marked the beginning of a process that could enable the Palestinians to have a state, in spite of it being only a partial realization of their national aspirations. It means a compromise in which the Palestinians settle for the Gaza Strip and most of the West Bank, receiving about a quarter of the territory they see as theirs. In that sense Israel will have to accept a Palestinian state, but Israel will manage to contain the Palestinians to a small part of the land that is in dispute.

The PA did all kinds of diplomatic maneuvers such as in the UN in order to be considered a state. Yet it was clear that if it tries to do it without Israel's consent, then Israel could do its best to contain and to make it very difficult for the new Palestinian state to exist. Israel might even invade and try to destroy that state, explaining that is was done in response to a security threat to Israel.

In September 30, 2015, Abu Mazen, the head of the PA, claimed in the UN that "the status quo cannot continue."[32] He supported a diplomatic-political campaign against Israel, such as approaching international institutes like the UN with a kind of "diplomatic intifada."[33] This is a way to contain Israel in the international arena as a response to the containment of the PA by Israel in the West Bank. The PA used for that the UN General Assembly, when overwhelming numbers of members supported the Palestinians in several cases, which showed how isolated Israel was. It could serve the PA by persuading Israel to restart the talks in terms that suit the PA, but it might also cause Israel to increase its containment of the PA.

Abu Mazen is known for opposing an armed confrontation against Israel. He managed to avoid a war with Israel in the West Bank. During his time in office, which started in 2005, there were confrontations between Israel and Palestinians, although they occurred not in the West Bank but in the Gaza Strip, which has been under the rule of his rivals, Hamas.[34]

On July 12, 2016, Nadav Agarman, the new head of the Shin Bet, Israel's main security service, told the Knesset Foreign Affairs and Defense Committee that there was often less tension because Abu Mazen publicly denounced terrorist attacks.[35] Although Abu Mazen certainly did not want to be contained by Israel, he tol-

erated that while continuing to support the security cooperation with Israel to contain Hamas. He did that because without
it he might have lost his rule if Hamas had toppled him or there
would have been an escalation with Israel that could have eventually destroyed the PA following a war with Israel. Abu Mazen
also tolerated and actually supported the containment of Hamas
in the Gaza Strip. He wanted Israel to topple Hamas as retribution
for kicking the PA, under his leadership, out of the Gaza Strip in
2007 and in order to pave the way for the PA to return there. Abu
Mazen did not want to do that while openly collaborating with
Israel against Hamas in the Gaza Strip, since it was too politically
sensitive. Instead he could have tried to influence Israel unofficially and indirectly, but mostly he waited for Israel to do all the
work alone, and then he would have considered his steps with
regard to the Gaza Strip. Overall much depends on whether the
PA survives if Abu Mazen is no longer its leader. He is the head of
the PA, the PLO, and the Fatah movement. In the future each of
those institutes might be under the control of a different figure.
Such a divide of power can make it more complicated to reach
an agreement with the Palestinians.

Mousa Abu Marzouk, a senior figure in Hamas, said on May
15, 2014, that "Hamas will not renounce violence until Israel is
destroyed."[36] "Hamas continues to adhere to its ideological rejection of Israel's right to exist."[37] Hamas therefore does not seek to
contain Israel but to annihilate it. Israel and the PA had several
rounds of talks that did not lead to an agreement, but at least the
two sides demonstrated in public that they were considering a
peace treaty. Any progress in the past, in the talks between the
PA and Israel, would have probably pushed Hamas to desperate
acts like confronting Israel, aiming at sabotaging the peace process. The last attempt to achieve an agreement, in 2014, reached
a dead end not because of Hamas but due to a lack of trust and
deep disputes between Israel and the PA. Still, if the PA and Israel
are about to sign an accord, they should take into consideration
how to contain Hamas so it will not disrupt their effort to reach
and carry out an agreement.

Khalid Meshaal, Hamas's political bureau chief, claimed on December 4, 2014, that "the path of negotiation has been proven to be a failure. . . . There has to be a change of strategy, and adoption of a program of national Palestinian struggle with various facets on the ground level, political level, diplomatic level, legal level, media level, public level—and the resistance, with all its aspects, including armed resistance."[38] The collapse of the talks in April 2014 and deadlock since then helped Hamas to present itself as the one that has been right all along in its approach to Israel. Hamas's strategy could be appealing, particularly for Palestinians who are frustrated with the political stalemate with Israel. Yet the price Palestinians paid, mostly those in the Gaza Strip, point out the abyss to which Hamas is dragging its people.

The containment of the Gaza Strip has foiled Hamas's efforts to gain a state.[39] On May 1, 2017, Hamas published a policy document in which the group claimed it drops its demand to destroy Israel but still rejects Israel's right to exist, while continuing an "armed struggle" against it. Fatah spokesman Osama al-Qawasme said that Hamas agrees to what Fatah accepted in 1988, a position for which Hamas has criticized Fatah since then. It was not clear if the document replaced Hamas's 1988 charter, which calls for Israel's destruction. Israel responded by saying this is an effort to "fool the world."[40] Fahad Shoqiran, a Saudi writer, said that "the new document does not express any realism."[41] It was kind of symbolic that the document was revealed one day before Israel celebrated its independence day. More important, it was an attempt to present Hamas in a more moderate way. It meant Hamas might not have disrupted and maybe would have considered participating in some kind of talks between Israel and Palestinians. This development was the result of the containment of the Gaza Strip that made it difficult for Hamas to rule there. Hamas was aware that Israel will not stop to contain the group because of that document. However, for Hamas it was another step, part of its effort to make it easier for the group to run the Gaza Strip.

Daoud Kuttab, a Palestinian journalist, claimed on June 7, 2017, that it is a waste of time to work on confidence-building steps, since some of them are just an attempt "to avoid dealing with the main issues." He added that some of the settlements will be "absorbed into Israel" while others stay "in the state of Palestine as long as they are not living on stolen Palestinian land and they abide fully to the sovereign Palestinian government."[42] In that sense the Palestinians can try to contain the Jewish settlers in the West Bank. The idea is to limit where the settlers can live and supervising and even bothering them in a way that will encourage settlers to leave the West Bank and convince other Jews not to come to reside there.

A survey that was conducted in the West Bank and the Gaza Strip in May 16–26, 2017, showed that Palestinians were more moderate than their leadership on issues such as Hamas's attacks against Israel. "However, many continue to hold maximalist aspirations against Israel in the long term, while rejecting its right to exist."[43] In another survey from late November and early December 2017, 47 percent of the Palestinians backed a two-state solution, which is a very complicated option.[44] Yet establishing one state is not feasible. In such a state, both the Jews and the Palestinians will strive to gain the majority so they can contain the other, and this struggle will lead sooner or later to a civil war. One state will have too many problems, some of them so big and dangerous that they will cripple and eventually bring down the state. It is enough to mention the impossible mission of building new security forces for the state. There has been security cooperation between Israel and the PA, yet having a joint police, let alone a military, composed of Israeli Jews and Palestinians, is such a tall order that it rules out one state to begin with.

Each side must take steps in teaching its public about the other. It is very important in order to increase the chances of achieving peaceful solution that is based on talks, compromise, and understanding the other side, while containing the radicals in both camps, those who oppose negotiations. Even during the current stalemate there should be a serious effort of preparing both sides to accept the other's rights to have its own state. It requires both sides to be flexible and not to be biased. There are all kinds of initiatives, like private ones, which try to encourage Israelis and Palestinians to better know each other. Those projects have to do, for example, with sport like organizing soccer games where Israelis and Palestinians are members of the same team. Yet this is not enough. There is a need for a vast and well organized project in this matter. Social media should also be used for this important goal.

Along the years Palestinians who have been citizens of the state of Israel since 1948, that is, Israeli Arabs, almost were not involved in guerrilla or terrorist attacks against their state. The long Israeli-Palestinian conflict did not push the Arab Israelis to stop their neutrality. It was because Israel contained them, but they also contained themselves.

The War of 2014 in the Gaza Strip

In 1994, as part of the Oslo Accords, Israel relinquished most of the Gaza Strip to the PA. In 2005, following its disengagement plan, Israel retreated from the rest of the Gaza Strip, handing it over to the PA, without signing on an official agreement in this matter. In 2007 Hamas forcefully seized all of the Gaza Strip, kicking the PA out. In response Israel contained the Gaza Strip, although it permitted people to get in and out of there, such as for receiving medical treatment in Israel. Israel also allowed basic needs to be sent into the Gaza Strip, so it was not a full siege, certainly not like the one Assad used against his foes in Syria.

The Gaza Strip borders mostly with Israel. It made it easier to enforce a siege by supervising and when it was needed to prevent anyone from entering or leaving the Gaza Strip. Israel has the right to do so, particularly in regard to its own territory and air space. The dispute with those who oppose this blockade is focused on the accesses from the Gaza Strip to the Mediterranean Sea. This ongoing struggle led to several attempts in which civilian ships challenged Israel by trying to break into the Gaza Strip. It brought collisions; the most violent one occurred on May 31, 2010, when an Israeli raid on a ship caused the death of nine people there. A much bigger clash took place between Hamas and Israel. In the December 2008–January 2009 campaign (Israel's Operation Cast Lead), Hamas clashed with Israel. Various skirmishes broke out periodically until another round occurred in November 2012 (Israel's Operation Pillar of Defense). Then again, after a relative period of calm, there was another escalation. This led to the war in July and August 2014 (Israel's Operation Protective Edge).

"The Israeli withdrawal from the Gaza Strip in 2005 was a golden opportunity for Hamas to rebuild itself militarily by arming itself."[45] Israel, as part of containing its foes in the Gaza Strip, mostly Hamas, tried to disrupt their military buildup. Israel often managed to prevent weapons and ammunition from reaching the Gaza Strip. Israel did it by bombing stockpiles in Sudan such as on October 23, 2012, and capturing ships carrying arsenal such as on March 15, 2011, in the Mediterranean Sea, and on March 5, 2014, in the Red Sea. For that purpose the Israeli navy also watched, around the clock, the access from the Gaza Strip to the Mediterranean Sea.

In mid-2014 Hamas ran into deep trouble in the Gaza Strip after losing its patrons in Syria, Egypt, and Iran. Furthermore, Egypt became a foe of Hamas, which caused Hamas severe economic problems, due to blocking of tunnels that led from Sinai, an Egyptian territory, to the Gaza Strip. Those underground passages served as delivery routes of supply, including military ones. Egypt basically joined the Israeli effort to contain Hamas. However, Hamas had in early July 2014 about 11,000 rockets. The combination of its economic low point and its military might urged Hamas to gamble on confronting Israel. The latter would have preferred to continue with deterring and containing Hamas, but Israel, against its will, was dragged into a war.[46]

A group of eleven senior officers, political leaders, and officials from the United States and other states, mostly from Europe, claimed that Israel did not want to engage in the 2014 war and tried to end that collision during the battles.[47] Hamas assumed that Israel just sought to degrade Hamas's rule in the Gaza Strip, not to destroy it. Some Israeli ministers publicly supported bringing down Hamas's regime, but this nonstate organization concluded it could "escalate the conflict without feeling it was risking its survival."[48] Israel stuck to containing Hamas, and Hamas used that to its advantage.

Hamas sought to break the siege by coercing Israel to open the naval and air routes to the Gaza Strip. Hamas was also eager to get access to Sinai. By fighting Israel, Hamas hoped to pressure Egypt in this matter. However, although Israel was the sole force clashing with Hamas, Egypt joined Israel somewhat in containing Hamas by blocking the paths from the Gaza Strip to Sinai and vice versa.

In previous confrontations, the IDF advanced less than 2 km into the Gaza Strip because of the resistance it faced but mostly because Israel contained its own steps. Not only that, throughout the confrontation in 2008–9, Israel captured a small part of the Gaza Strip, but the IDF withdrew from it after the fight was over. In the clash in 2012 Israel did not conquer any land. In the 2014 war Israel could have seized all of the Gaza Strip and toppled Hamas. Israel might have seized the entire Gaza Strip for several months, as it did following the 1956 war, and even to try to stay there for a few decades as it was after the 1967 war. Yet from political, security, and economic perspectives, it was not worth it for Israel, due to the cost both Israel and the Palestinian population would have had to pay. Israel would have also absorbed severe criticism from the international community. In any case, the IDF would have sooner or later left the Gaza Strip, and had Hamas been too frail to regain control of it, the results from Israel's point of view might have been worse. The alternative to Hamas could be either chaos or other outfits more radical than Hamas, such as ISIS, taking over the Gaza Strip or part of it. Another radical group, the pro-Iranian Islamic Jihad, would have grabbed territory there, too, which would have increased Iran's influence there. Hamas is also pro-Iranian, but it has been quite independent, which increases the chances of weakening the ties between that group and Iran.

Furthermore, in a post-Hamas era in the Gaza Strip, non-Hamas groups might attack Israel. The latter will try to stop them or at least to retaliate, but it might not be easy for Israel to find out which outfit attacked and to confront that group. In this sense Hamas is a well-known entity, and this fact facilitates their handling as far as Israel goes. Israel therefore preferred to go on containing Hamas in each of the wars that occurred in the Gaza Strip.

During the war of 2014 the IDF attacked more than five thousands targets in the Gaza Strip.[49] The IDF relied on its clear advantages such as airpower and data gathering from the air, ground, and sea. (The Gaza Strip is highly monitored due to its small size, 365 km2, and also since that area is surrounded almost completely by Israel.) It was not enough to prevent fire from the Gaza Strip. This goal required destroying all the rockets and mortar shells and their launchers, or forcing Hamas to stop firing. IDF's impressive firepower could have only contained to a certain degree Hamas's ability to strike Israel.

Khalid Meshaal claimed that "we are committed to target military posts."[50] Yet during the war of 2014, Hamas "deliberately and indiscriminately targeted Israeli civilian population centers. . . . There is no doubt that all of these attacks constitute war crimes."[51] Hamas therefore did not confine its fire to military objectives solely. Hamas did not inflict many casualties or damages, since many of its rockets missed their targets or were intercepted by Israel's Iron Dome system. Several rockets landed in and around Tel Aviv, the most vital and populated area in Israel. Nevertheless, the alarm sirens exposed millions of Israelis to the reality that people in the south of Israel have been living in since 2001, where a small percentage of the Israeli population had absorbed thousands of rockets and mortar shells. Israel does not have population centers very near to the Gaza Strip besides the city of Shedrot. About 24,000 people lived there in 2018. The relatively short range of Hamas's rockets and mortars meant that for most of the time Israel could have contained the clashes to the south of Israel. There was also the danger of a possible penetration into Israel from the Gaza Strip through the tunnels, which was contained to the border area, but it might have been more deadly than the rockets.

Anthony H. Cordesman argued that "the real revolution in military affairs is forcing modern states to use the advancements in military technology to focus on minimizing civilian casualties and collateral damage rather than destroying the enemy."[52] This was a major challenge for Israel during the war of 2014 because "Hamas made no effort to evacuate civilians; on the contrary, there are documented cases of them compelling civilians to remain or return to places where they expected Israeli attacks."[53] Uzi Rabi and Harel Chorev explained that Hamas put at risk its population in order to protect weapons caches and to "win over public opinion in the Arab world and in the West."[54] A UN commission that studied the 2014 war condemned both sides for their activities. The commission called Israel in particular to "conduct a thorough, transparent, objective, and credible review of policies governing military operations and of law enforcement activities" such as "the use of explosive weapons with wide-area effects in densely populated areas."[55] Hamas managed to contain Israeli operations during the wars, since Israel had to be careful not to harm noncombatants. Hamas also hoped that the war would make Israel wonder whether or not to continue with its containment of the Gaza Strip, fearing it might ignite another war with all its cost and constraints.

After fifty days of combat, the two sides, mostly the Palestinians, were exhausted. As in former rounds there were no direct negotiations between Israel and Hamas. Yet in 2014, as in 2009 and 2012, the two sides accepted an unofficial agreement that kept the containment of the Gaza Strip. The Gaza Strip paid an enormous price in blood and treasure, more than two thousand dead, including hundreds of Hamas fighters, together with vast destruction. Israel lost seventy-two people, almost all of them troops. It might not seem much, compared with the Palestinian casualties, but for Israel it was quite a cost, considering the relatively weak foe, the limited scale of the war, and the results: the continuance of the containment, for lack of a better option.

Following the war of 2014, Hamas assumed that rebuilding its forces would take years.[56] Hamas needed weapons like antitank missiles, yet they couldn't stop the IDF from seizing the Gaza Strip and toppling the rule there. Furthermore Egypt goes on with its effort to cut off the Gaza Strip from Sinai. The containment of the Gaza Strip by both Israel and Egypt make it harder for Hamas to rearm, which affects its ability to confront Israel in order to break the containment. Yet Hamas still managed to recover enough to start another war, if it wishes to do that.

Israel might argue that manufacturing rockets and digging tunnels by Hamas "are a casus belli for Israel, and that these are legitimate reasons for Israel to take military action in Gaza."[57] In 2017–18 the IDF wiped out several tunnels without entering the Gaza Strip, which prevented an escalation. Yet there are many other tunnels inside the Gaza Strip. If the IDF tries to reach them, it will bring a war. A war will also happen if the IDF tries to put an end to the production of rockets, which requires the conquest of the entire Gaza Strip. Even if Israel strives to destroy rocket factories by launching air strikes solely, it will ignite another war with Hamas. Israel's containment therefore has its limits, since it does not prevent Hamas from getting ready for combat.

Israel can capture or kill leaders of Hamas's military wing.[58] In the past Israel assassinated Hamas's senior leaders such as the founder of that group, Sheikh Ahmed Ismail Hassan Yassin, in March 2004, and the head of Hamas's military wing, Ahmed al-Jabari, in November 2012. Hamas was rattled but continued its activities. If Israel repeats this approach, the results will probably be the same. Israel can't prevent Hamas from putting someone else in charge. It is a gamble for Israel, since the next leader might be more extreme or more capable of planning attacks against Israel. Hamas might also go after high-profile figures in Israel. Assassinations could be part of containment but not to serve as an alternative. Decapitation might even make the situation much worse for Israel.

Following the war of 2014, Egypt wanted to increase the involvement of the PA in the Gaza Strip at the expense of Hamas.[59] Israel's defense minister, Moshe Ya'alon, said on October 24, 2014, that "part of our interest is to pave the way for the Palestinian Authority to get into the Gaza Strip. I'm not sure Abu Mazen is ready to take responsibility."[60] Khaled Elgindy claimed there is a need "to avoid the perception that the PA is returning to Gaza on the backs of Israeli tanks." This required the PA and Hamas to reach common ground.[61] In early November 2014 there was no "effective or united Palestinian government in place in Gaza."[62] Khalid Meshaal argued in December 2014 that "reconciliation is a national necessity, and we must hold onto it. We in Hamas are committed to it."[63] In mid-2015 the Palestinian unity government did not work.[64] "There is nothing more we can do, no more that we can do to facilitate reconciliation," said Hamas spokesman Sami Abu Zuhri in early May 2015. Furthermore, if elections were held in the PA and Hamas got both the parliament and the presidency, "it would be extremely difficult to engage, with Hamas listed as a terrorist organization by the United States and EU."[65] In the upcoming years the PA and Hamas failed again and again to fix the rift between them. Without a united Palestinian front, it was harder for each of the factions there to break the containment against them.

The Humanitarian Crisis in the Gaza Strip

According to the World Bank in May 2015, "Gaza's real GDP is only a couple of percentage points higher now than it was 20 years ago in 1994, while the population growth is estimated to have increased by about 230 percent over the same period. Consequently, real per capita income in Gaza is 31 percent lower now than in 1994. Gaza became a major source of deficit and the fiscal burden on the Palestinian Authority's finances amplified by the internal divide. While about 43 percent of PA's expenditures are spent in Gaza, only 13 percent of its revenues come from Gaza."[66] On September 1, 2015, according to the United Nations Conference on Trade and Development (UNCTAD), assistance to the Palestinian people, the Gaza Strip "could become uninhabitable by 2020 if current economic trends persist." There were enormous problems there in regard to fresh water, electricity, and lack of jobs. Almost half of the 1.8 million people who live in the Gaza Strip depended on food distribution from United Nations agencies.[67] Christoph Duenwald, who led a mission from the IMF in early February 2016, made a report in which he claimed that in the Gaza Strip the reconstruction suffered from delays, although it "provided some boost to the Gazan economy . . . the humanitarian situation remains dire." Unemployment was higher than in the West Bank.[68]

In early June 2016 about 400 tons of food and "all the trappings of daily life" went from Israel into the Gaza Strip, twice the amount compared to a year before. It was delivered after an "arduous process that involves three stages—screening the goods in Israel, loading them onto trucks that carry them into Gaza, and finally distributing the goods via Palestinian drivers." There were also exports from the Gaza Strip, yet not enough to help the crumbling economy there to recover.[69] All of that was the price of the containment of the Gaza Strip. At first, after Hamas took over in 2007, Israel assumed that the hardships of the containment would turn the population there against Hamas, but this did not happen. Israel therefore allowed sending more supply into the Gaza Strip while continuing with the containment. Israel suspects that without the containment, large numbers of weapons such as long-range rockets will pour into the Gaza Strip and sooner or later they will be launched at Israel. The latter will then have to conduct a major operation in the Gaza Strip. The containment is therefore supposed to prevent a war, one that will cost both sides, particularly the Gaza Strip, dearly. Israel might even topple Hamas during such a war. In that sense the containment is meant to save Hamas from itself.

On July 9, 2015, Lior Akerman, who served as a head of a division in the Shin Bet, claimed that Hamas in the Gaza Strip becomes less popular because of the "atrocious conditions" and poverty there. "Although Hamas's financial situation is dire," it spent its budget on military buildup.[70] In spite of the containment, Hamas did not change its policy toward Israel, which could have helped its people. Hamas stuck to its stiff and hostile strategy toward Israel. Even with the limited resources it had, instead of investing its efforts in helping the Gaza Strip to recover, Hamas decided to focus on preparing for another round against Israel. This approach was demonstrated in the huge resources that were given to digging tunnels; some of them were aimed at penetrating into Israel. The tunnels were not supposed to assist in ending the containment or starting talks with Israel but in killing and capturing Israelis so they could be replaced with Palestinians prisoners. Hamas's obsession regarding those paths below the ground literally undermined the hope for rebuilding and saving the Gaza Strip.

In early September 2015, the head of IDF's Southern Command, Maj. Gen. Sami Turgeman, argued that Israel and Hamas shared "three temporary interests." One was to avoid a humanitarian crisis in the Gaza Strip, following the decline of infrastructure there. The second was to contain the spreading of Islamic organizations that are more extreme than Hamas. The third was to prevent a political vacuum in the Gaza Strip. Hamas was worried also about losing some of its members who joined other groups in the Gaza Strip. Hamas dealt with this problem by gathering intelligence and carrying out arrests.[71] Therefore Israel contained Hamas, and both of them strove to contain their common enemies in the Gaza Strip.

In late February 2016 the head of IDF's Intelligence, Maj. Gen. Herzl Halevi, spoke in the Knesset to the Foreign Affairs and Defense Committee. He argued that there is a growing humanitarian crisis in the Gaza Strip and that the reconstruction of the Gaza Strip, following the war of 2014, is advancing slowly. According to Halevi, the success of the reconstruction of the Gaza Strip is vital in preventing another confrontation.[72] The war of 2014 occurred largely because Hamas was in distress due to the deep economic problems of the Gaza Strip, following Hamas's policy and the containment of the Gaza Strip. This scenario could have happened again, particularly if Hamas assumes that because of economic hardships there is a danger to its rule. A growing frustration in the Gaza Strip might cause the population there to turn against Hamas, even openly, by having mass demonstrations. Hamas would suppress them, using its guns. At the same time Hamas would try to divert public anger toward Israel. Yet the people of the Gaza Strip might oppose another destructive war against Israel and instead, with all the risks to their safety, they could focus on toppling Hamas. Like other Arab dictatorships, Hamas might be brought down by its people. If such an uprising would be seen as one that is not controlled by a radical Islamic group, then Israel could consider assisting the rebels. Israel will not put its troops in harm's way by entering the Gaza Strip, but Israeli air power could help, for example, by neutralizing Hamas fighters who would try to suppress the mutiny.

According to the UN, by 2017 "basic services and private sectors have been gradually debilitated" in the Gaza Strip, which caused a "steady deterioration in living standard," and over the past decade more than a million people there required humanitarian aid.[73] The low point of the Gaza Strip continued as long as Israel went on with containment, following Hamas's hostile approach and the conflict between them.

On March 30, 2018, about 17,000 Palestinians confronted the IDF and other security units on the border of the Gaza Strip. As a result, sixteen Palestinians were killed and hundreds were wounded, the deadliest day since the 2014 war.[74] Similar events soon occurred, with fewer casualties to the Palestinians and none to Israel. Yet on May 14 there was a peak when fifty-two Palestinians were killed and hundreds were wounded. This strategy was supposed to help Hamas break the siege and demonstrate the despair among Palestinians in the Gaza Strip due to their grim economic situation. Yet only a tiny percentage of them came to face the Israeli military and police, because of their fear of the Israeli response and also because they assumed there was not much point to such a clash. Therefore Israel managed to relatively contain both the number of the Palestinians who participated in the event and the skirmishes themselves.

Hamas's Preparations for War

In 2016 Hamas implemented decentralized deployment of its units "with the idea of not presenting targets and "centers of gravity," instead creating autonomous fighting cells capable of operating effectively as independent combat groups for extended periods."

They used tunnels to move undetected for offense and defense purposes such as when conducting raids and launching rockets. Digging a tunnel is easy due to the terrain of the Gaza Strip and the low cost of both manpower and tools needed. Hamas also has been skilled in deploying IEDs that are cheap to produce, easy to make, and quite effective, particularly when they are located along routes where the IDF has to move inside the Gaza Strip. There are also special land and marine units to carry out raids that would both cause physical damage and affect public mind-set such as by capturing Israeli troops. In addition, Hamas has been watching Israeli troop movements deep inside Israel by using various technological measures.[75] All of that was meant, during a war, to delay, disrupt, damage, and inflict casualties among Israeli forces and to harm the Israeli population in order to contain Israeli operations, especially inside the Gaza Strip.

In the war of 2014, Hamas had short- and long-range rockets that were positioned in such a way that allowed firing across the entire campaign by looking for weak spots in the Israeli Iron Dome system that intercepts rockets. During the Israeli land offensive, "there was no significant decline in the fire of rockets." When it did happen, it was because Hamas wanted to save its rockets so they would last longer.[76] Therefore the IDF did not succeed much in containing rocket launches. Since then Hamas worked on upgrading its firepower. Yet the containment of the Gaza Strip by both Israel and Egypt made it difficult for Hamas to receive materials for its war industry.

On April 14, 2016, a senior IDF officer said that Hamas in the Gaza Strip has 5,000 men in its elite unit, which conducts special missions. He added, "Hamas is a highly intelligent enemy. They surprise me and learn their lessons very quickly."[77] Hamas had twenty-five regional battalions. IDF Southern Command watched them carefully and prepared detailed files on each of them. Early that month IDF battalion commanders participated in courses that were aimed at teaching the officers how to defeat Hamas in urban warfare.[78] Hamas's battalions are not like those of the IDF because Hamas is a nonstate organization that has fewer resources than Israel. There are major differences starting with personal equipment of the Israeli troops like body armor and all the way to the support they receive from other corps, ones that Hamas does not have, like armor and an air force. Hamas relies on light arms and antitank missiles, those that Hamas manages to smuggle into the Gaza Strip in spite of the containment there.

Hamas assumes that in future war sooner or later, Israeli forces, those that will penetrate the Gaza Strip, will leave that area, as it was in former wars. Until then Israeli troops will be exposed, since Hamas could exploit its familiarity with the terrain to strike its foe. In that sense maybe even Hamas wants to drag the IDF into the Gaza Strip, "hiding and blending in with civilians, moving freely through underground tunnels, able to conduct pinpoint surprise attacks in short bursts—all of it with no intention of repelling IDF forces from their territory, but rather aimed at inflicting casualties, degrading IDF forces' morale and physical condition, and undermining belief in their ability to complete the operation and achieve its ends."[79] In that way Hamas hopes to contain the Israeli penetration into the Gaza Strip.

Cease-fires during confrontation "provide an opportunity to convey messages to the enemy and to increase efforts to affect public awareness . . . threatening increased levels of firepower in the next phase, alongside the possible benefits for the enemy of reaching a quick end to the operation."[80] Those are methods to contain the scale or length of a war.

On July 12, 2016, Nadav Agarman, the head of the Shin Bet, claimed Hamas was not responsible for the sporadic rocket fire from the Gaza Strip in recent months.[81] Other groups that oppose both Israel and Hamas launched rockets from the Gaza Strip, aiming to drag Israel to confront Hamas. Hamas tried to contain both the fire at Israel and those groups, including by using force, in order not to be entangled in war when it did not serve its purpose.

On April 14, 2016, a senior IDF officer said that "Hamas fears a surprise attack." According to the officer, Israel has different options "from a deterring strike to a full occupation of the Strip."[82] In early 2017 Hamas tried "to reach a state of constant readiness in fear that Israel will strike it first in a surprise attack."[83] Neither side sought a war. However, a war might still occur any time because of miscalculations. Israel might also change its policy, if it assumes that containment does not work anymore or if Hamas decides it has nothing to lose following the containment of the Gaza Strip.

In early 2017 Hamas seemed to restore the military capabilities it had prior to the 2014 war.[84] Hamas also acquired dozens of rockets; each one contains hundreds of kilograms of explosive material, which are more powerful than its other arsenal. Those rockets are short range, but they could devastate villages near the Gaza Strip.[85] Israel has contingency plans to evacuate up to a quarter million civilians from areas near the border to protect them from attacks by Hamas.[86] Actually both sides have an interest in containing the campaign to areas near the Gaza Strip. Israel, of course, does not want to run any battles on its own soil, but if it happens, then Israel seeks that the clashes will occur near the Gaza Strip so that most of the state will be left out of the war. For Hamas it is easier to strike close to the Gaza Strip, compared with attacking areas that are deeper inside Israel.

In the Gaza Strip "with some up to 50 meters deep, many tunnels are supported by more than 500 tons of cement arches and come equipped with communications lines, filtration systems, and hydraulic cables to transport weaponry. And at 2 meters high and 1.5 meters wide, gear-laden fighters are able to walk or run through such tunnels to kill or kidnap unwitting soldiers or civilians."[87] The IDF's Gaza Division had "placed counter-tunnel measures—detecting and destroying them—as its No. 1 priority in 2016. Many units, some of them technical, have been engaged in employing overt and covert capabilities as part of the effort."[88] The Gaza Division ran its largest annual exercise in early February 2017. The five-day drill simulated scenarios such as how "large numbers of Hamas commandos managed to infiltrate Israeli communities via tunnels, by para-gliders, and from the sea."[89] Israel's minister of defense, Avigdor Lieberman, said on March 26, 2017, that Hamas has fewer than fifteen tunnels that lead into Israel.[90]

In September 2017 the IDF assumed that Hamas had shifted its approach from digging tunnels that will penetrate into Israel to those aimed at ferrying men and weapons across the Gaza Strip for defensive purposes.[91] It followed a huge Israeli project: building an underground wall, full of sensors, aimed at discovering and blocking tunnels that lead into Israel. Israel managed to detect and annihilate several tunnels, following a massive effort in this matter. Israel was eager to contain the threat from the tunnels, investing in it more than a half billion dollars. Although in the 2014 war the tunnels caused relatively low casualties among Israelis, they were remembered in Israel as a major threat.

The West Bank

Ninety-five percent of the Palestinians who live in the West Bank are under the rule of the PA, although Israel's presence disrupts their day-to-day routine.[92] Israel's security cost from 2001 through 2016 in the West Bank and East Jerusalem was about $3.6 billion.[93] It was the price of containing guerrilla and terrorist attacks in that area.

The war of 2014 started after three Israeli teenagers were kidnapped and murdered in the West Bank. Israel blamed Hamas and launched a major operation. Hamas responded from the Gaza Strip, and the escalation ended in a confrontation. During the battles in the Gaza Strip the West Bank continued to remain relatively quiet, as in the 2008–9 war in the Gaza Strip. Israel managed to contain the West Bank by keeping it out of the war, although this was achieved also due to the policy of the PA, which also did not want to be involved in the war in the Gaza Strip.

In October 2014 Israel stopped an attempt by Hamas to overthrow the PA in the West Bank.[94] Actions such as arrests of newly established cells prevented Hamas from translating "their large following and support in the West Bank into operational networks."[95] Israel and the PA have been working on containing Hamas in the West Bank. After Hamas seized the Gaza Strip in 2007, it did not moderate its policy toward Israel. The same will be if Hamas manages to topple the PA and take over the West Bank or part of it. Since 2007 Israel has been tolerating the PA's loss of the Gaza Strip to Hamas. However, if Hamas takes control of areas in the West Bank as well, it will be too much for Israel. The risk to Israelis living in the West Bank and the proximity of that area to Israel's main population centers will cause Israel not to contain but to forcefully prevent Hamas from creating an entity in the West Bank.

Abu Mazen's term as the head of the PA was supposed to end in January 2009, but he had "unilaterally extended it." He also repressed his opponents, while corruption in the PA continued to flourish.[96] A poll by the Palestinian Center for Policy and Survey Research, from early June 2015, claimed that in the Gaza Strip only 30 percent said they could criticize Hamas without fear, and in the West Bank 32 percent said they could freely criticize Abu Mazen.[97] In that sense Hamas and the PA are similar, in spite of all their differences, for it demonstrates how both of them act as a dictatorship. For Israel it is not that important if a Palestinian or any other Arab rule for that matter is not a democracy, as long as they don't operate against Israel. Therefore Israel prefers the PA, with all its drawbacks, to Hamas. Israel contains the PA but in a much softer way than it contains Hamas.

In August 2015, according to Daniel Byman, following the collapse of the peace talks between Israel and the PA, there were more calls for "resistance." There were those in the West Bank who supported Hamas for confronting Israel in the Gaza Strip, as long as the West Bank was kept safe from an Israeli offensive.[98] Containing the wars between Hamas and Israel to the Gaza Strip was a good compromise for those among the Palestinians in the West Bank who seek a clash with Israel if they don't pay the price. Yet other Palestinians suffered, including civilians, in the Gaza Strip. In that sense those Palestinians from the West Bank were like others in the Arab world who seek a war with Israel if it is not at their expense and limited to other Arab territories.

In a poll from mid-September 2015, Palestinians from the West Bank and the Gaza Strip were asked what "is the most effective way of establishing an independent Palestinian state next to Israel." Forty-two percent said armed action, and 29 percent supported negotiation. However, the survey showed that 78 percent of Palestinians think the chances of getting their own state in the next five years are "slim to nonexistent."[99] By that they recognized that Palestinians can't, by force or talks, persuade Israel to end its containment of the PA by allowing the establishment of a Palestinian state, unless it is done on Israel's terms.

The unrest in Jerusalem in October and November 2014 occurred after the Israeli government took a gamble by building in east Jerusalem. Abu Mazen was also heavily responsible for that collision, since the PA encouraged aggressive actions against Israel. The PA tried to exploit the unstable situation in its favor, but the PA might have gotten more than it had bargained for if events had run out of control. Eventually the tension was contained, and this circle of violence ended.

Since October 2015 there has been another round of unrest in the West Bank, much longer than the former one. This started in Jerusalem, following Palestinian accusations that Israel breached the arrangements concerning the Temple Mount, the third holiest site in Islam. Yet this dispute joined other issues, including accusations by Palestinians that both their own government and Israel are to blame for the economic hardships and political stalemate in the West Bank. This low point pushed Palestinians to express their anger by clashing with Israeli troops and civilians. It was the result of the ongoing containment of the PA by Israel, since both sides were unwilling or incapable of changing it due to the problems and risks it involved.

Between October 2015 and February 2018, following Palestinian attacks, 62 people were killed and 899 were wounded; almost all were Israeli citizens. Most of the assaults were stabbing and shooting attacks, while vehicular (ramming) were less. There were also several thousand violent incidents in which Palestinians threw rocks. Tossing of cocktails/grenades happened less often. There were also about 200 cases of roadside/pipe bombs.[100] It could have been much worse for Israel, if there had not been a huge effort by Israel's security forces to contain those attacks.

Following the Oslo Accords, the IDF was not permitted to penetrate "A" areas, zones in the West Bank that were under complete control of the PA. During the 2000–2005 confrontation (the second Intifada), assaults like suicide bombers eventually brought the IDF to seize "A" areas. This deterioration might repeat itself if there is another confrontation in the West Bank, a third Intifada. Israel might not wish to bring down the PA, just restore more or less the former situation: the containment of both the PA and Hamas, possibly in a better way than before.

Ilan Goldenberg explained on May 2016 that it is possible, as part of a two-state solution, to secure both Israelis and Palestinians in a way that will be "equal or greater to that provided today by Israel's deployment into the West Bank, and that such measures can be consistent with Palestinian needs for sovereignty and dignity." Israel will be able to defend itself, but a multilayered system can make unilateral Israeli operations "reduced to rare emergency situations."[101] Yet Israel wants to continue to contain Hamas and other radical groups in the West Bank, according to methods that have been working quite well for many years now. Israel, as part of establishing a Palestinian state, might be very reluctant to change its current strategy in favor of a new policy, one that was not tested in the West Bank, even if it is based on highly advanced technology.

In 2016 the economy of the city of Nablus was considered to be the strongest in the West Bank, which includes a lot of trade with Israel. Furthermore, since October 2015 the area of Nablus was quiet as far as attacks on Israelis.[102] In July 2016 around 140,000 Palestinians were employed in Israel, legally or not. They provided for one-third of the Palestinian population in the West Bank.[103] It shows the importance of allowing Palestinians to get jobs in Israel, since they can't find it in the West Bank. Israel tries to stop those who come without permission to work inside Israel. Although they just want to earn money, they present more of a security risk than those who enter Israel legally. Overall both sides benefit from that situation, although it demonstrates how the PA depends on Israel, which allows Israel to contain the PA.

It will go on until the Palestinian economy is more developed. It did not happen until now because of Israel, the PA, and other states. Israel is willing to boost and help the PA's economy. The PA needs that, but mixing it with the demand to establish a Palestinian state complicates this process.

In September 2016 a report by the UNCTAD claimed that Israel deprives the Palestinians in the West Bank of "their human right to development and hollows out the Palestinian economy. Chief among these are the confiscation of Palestinian land, water, and other natural resources; loss of policy space; restrictions on the movement of people and goods; destruction of assets and the productive base; expansion of Israeli settlements; fragmentation of domestic markets; separation from international markets and forced dependence on the Israeli economy. Moreover, a continuous process of de-agriculturalization and de-industrialization has deformed the structure of the Palestinian economy."[104] These were the results of the Israeli containment of the PA, following the policy of both sides.

Marwan Muasher claimed in late June 2017 that "young people and civil-society groups are increasingly focused on how to secure individual rights, and regard their civil liberties as a precursor to, rather than the result of, statehood. In fact, two-thirds of Palestinians believe that the two-state solution is no longer feasible."[105] In that sense they accepted the ongoing containment of the PA as a permanent reality. This is not necessarily an Israeli success if it leads to increasing international pressure on Israel to try a one-state solution or if another confrontation starts, let alone if it is like the one that occurred between 2000 and 2005.

On July 12, 2017, the PA and Israel signed a water-sharing deal to help Palestinian communities. The PA made it clear that this issue still has to be discussed in talks about the final settlement. The hope was that the deal could pave the way for a return to negotiations.[106] Yet this did not happen. It also demonstrated how Israel can help strengthen the PA in spite of the containment. On the other hand, it was not an alternative for establishing a Palestinian state, as far as the PA was concerned.

If the PA gets weaker or collapses, then Hamas would try to seize, if only unofficially, areas in the West Bank, for example, Hebron, where Hamas is known to have a strong base of support. Israel will prevent that, not only in Hebron, while considering allowing moderate Palestinians to be in charge of some areas in the West Bank. Israel will claim it must enforce law and order and secure the population in all the West Bank, both Palestinians and Israelis. Israel will not want to run the West Bank, as it did before the Oslo Accords, but to be more in the background. From Israel's perspective this might mean creating cantons.

The Security Cooperation

In August 2014, following the fight in the Gaza Strip, according to Martin Indyk, Abu Mazen "gained some credibility in some quarters in Israel" because he "prevented a third intifada from breaking out in the West Bank."[107] In October 2014 "more than 90 percent of the arrests of Hamas operatives in the West Bank" were carried out by Israeli security forces while their Palestinian counterparts were "primarily tasked with maintaining law and order."[108] In the following month, from Israel's perspective, the PA and its security units "are a security asset for Israel." Yet at the same time the PA ran a "wild" incitement against Jews.[109] In late November 2014 the Palestinian security forces seemed to suffer from lack of motivation, and they were not as helpful as they used to be.[110] However, at that time "as one senior Palestinian security official described it, never before has security cooperation been as intense, elaborate, and effective as it is today."[111] This was essential in containing Hamas in the West Bank.

On July 9, 2015, Lior Akerman, who served as the head of a division in the Shin Bet, claimed Hamas tried to seize control of the West Bank but failed due to the "successful cooperation between the Shin Bet and Palestinian Authority security forces."[112] The buildup of the Palestinian security forces "has been an unquestioned operational success," yet in October 2015 "there can be no doubt that security cooperation, and with it a shared Israeli and Palestinian interest in the survival of the PA, is living on borrowed time."[113] Former chief of staff and defense minister Shaol Mofaz warned in early January 2016 that a collapse of the PA and its security forces would mean that the IDF would have to dramatically increase its presence in the West Bank. "The IDF will be the entity in charge of all civilian matters and that will be terrible." It could lead to another uprising.[114] In February 2016 the IDF had more than a hundred companies in the West Bank.[115] The IDF will need many more troops if Israel has to control Palestinian areas, as part of containing Hamas and others who might attack Israelis.

In 2016, in two major cities in the West Bank, Jenin and Tulkarem, Palestinian security forces have foiled many assaults against Israelis. The IDF could have focused there on counterterrorism and less on securing settlements. The Israeli military presence in Jenin and Tulkarem was also smaller than in other areas, so there were fewer targets for Palestinians who seek to harm the Israeli security forces.[116] The Palestinian security forces helped Israel to contain their common foes in Jenin and Tulkarem, and the relative quiet there allowed the IDF to send forces to more problematic sectors in the West Bank.

On June 5, 2017, the Palestinian prime minister, Rami Hamdallah, admitted in a closed session that Israel's limited response to the clashes that have occurred since October 2015 helped to prevent a third intifada. The IDF avoided collective punishment such as blocking Palestinians from getting access to roads, and by that the IDF reduced the chances of an escalation. Instead the IDF concentrated on the actual suspects.[117] On June 20, 2017, IDF chief of staff Gadi Eisenkot praised the Palestinian security forces, saying they "deserved recognition" for their contribution to stopping terrorist attacks.[118] The approach of the Israeli and Palestinian security forces managed to contain those who wished to attack Israelis and to start an uprising.

In 2017 "the forces available to the Palestinian Authority to regain and secure control of Gaza are clearly inadequate. The backbone of the Palestinian National Security Forces are the nine battalions of national security forces based on the West Bank and the two battalions of presidential guards that have been trained in international assistance under the guidance of the U.S. security coordinator to the Palestinian Authority. These forces (approximately six thousand personnel) are barely sufficient for the maintenance of security in the West Bank. To date, no forces for a mission in Gaza have been built."[119] In July 2017 "the PA exercised varying degrees of authority over the West Bank due to the IDF's continuing presence in certain areas, per Oslo-era agreements."[120] The small scale of the Palestinian security forces proved how important it was for them to have the IDF near them while cooperating with it, in order to contain Hamas in the West Bank. Another solution is to expand the Palestinian security forces so they can take more responsibility in the West Bank, which will allow Israel to reduce its security presence there. Israel could permit that while continuing to contain the PA, until both sides are ready to negotiate.

Israel agrees that some Palestinian security forces must be armed, yet not with weapon systems like tanks. Israel wants to make them sufficiently strong to fight guerrillas and terrorists, but not more than that. However, a part of the Palestinian security forces might be upgraded, in order to prepare them to be able to retake the Gaza Strip. They can be fit enough for that task, since Hamas is not that powerful, especially if Hamas becomes weaker in the future. There might be even anarchy in the Gaza Strip, so the mission will be less to reoccupy it and more to enforce law and order in a Palestinian area while containing guerrilla and terror there, a field where the PA gained much experience in the West Bank. Israel could assist the PA in resizing the Gaza Strip, as long as it will not be counterproductive. Although the PA can't survive in the West Bank without the Israeli security forces, if they capture the Gaza Strip together it might cause more harm than good, as far as Arab and particularly Palestinian public opinion is concerned. The PA has to retake the Gaza Strip by itself, since the Gaza Strip is its territory, let alone if this step is part of establishing a Palestinian state.

In late October 2017 Israel and the PA fully resumed the security coordination between them, after three months in which it was suspended by the PA.[121] Overall it has almost been a miracle; security cooperation existed in spite of the containment of the PA, the stalemate in the peace talks, and the outbursts of violence in the West Bank. The security cooperation and its positive results provided a base on which peace talks could be resumed, but it also enabled the containment of the PA to continue. However, without this security activity the PA would have been destabilized by interior chaos, which did not swerve the interest of both Israel and the PA. Increasing and at least keeping the current security cooperation is essential to prevent a fragile situation from becoming much worse.

"Whether due to the promise of steady employment or patriotism, or some combination of both," the Palestinian security forces remained in early 2018 "for many, a compelling proposition—notwithstanding tenuous legalities, inchoate reform efforts, and overall sustainability." There was also the challenge of explaining to the Palestinian public why the security cooperation with Israel is so vital.[122] This is particularly important when the security arrangement gets more complicated in times of unrest in the West Bank, which increases the probability of a confrontation.

The Role of the United States and the European Union

Following the collapse of the peace negotiations in April 2014, the United States accused the Israeli government of undermining the talks by continuing with settlement activity. The U.S. government had also disputes with the PA.[123] Secretary of State John Kerry said on October 22, 2014, that "the current situation, the status quo, is unsustainable."[124] On May 14, 2015, the United States and Arab Gulf states "strongly affirmed" the need for a two-state solution.[125]

The United States have been giving aid to the PA.[126] During 2016 "the PA continued to develop its civilian justice institutions (e.g., judiciary, police, prosecutors) to improve both investigative and prosecutorial functions. The United States provided assistance to enable the PA to reduce case backlogs, improve warrant executions, and upgrade forensic services."[127] In that sense the United States helped the PA to turn into a state in the future without affecting the current containment on the PA, which prevented the PA from becoming a state.

According to a Gallup poll from late February 2016, "American" views about the Israeli-Palestinian conflict remained steady over the past year, with 62 percent of Americans saying their sympathies lie more with the Israelis and 15 percent favoring the Palestinians. About one in four continue to be neutral, including 9 percent who sympathize with neither."[128] In that sense the United States accepted the containment of the PA by Israel, because there was no public demand in the United States to force Israel to change that.

Some assumed that Obama's legacy "could well be the death of the two-state solution itself."[129] It seemed that at a certain point the Obama administration gave up the attempts to establish a Palestinian state and instead focused on containing ISIS. In 2015–16 ISIS was indeed a bigger problem, not only for the United States but also for Israel and the PA. None of them wanted to see ISIS becoming stronger. So the United States tolerated the containment of the PA by Israel.

In 2017 the Trump administration continued to support the Palestinian security forces as part of helping both the PA and Israel to contain Hamas in the West Bank.[130] The United States also worked on a peace initiative. However, on December 6, 2017, the Trump administration decided to recognize Jerusalem as the capital city of Israel. Although it left enough room for negotiations, the PA strongly objected to that step, which caused a rift with the United States. The PA assumed it is part of an overall plan to contain the Palestinians in the West Bank in a way that forces them to accept Israel's terms and not only with regard to Jerusalem.

Breaking the standstill and with it the containment of the PA requires easing the tension and building trust between the United States and the PA, if the United States goes back to be the broker between Israel and the PA. Yet the current U.S. administration, like the former one, might hesitate to play that role due to the complications of the conflict. Furthermore the United States has other important priorities in the Middle East, such as containing Russia and ISIS. Meanwhile, the United States allowed Israel to go on with containing the PA.

In mid-November 2014 the European Union did not intend to impose sanctions on Israel "if it takes steps to block a two-state solution."[131] It was at a time when several European states recognized a Palestinian state. Although this decision was sometimes symbolic, it was still a clear sign and a warning to Israel that the containment of the PA might bring growing pressure, if talks with the PA are not resumed.

In early September 2015 EU foreign policy chief Federica Mogherini said that Europe hopes to restart the talks between Israel and the Palestinians.[132] On March 20, 2018, she emphasized that together with the West Bank, the Gaza Strip and East Jerusalem must be part of a Palestinian state.[133]

Overall the EU is busy with its internal problems. Even if the EU focuses on the Middle East without the United States, the EU does not have enough leverage to restart the talks between Israel and the PA.

The Role of Middle Eastern States

There is the famous Arab Peace Initiative to end the Arab-Israeli conflict.[134] Yet in 2014 Henry Kissinger claimed that "considering the widespread upheaval in the Middle East, it is a mistake for Israel to pursue a comprehensive peace deal with the Palestinians."[135] Indeed the Arab turmoil might destabilize and even bring down more Arab regimes, including those whose support is required in reaching and keeping a peace between Israel and the Palestinians. In that sense Israel continues to contain the PA, although if the peace process fails, Israel can return to contain the PA or even a Palestinian state, if it is established.

In September 2015, following clashes between Israeli security forces and Palestinians at Al-Aqsa mosque in Jerusalem, King Abdullah II said that "any more provocations in Jerusalem will affect the relationship between Jordan and Israel."[136] Jordan is very sensitive about the Palestinian-Israeli conflict, since a large part of its population is Palestinian and the Hashemite kingdom has a border with Israel, including in the West Bank, where the PA is located. Jordan seeks to contain the problems in the West Bank, like in Jerusalem, so they will not spill over into the kingdom.

Jordan's deep economic and political hardships got worse after more than 1.2 million refugees fled into that country from Syria. Those challenges might undermine the Hashemite Kingdom, and its endorsement is essential in both reaching and preserving an agreement between the PA and Israel. Meanwhile Israel has been collaborating with Jordan in securing the long border between them, which helps both states to contain common foes such as radical Islamists. If Jordan crumbles and become lawless, then Israel will be exposed to incursions such as in the Jordan rift valley, which connects Jordan and the West Bank. Israel refused to surrender that vital area to the PA as part of a peace treaty because of Israel's concerns about the future of Jordan. If the latter collapses, then Israel will use its control in the Jordan rift valley to contain the West Bank.

On December 7, 2014, Israel's defense minister, Moshe Ya'alon, argued that terrorist activity in the West Bank "is mostly operated from the outside, whether from the Gaza Strip or Turkey."[137] In June 2015 a senior member of Hamas, who was based in Turkey, was asked by the authorities there to reduce the scale of its operations against Israel. Turkey feared the United States would blame it for supporting terror.[138] Although the leader of Turkey, Recep Tayyip Erdogan, has severely criticized Israel over the years, Turkey might still play a positive role by moderating its Palestinian partner, Hamas, as part of both improving Turkey's shaky ties with Israel and promoting the peace process. Turkey has also called again and again for an end to the siege on the Gaza Strip. Turkey served as a broker between Israel and Syria in the attempt to sign a peace accord in 2008. As both a non-Arab state and a powerful one, Turkey could help end the containment of both the PA and the Gaza Strip.

In late November 2014 the Egyptian president, Abdel Fattah el-Sisi, said that if there is a Palestinian state, Egypt is willing to send forces there to "help the local police and reassure the

Israelis through our role as guarantor."[139] Yet an Egyptian military presence in the West Bank or the Gaza Strip might cause complications. If clashes occur there between Palestinians and Israel, Egyptian troops might be caught in the middle. If Egyptian troops were harmed, it would create a crisis between Israel and those in Egypt who would see Israel as responsible for these casualties. Furthermore Egypt has huge economic problems and in the worst case scenario it might turn into a failed state, which raises serious doubts about relying on it in containing terrorism in a Palestinian state.

Efraim Inbar claimed in mid-2017 that if "the Palestinians are politically incapable of engaging in state building, then it might be helpful to place them under the tutelage of the neighboring Arab states—Egypt in Gaza, Jordan in the West Bank."[140] This concept was raised many times in the past. It could be a way for Israel to contain the Palestinians, if the latter are controlled by Arab states. Yet it seems that neither Egypt nor Jordan nor the PA is willing to consider that. This option might be more relevant if Egypt or Jordan, due to their enormous internal problems, became a failed state. Then there is a chance to allow Palestinians from the overcrowded Gaza Strip to move to northern Sinai, which has large empty areas. In Jordan the Palestinians there might exploit the opportunity, if the kingdom there crumbles, to establish their own state. The latter could include parts of the West Bank, particularly where there are concentrations of Palestinians.

6

Egypt's Security and Stability Problems

Egypt and Israel ended the conflict between them in 1979. The relations were called a "cold peace," yet the 1979 peace treaty survived. Abdel Fattah el-Sisi, who became the Egyptian president in 2014, has plenty on his plate. Israel strives to help Egypt in order to contain the problems inside Egypt so they will not affect Israel. It has to do with the fight against ISIS in Sinai. Israel wants to defeat and at least to contain ISIS so that it will not attack Israel.

The United States objects to the tough suppressing of the Egyptian opposition, due to violation of human rights. Yet the United States tolerates the way Sisi contains its internal rivals, in order not to harm U.S.-Egyptian relations. Egypt also has been trying to contain its enormous economic problems, which does not stop Egypt from investing heavily in military buildup. This process and the hostility toward Israel by many Egyptians worry Israel. A war between Israel and Palestinians could lead to a crisis between Israel and Egypt, and if this is not contained, then in the worst case there might be a clash between Israel and Egypt as well.

The Battle in Sinai

The Egyptian military has to defend its country from external and internal enemies. Over the years its main mission was to get ready to fight its Israeli counterpart. The two militaries clashed many times until 1974. Following the 1979 peace treaty, the Egyptian military continued to prepare for a possible war against Israel, but in recent years it became clear that Egypt's top security priority has been to suppress insurgents. Actually Israel and Egypt share a common foe, ISIS, which operates inside Egypt and particularly in the Sinai Peninsula, an Egyptian territory that has a border with Israel. The peace between Israel and Egypt has been quite cold, but there has been tight security cooperation between the two states against ISIS.

Egypt has been struggling to win in Sinai.[1] It faces armed groups of Islamic extremists such as Ansar Bayt al-Maqdis, which in November 2014 joined ISIS. Over the years there were some severe incidents, such as one that occurred on October 25, 2014, when a car bomb killed twenty-eight Egyptian soldiers in northeastern Sinai. It was the deadliest assault against Egyptian security forces in Sinai since the one that happened on August 19, 2013, when twenty-five Egyptian officers were caught and executed. The attack on October 25 came after it seemed that Egypt had managed to stabilize the Sinai. Yet Egyptian security forces assumed that it would take up to three years to accomplish this mission.[2] Following that attack, Egypt created a buffer zone on the border with the Gaza Strip, aiming at blocking the tunnels, which were used to smuggle weapons and combatants between the Gaza Strip and Sinai. This Egyptian effort to contain the Gaza Strip led to thousands of people losing their houses.[3]

By November 2015 "against all available data," the Egyptian military insisted that victory was near, but it seemed more like Egypt had managed only to contain its foes.[4] "The Egyptian military's narrow security lens and harsh tactics have, in effect, further alienated local residents and helped fuel the insurgency."[5] Egypt's military lacked the right weapon systems for counterterrorism, and its tactics in Sinai ignored "hard-learned modern counterinsurgency techniques, employing (frequently excessive) kinetic strategies, rather than economic ones."[6] Another problem was failing to encourage "initiative at the lower levels" inside the Egyptian armed forces.[7] Egypt's military was therefore "neither well prepared nor well equipped to take on an insurgency."[8]

Insurgents in Sinai don't have any aircraft, so the Egyptian military has been enjoying air supremacy. Gunships are useful in striking positions, although some factors like the weather could affect the effectiveness of air bombardments, like when there is a sandstorm. The Egyptian military has other major advantages, such as overwhelming superiority in the number of troops. Nevertheless, the size of Sinai is about 60,000 km2, which gives insurgents plenty of room to maneuver and to hide. Insurgents found cover mostly in the northeast of Sinai, including in urban areas, where the Egyptian armed forces had to be careful not to cause collateral damage.

There is no need to train Egyptian troops in basic aspects of high-intensity warfare such as how to fight tanks, since insurgents have no armored vehicles at all. However, the Egyptian military could still use tactics that are effective in both high- and low-intensity wars such as vertical flanking from the air and sea for laying down ambushes and launching raids. Until the Egyptian armed forces improve and focus on counterinsurgency, it will be difficult to beat ISIS, and at most ISIS could be contained.

"Egypt is the birthplace of both moderate and extremist Islamic thought, the hub of Sunni scholarship, and home to Al-Azhar University, the center of moderate Islamic teaching. For these reasons, Egypt can play a key role in countering ISIS's extremist ideology."[9] Nabil Naeem, the founder of the Islamic Jihad organization in Egypt, said in early April 2016, in response to a suggestion calling for reconciliation with guerrilla and terror groups, that "these groups cannot be trusted. You either annihilate them or they annihilate you. There is no third choice."[10] Yet there has been an ongoing neglect of hundreds of thousands of Bedouins in Sinai. The Egyptian government has been humiliating them, such as by not classifying them as permanent residents, and has not improved their poor economic situation. This grim reality drove some of the Bedouins to support ISIS.[11] Egypt has to implement not only military measures but also economic, social, and political ones in order to reduce the motivation of the population in Sinai to support ISIS.

By June 2015 about 1,000 Egyptian troops and policemen were killed in Sinai.[12] In recent years Egypt has continued to suffer heavy losses. On March 23, 2017, a roadside bomb killed ten Egyptian troops in Sinai. At the time Sisi doubled the budget of the military association that takes care of families of fallen soldiers and provides physical therapy for disabled troops.[13] On July 7, 2017, an attack killed twenty-three Egyptian troops in a checkpoint in northern Sinai.[14] Those strikes showed that Egypt was not able to suppress this insurgency. From the Israeli perspective, the fight in Sinai was at least restricted to the peninsula. Egypt's efforts were not very successful, but they occupied ISIS, bothering it enough so it did not turn to focus on Israel.

Egypt has to secure not only the Sinai but also its 1,100 km border with Libya, where there were several attacks against Egypt's security forces. In one of them, on July 19, 2014, twenty-two border guards were killed at a remote checkpoint.[15] On May 27, 2017, Egypt launched air strikes against camps in Libya, which served to train those who murdered twenty-nine Coptic Christians in Egypt a day before.[16] It was not the first time Egypt bombed inside Libya. Egypt therefore has to fight on two fronts, in Libya and Sinai, which are hundreds of kilometers from each other, and this makes it difficult to send troops from one front to another. The size of each front is also quite large, another factor that forces Egypt to overextend its units. However, the insurgents on both fronts are sometimes located in specific areas, and they are not that strong. Libya also serves as a reminder for Egypt of what could happen if Egypt becomes a failed state following a failure to overcome the insurgents.

In late November 2017, after an extremely deadly attack cost the lives of more than 300 noncombatants in a mosque in northeast Sinai, Sisi ordered his military command to use whatever force was needed to secure the Sinai within three months.[17] Egypt's armed forces carried out a major campaign, Comprehensive Operation Sinai 2018, which inflicted casualties on ISIS but did not bring final victory. Egypt has to upgrade and change its methods and meanwhile to accept that it can't defeat ISIS but only contain it as much as possible. It intends to inflict maximum casualties on ISIS and disrupt their operations while trying to limit the group's grip in Sinai.

Israel's Role in the Fight on Sinai

The campaign in Sinai affects Israel, which has a border with Egypt about 240 km long. There have been several skirmishes along that border. The most lethal happened on August 18, 2011, when eight Israelis were killed. Also, rockets were fired from Sinai toward the city of Eilat, which is on the border. The IDF deployed near that city an Iron Dome battery to intercept rockets. The rockets did not cause casualties, but they might if this fire becomes more massive. There are about 60,000 people living in Eilat.

Israel's problems with its border in Sinai do not only concern security. They include also illegal immigrants from Africa and drag trafficking. Israel built a high, strong fence and stationed troops and surveillance measures. This barrier has been very effective in stopping almost completely illegal immigrants, although infiltration of insurgents and certainly fire from Sinai are possible, as it was proven in the past.

Following the chaos in Sinai, the Israeli Intelligence increased its monitoring of the peninsula.[18] The main goal has been to find out in advance about an attempt to strike Israel. The Intelligence can also expose upcoming attacks against Egyptian objectives and by that to assist Egypt in containing ISIS. Here Israel has to be careful in updating its Egyptian partner without revealing sources and admitting publicly that Israel is spying inside sovereign Egyptian territory.

According to the 1979 peace treaty, most of the Sinai is demilitarized. Egypt could deploy in the demilitarized zone small units of border guards and police. Yet Israel, in order to help Egypt to confront ISIS, allowed Egypt to send reinforcements there. By early 2018 there were eighty-eight battalions with 42,000 soldiers stationed in Sinai.[19] They possess armored vehicles like tanks. Israel also authorized Egypt to use aircraft there such as AH-64 gunships. Israel strives to find a compromise between keeping the demilitarization and permitting the Egyptian military to gather enough forces to crush and at least to contain ISIS in Sinai.

A major component of the peace treaty is that Egypt could not have fortifications in most of Sinai. Nevertheless in 2014, while coordinating with Israel, Egypt built a series of small posts on the border. Each Egyptian site has fortification strong enough to protect the troops there from antitank missiles, since the insurgents have those kinds of projectiles.[20] This is another Israeli concession in regard to the peace treaty, meant to help Egypt to handle the insurgents.

Islamic extremists attack targets not only in Sinai but all over Egypt. They hide roadside bombs, shoot security forces, and assassinate high officials. If there is chaos inside Egypt, parts of that state might fall into the hands of armed groups.

Israel and Egypt cooperate with each other against ISIS. One of the terrorists' aims is to attack Israel and by that to spark a dispute between Israel and Egypt, which could jeopardize the peace treaty.[21] Daniel Byman and Khaled Elgindy warned in 2013 that, following the anarchy in Sinai, there is a probability of a military collision between Egypt and Israel.[22] It was one of the most important reasons why both Egypt and Israel had to contain ISIS in Sinai.

In July 2015 Geoffrey Aronson assumed that the Egyptian failures in the peninsula might push Israel to be more involved in Sinai, which might show "Israel's impatience or perhaps even disenchantment with Sisi's leadership on this issue."[23] Since 2015 "unmarked Israeli drones, helicopters, and jets have carried out a covert air campaign, conducting more than 100 airstrikes inside Egypt, frequently more than once a week" with Egyptian approval. Some of the aircraft follow "circuitous routes to create the impression that they are based in the Egyptian mainland."[24] In spite of its desire to contain ISIS in Sinai, Israel has to be very careful not to officially conduct operations there. Israel must not make Egypt look weak, one that needs help. It will humiliate the Egyptian regime both inside Egypt and around the Arab world. Egypt will have to respond in a way that might damage its relations with Israel and harm their joint struggle against ISIS.

In late March 2017 Israel's Sagi Territorial Brigade, which guards the border with Egypt, ran an exercise in case ISIS attacks a military or civilian site in the Negev by foot or cars or by launching rockets.[25] There were already some clashes on that border in recent years. The IDF therefore has to prepare in case ISIS increases its activities against Israel, particularly if the group is not confined to operating in Sinai.

Israelis continued to visit Egypt and mostly the Sinai. For example, in 2015 134,455 Israelis entered Sinai through the Taba Border Crossing.[26] In 2017 almost a quarter of a million Israelis visited Egypt. They went to areas that were relatively safe, far from where ISIS was. It proved how even in Sinai there was a place for tourism, literally, as long as ISIS was contained in other areas.

Egypt's Other Internal Issues

Unlike other Arab countries, "Egypt still has a coherent state, as well as a coherent military that enjoys significant public support" while controlling all of Egypt's territory.[27] Nevertheless, Egypt's security institutions—military, police, and intelligence forces— have been trying since the 2011 uprising to prevent what they see as a threat to Egypt's "entire social and political order."[28] As long as insurgents strike Egyptian targets, most Egyptians seem to accept their government's heavy-handed policy out of fear of losing stability and becoming like Libya, Syria or Yemen.

Cairo University professor Mostafa Kamel al-Sayed said in June 2015 that there had been improvement in personal security in Egypt.[29] In the same month, according to polls, Sisi enjoyed "ratings close to 80 percent."[30] In July 2015, according to Eric Trager, "Egypt is more politically stable than it's been in years . . . the Sisi regime is internally unified," which prevents chaos as the one that occurs in other Arab countries. This is a regime where Sisi, with all his power, is "the CEO of the loose coalition of state bodies" such as the military and other security forces, judiciary, powerful tribes and clans, business community, and private media.[31] However, Steven Cook claimed in December 2015 that Sisi's rule is based on violence, coercion, and patronage, and they are an "inefficient means of establishing and ensuring stability."[32] It was the price of containing the unrest in Egypt.

The Muslim Brotherhood (MB) was in power in 2012–13 but lost it for several reasons.[33] During the short period when Mohamed Morsi from the MB was Egypt's president (2012–13), school textbooks promoted their ideology by including pictures of women wearing veils. After Morsi was toppled, the curriculum described them "as corrupt and power hungry" while justifying their ousting.[34] In early 2016 the MB was "no longer deeply embedded in society" and "no longer has a robust internal organization, vast financial resources, a clearly defined ideology, or a tightly disciplined membership." His leaders were in prison, in exile, or dead.[35] It seems that the Egyptian government managed to overcome and certainly to contain the MB, which was the biggest opposition force.

One of Egypt's main income sources is tourism, which reached a low point following the unrest and particularly terrorist assaults that took place in Egypt after 2011. Egypt tried to secure its territory by fighting and containing terrorists, and the tourism did recover to some degree. Yet when 224 tourists from Russia were killed in midair after their plane left Sinai in October 31, 2015, with a bomb on board it was a major setback for Egypt's tourism industry.

In spite of the upgrading of the Suez Canal, maritime shipping experts doubted that it would increase the revenues significantly. In addition in late 2015, Egypt needed "a GDP growth rate of about 7 percent to create the approximately 700,000 annual jobs just to maintain the 12 percent (official) unemployment rate." Maybe the country's biggest concern has been its growing population, which is now about 90 million and might reach 150 to 180 million by 2050. Feeding all of them would be a huge challenge.[36] Egypt tried to contain this issue by persuading its people to have fewer children, but without much success so far.

Jon Alterman explained in early February 2016 that in Egypt, "Foreign investment is less than 20 percent of its pre-revolutionary high, and domestic investors wonder how they can invest when they have no sense of what the economic and regulatory environment will be like in three years, let alone in a decade. . . . Tourism is way down. . . . Suez Canal tolls are flat amidst a global trade slowdown. Low oil prices produce a double-whammy, reducing remittances flowing into Egypt. . . . The Egyptian pound is over-valued, pushing businessmen into the black market for dollars and raising the prices of Egyptian exports on international markets."[37] In early April 2017 there was a danger of a "state failure."[38] This can bring down the country and with it its peace treaty with Israel. Furthermore hundreds of thousands and maybe millions of desperate and poor Egyptian might try to immigrate to Israel illegally, hoping to find a better future by looking for jobs and at least food and basic medical services. Israel therefore should help Egypt's economy as much as possible in order to contain the problems there before they reach Israel.

Egypt received praise from the International Monetary Fund for carrying out reforms. Yet in 2017 after the currency lost half its value, members of the middle class were struggling, so they replaced new cars with cheaper ones, bought less pricy products, and did not go abroad for the holidays.[39] It was the outcome of Egypt's effort to contain its economic crisis.

Relations with the United States

A major turning point occurred in the Middle East in 1979. Israel and Egypt became peace partners, and Iran decided to see Israel as an enemy. The United States served as a broker to the Israeli-Egyptian peace accord. The superpower also developed its ties with Egypt and gave it tens of billions of dollars in military aid.

Michele Dunne said on June 23, 2015, that after all the American investment in Egypt in the last decades, the United States does not want to have friction with Sisi, but U.S. officials "are concerned that the course that the regime is on is leading toward greater instability, even state failure, down the road." This criticism is due to massive human rights abuses with more than 40,000 political prisoners. "Political life, media, and civil society have largely been closed off . . . it's a pressure cooker." The United States could give more civil than military aid and also to support human rights, or else the United States looks like it is for repression.[40]

The Obama administration, which assumed that Egypt's way to contain its internal troubles was wrong and too costly, strove to advise the Egyptian government without causing too much tension between the two states.

Some senior Egyptian officials did not trust the United States. In late 2015 they rejected "the notion that the crackdown on the Muslim Brotherhood in August 2013 produced the insurgency in the Sinai Peninsula, an argument that has been popularized in Washington."[41] In June 2016 Egypt saw "ongoing U.S. criticism of Cairo's deteriorating human rights record as interference in their country's domestic affairs."[42]

In October 2016 it was argued that the United States should have continued giving economic aid to Egypt, although that program had to be reformed "to enable the assistance to achieve its objectives in an extremely difficult context."[43] Meanwhile, the United States actually returned to the era of Mubarak, ignoring massive civil rights violations in Egypt, in order to keep its ties with Egypt. By that the United States, for lack of a better choice, accepted Egypt's containment of its opposition.

In July 2015 Adm. Jon Greenert, chief of naval operations, visited Egypt and praised "their attention to U.S. security needs" by allowing U.S. ships to pass in the Suez Canal.[44] It was a major reason for the United States to assist Egypt and to tolerate the suppressing of civil rights there.

Since the early 1980s the United States has provided Egypt with thousands of weapon systems such as F-16 fighter-bombers, AH-64 gunships, and M1A1 tanks. In 1991 Egypt sent two divisions to join a vast coalition, under U.S. leadership, in a high-intensity war against Iraq. In more than a decade now the United States has been urging Egypt to reform its military so it can run hybrid and low-intensity wars. According to this approach, the Obama administration tried to adjust its military aid to Egypt. Tamara Cofman Wittes said on April 19, 2016, that the Obama administration was "redirecting U.S. military assistance to Egypt away from long-term commitments to major weapons systems, and toward effective counterterror and border security capabilities."[45] In this sense the United States tried to help Egypt to contain insurgents like ISIS.

Israel has been supporting the American military aid to Egypt since those weapon deliveries were seen by Egypt as part of the 1979 peace accord. Therefore Israel is worried that stopping aid might jeopardize the peace treaty. In addition Israel should be pleased if Egypt's military gets weapons and gear like surveillance equipment that will upgrade its ability to contain insurgents. Egypt's aircraft and tanks could still be used for containing ISIS, although for that Egypt does not need thousands of those platforms. Even during a major operation against insurgents, at most a few dozen F-16 and several hundred armored vehicles should be enough to accomplish the mission.

Following the toppling of President Mohamed Morsi by Sisi in July 2013, the United States cut aid to Egypt. A large part of it was restored in June 2014.[46] On November 1, 2015, the U.S. and Egyptian governments agreed to resume production of M1A1 tanks in Egypt. Egypt was also about to assimilate twenty Harpoon missiles and some Hellfire missiles as part of confronting terror inside the country and across the region.[47] However, on November 7, 2015, Egypt's foreign minister, Sameh Shoukry, complained that western states had not sufficiently assisted Egypt in its war against terror.[48] The United States has the resources and experience to assist Egypt to fight in Sinai. According to Robert Springborg, "The U.S. should not become directly involved in Egyptian counterinsurgency efforts in Sinai or elsewhere in the country. That would be counterproductive" because it would undermine the legitimacy of the Egyptian regime "while providing justification for terrorist acts on the basis that they are directed against Americans."[49] Indeed, U.S. support to Egypt in containing ISIS has to be limited to training and providing weapons and equipment.

In September 2017, for the first time since 2009, the United States and Egypt carried out Bright Star, their joint exercises that started in 1981. It was "a combined command-post and field-training exercise aimed at enhancing regional security and stability" by following scenarios that concern Egypt.[50] It could have helped Egypt in containing ISIS.

In 2015 the Obama administration reviewed America's contribution to the multinational force and observers (MFO) in Sinai, which monitors the demilitarization of the peninsula, as part of the 1979 peace treaty. Its troops were exposed to assaults, and they lacked weapons and armored vehicles. One option was to pull them out, but this might have had major implications.[51] Eventually in September it was decided that 75 U.S. troops would be added to the 650 troops the United States already had in the MFO, which has about 1,600 soldiers.[52] In April 2016 Israel and Egypt were notified that the United States was considering reducing the number of its troops in the MFO.[53] The goal had to be keeping the MFO operating in spite of the battles in Sinai. It was also possible because ISIS focused on Egyptian security forces and not on the MFO.

On July 25, 2017, the EU and Egypt announced the ratification of their partnership priorities for 2017–20. They will "increase cooperation in trade, investment, social justice, and climate action" and will "work to promote democracy, fundamental freedoms, and human rights as constitutional rights of all citizens as stated in Egypt's constitution and international commitments."[54] The EU could not have replaced the United States, certainly not in providing the same military aid, but the EU has been important to Egypt's economy. Egypt therefore has to consider European interests, such as respecting human rights, in spite of the effort to contain insurgents.

Reasons for a Clash between Israel and Egypt

In late September 2015 a poll published in Egypt revealed that its people consider Israel to be their worst enemy, far more than any other state.[55] In November 2015 many in Egypt saw Israel as their foe.[56] Bruce Maddy-Weitzman said on March 7, 2016, that the scale of trade and investment by Israel in Egypt and vice versa remained low. Furthermore, "on cultural and ideological levels, the dominant view among Egypt's political classes has long been one that views Israel as an aggressive geopolitical rival and competitor. 'Normalization' (*tatbi*) in the social and cultural realms remains a taboo for most Egyptians. . . . Israel's success holds up a mirror to Egypt's regional and domestic weaknesses, reinforcing long extant tendencies to view Israel in a negative light."[57] Many in Egypt wish to contain Israel in order to make the latter vulnerable and inferior to Egypt. Yet the reality seems to show the opposite: Israel's strength presents it as a powerful state but also demonstrates Egypt's low point.

In 2017 Egypt's elite were basically divided into Islamists and non-Islamists who are both against Israel. Islamists do it in their religious sermons and non-Islamists like the Nasserists, pan-Arabists, liberals, and so forth, use the media where they are dominant. Egyptian elites fear that Israel wants to take over the region and to replace Egypt. The Egyptian military used in its propaganda "anti-Israel sentiment to legitimize its role politically and economically."[58] In spite of Egypt's frustration and deep suspicion, Israel has neither the intention nor the capability to control the Middle East. Only powerful Arab states like Saudi Arabia and maybe Iran could try to do that while containing Egypt.

When Sisi ran for office in 2014, some MB claimed that Sisi was Jewish. Sisi supporters argued that the founder of the MB, Hasan al-Banna, was Jewish.[59] Hence both sides tried to slander their political rival by claiming he was Jewish. In June 2017, during the Ramadan, Egyptian TV continued to portray Israel and Jews "very negatively—as spies, thieves, killers, and socially immoral individuals, which is against the essence of this Islamic holy month, when Muslims are supposed to be tolerant and accepting of others." It occurred because the Egyptian regime kept building "the public's fear of Israel as a tool to maintain its internal control."[60] Egypt presents Jews and Israel in a negative way as part of the effort to strengthen the regime, which makes it easier to contain its opposition.

The Egyptian government might exploit an anti-Israel environment to distract its population from the huge troubles at home. It might be also the opposite, as the Egyptian public might drag its leadership to provoke Israel. In both cases the goal of the Egyptian government might not be to actually confront Israel, but it might lead to that outcome.

Egyptians are not allowed to visit Israel "without a permit from national security authorities. As a consequence, Egyptians do not travel to Israel except in three cases: diplomats at the embassy in Tel Aviv, Christian pilgrims and a few journalists trusted by the security apparatus."[61] Such strict policy means that most Egyptians cannot know Israel better, which might contribute in reducing the suspicions among Egyptians toward their northern neighbor. It is part of Egypt's strategy for containing Israel.

Paul Salem, the vice president for policy and research at the Middle East Institute, mentioned in January 2016 that Egypt remained "an important actor in regional affairs."[62] In spite of its major economic and security hardships, Egypt remains a key Arab state due to its historic role and strategic location like controlling the Suez Canal and because Egypt possesses both the strongest Arab military and the largest Sunni population among Arab countries. Such status might encourage Egypt to restore what it sees as its role in taking a leading position in the Middle East. A more ambitious Egyptian foreign policy might consider Israel an obstacle and increase Egypt's effort to contain it.

Iran, which strives for hegemony in the Middle East, considers both Egypt and Israel as strategic rivals. Iran could try to push the Islamic Jihad, a pro-Iranian terrorist organization in the Gaza Strip, to provoke Israel in order to bring a confrontation not only between Hamas and Israel but between Israel and Egypt as well. Such a war might make both states weaker, which would help Iran to contain them.

Egypt, which does not have nuclear weapons, has been trying for years to create a nuclear-free zone in the Middle East by disarming Israel.[63] In May 2015 several states, including Egypt, failed in a move to convene a UN conference in which Israel might have had to acknowledge it has nuclear weapons.[64] Egypt seeks to contain Israel's nuclear capabilities, which causes an ongoing tension between the two states. Besides that, there is the conventional arms race between the two states, which over the years did not get much public attention, yet both states are aware of the military might of their neighbor. Each state hopes to contain the military buildup of the other. Those factors might increase the suspicion on both sides, particularly in a time of crisis.

Egypt has been planning to build, with enormous Russian aid, a nuclear "power facility near Dabaa on the Mediterranean coast." The goal is not only to provide energy but also to bolster the regime's image. The project is not supposed to have any military goals. Yet "Egypt's calculus may change if Iran acquires nuclear weapon capabilities, especially since Sisi has declared his commitment to securing Gulf allies against external threats." Therefore, the United States should watch the nuclear program in both Egypt and Iran in order to stop proliferation as part of containing a nuclear arms race.[65] Israel wants the same. If Israel suspects that Egypt is trying to build a nuclear weapon, then Israel will try to stop it by putting massive political and economic pressure on Egypt. As long as there is peace between the two states, Israel will not bomb Egypt's nuclear sites, but it might use other methods like cyber warfare and sabotage. With all the risks of such actions considering the possible threat to Israel, those steps might be taken.

The United States has lost much of its influence in Egypt, which might have severe ramifications if the United States tries to reach a compromise between Egypt and Israel during a serious crisis between Israel and Egypt. Growing tensions between the United States and Egypt might reflect also on Egypt's policy toward Israel because the latter is a close U.S. partner.

All in all there are several reasons for friction between Israel and Egypt. If some of them materialize in a certain period, in a kind of "perfect storm," they might bring a severe crisis. If this is not contained in time, it can end in a clash between the two states.

Presidential Approach

In the era of two Egyptian presidents, Anwar Sadat (1970–1981) and Hosni Mubarak (1981–2011), Egyptian textbooks in schools glorified their role in the wars against Israel.[66] It happened even though those two leaders supported the peace with Israel. It could be explained as a way to demonstrate to the Egyptian people that Sadat and Mubarak were willing to fight Israel in the past but had decided to change Egypt's strategy to one that calls for peace. Those two leaders did keep some components from Egypt's policy during its conflict with Israel, such as the desire to contain Israel.

Mohamad Morsi became president in June 2012, which concerned Israel because he presented the MB. The MB could have joined others like Hamas and Iran against Israel.[67] Morsi's failure to deal with Egypt's enormous economic problems might have tempted him to change or even to abolish the peace treaty.[68] Either way he was toppled by Sisi. In December 2015 Steven Cook said that Sisi did not consolidate his power. His "reliance on coercion and patronage is an ineffective way to ensure stability, and has in turn created a more authoritarian and more unstable country."[69] Andrew Exum claimed in early April 2017 that 'Sisi's regime is very, very weak."[70] However, Sisi managed to "preserve his popularity among a significant section of the Egyptian public" in spite of the hardships of the country.[71]

There is a certain resemblance between Gamal Abdel Nasser and Sisi in their nationalistic approach.[72] From Nasser's perspective, Israel stood in his way, literally, to reach and by that to dominate Arab states like Jordan. Nasser also wished to contain Israel. In the high-intensity wars in 1956 and 1967, Israel was the one that attacked Egypt, following Nasser's provocations. Sisi seems to want the same reputation that the legendary Nasser had, but Sisi seeks that without confronting Israel. He actually collaborates with it such as against ISIS, but this could change. He might follow the traditional Egyptian goal of striving to contain Israel. There are signs to that such as Sisi's heavy investments in his military.

The Palestinian Factor

On February 13, 2016, in a speech to the Egyptian parliament, Sisi emphasized the need to solve "the Palestinian issue," which is Egypt's problem, too.[73] On May 17 Sisi again called for Israel and the Palestinians to reach an agreement. He claimed that this could warm the peace between Israel and Egypt.[74] On July 10 Egypt's foreign minister Sameh Shoukry came for a visit to Israel, the first an Egyptian foreign minister had made in nine years. He called for restarting the negotiations between Israel and the Palestinians.[75] On July 21 Sisi called for renewing the talks between Israel and the Palestinians and warned of the consequences if there were delays in this matter.[76] On September 18, 2017, Sisi met with Netanyahu in New York. The Egyptian president stressed the need to resume talks between the Palestinians and Israelis, aiming at reaching "a fair two-state solution based on international treaties."[77]

Meanwhile, there is no Palestinian state, and so there might be another confrontation between Israel and the Palestinians. It might start because of a deadly incident as it almost happened during unrest in the past. The confrontation might start with massive protests by Palestinians, but the next stage might be assaults like shooting and suicide bombers against Israelis. If the PA does not do enough to stop those attacks, Israel might regain full control of all the West Bank. If the PA is at risk, Egypt, to prove it plays a center role in the region, might try to deter Israel from bringing down the PA. Miscalculations by Egypt or Israel might lead to a collision between the two states. Such a danger makes it clear how vital it is to solve and at least to contain the Israeli-Palestinian conflict.

Egypt's government sees Hamas as a foe.[78] Israel has the same view. In the 2014 war in the Gaza Strip, it looked like Israel and Egypt were close allies. Yet the interests of Egypt and Israel were not always identical, and sometimes there was a contradiction between them. Egypt, which was the broker between Hamas and Israel, had its own terms for a cease-fire, so the fight dragged on at the expense of both Hamas and Israel. Israel wanted to end the confrontation as soon as possible, even if it has to tolerate that Hamas will be only contained, not defeated. If Egypt had shown more flexibility and creativity, the 2014 war might not have lasted so long, which would have saved lives on both sides.

Egypt has to normalize relations with Hamas so it can be a mediator between Hamas, Israel, and the PA. Egypt also needs Hamas's cooperation as part of the fight in Sinai.[79] If there is another war between Israel and Hamas, it might cause severe casualties among Palestinian civilians, which might create deep resentment in Egypt against Israel. Egypt might demand that Israel limit and even stop its actions. However, there could be collateral damage in the Gaza Strip. In such a case, growing pressure from the Arab world and inside Egypt might cause Egypt to be more aggressive toward Israel, which might ignite a serious crisis between them. Therefore Israel has to continue to contain Hamas without getting dragged into another war in the Gaza Strip.

Egypt's Military Buildup

In 2015 Egypt was aware of the need to fight guerrillas and terrorists inside its territory, but past wars against Israel still weighed "heavily in the military's calculations," and Egypt did "not discount a conventional military attack as a potential threat."[80] It is well known that "Egypt's public military exercises sometimes show troops fighting a "blue" team that seems an obvious stand-in for Israel."[81] In 2017 the Egyptian military remained "a force designed to conduct conventional war—against Israel. Major military exercises continue to presume Israel is the enemy."[82]

In early February 2015 Egypt bought twenty-four Rafale jets from France. Israel watched Egypt's military buildup, wondering about its intentions.[83] A year later a senior Israeli defense official warned that in spite of the peace with Egypt, the latter was not buying weapons as part of its struggle against ISIS because Egypt has been focused on Israel. Therefore Israel must be prepared for all kinds of scenarios "and every radical strategic shift."[84] At the same time Israel has a clear interest in containing the buildup of the Egyptian armed forces.

How Might a War Look?

In a clash between Israel and Egypt there will be many factors like cyber warfare. Other factors will be based on lessons learned from the 1948–73 Arab-Israeli wars, especially on the Egyptian front.[85] Although almost four decades later, the same sides will fight on the same ground, conducting land, air, and sea maneuvers that will resemble those of the 1948–73 wars. Naturally, military technology and weapon systems have improved dramatically, but the fundamental rules of conventional warfare that existed in the wars between Israel and Egypt from the 1940s to the 1970s would not change; in other words, the way the Israeli and Egyptian armies would maneuver and operate against each other in the wide open area of Sinai will basically be as it was in the past. Israel's hybrid wars would also affect the way the IDF might run a high-intensity war in Sinai.

Whatever the reason will be for a war, each side, because of its foe's military strength, might strive to push the frontline as far as possible from their border. The aim will be to reduce the threat to their homeland by increasing their strategic depth and also for political reasons and national pride. Egypt particularly might not be able to tolerate any presence of IDF troops in Sinai, its sovereign land. Therefore during the early stages of a clash, Israel and Egypt could seek to deploy large forces deep in Sinai. Yet Israel might avoid that, knowing Egypt's sensitivity in this matter, which might escalate the war. Reducing the number of Israeli troops sent to Sinai could help in containing the war.

The last time the IDF invaded, in a massive way, deep into enemy's territory was in 1982, when Israeli forces advanced up to 90 km inside Lebanon. Israel's foes were some Syrian units and a Palestinian hybrid force from the PLO. Since 1982, the IDF has penetrated at most several dozen kilometers into enemy's land in the hybrid war in 2006 in Lebanon. In the hybrid wars of 2008–9 and 2014 in the Gaza Strip, the IDF penetrated only a few kilometers for military and political reasons. In all those collisions Israel's foes were much weaker than the Egyptian military, yet Israel's hybrid foes exploited urban and natural obstacles such as rugged terrain to slow down and contain the Israeli offensive. The Egyptian military will have to do that in Sinai, where there are vast open areas.

In a collision in Sinai, it is possible that unlike the 1956 and the

1967 wars, there will not be a fast decision early in the campaign. In this situation an army that advances 100–150 kilometers into Sinai and then faces a very stiff resistance would have a dilemma: adopting forward defense, which demands deployment far from its bases while fighting a fully functional army whose supply lines are much shorter, or choosing defense in depth, giving up ground until an opportunity enables launching a counterattack.

Egypt's military obviously knows the Sinai, since the peninsula is Egyptian soil, and in recent years it has been a battlefield against ISIS. While Egypt learns how to fight in Sinai, although it is against ISIS and not against the IDF, the IDF is not familiar with the peninsula at all, since its withdrawal from there in the early 1980s. The IDF does train in areas similar to Sinai, that is, open desert in the Negev in the south of Israel. Still, some of its exercises take place in the north of the country, where the terrain is quite different. It resembles that of Lebanon. This is part of IDF's preparations for a hybrid war against Hezbollah. The IDF also conducts many drills in urban areas that are meant to get the IDF ready to fight hybrid wars in the houses and streets of Lebanon, the Gaza Strip, and the West Bank. In Sinai there are relatively few cities and towns, so urban warfare would not be a major factor there. However, the war might be limited to northeast Sinai, where there are towns and the city of Rafah.

Gaining air superiority will be essential. This goal could be achieved by attacking the enemy's airfields as the Israeli air force did in 1967, although advanced air defense and underground hangers will make it more difficult to conduct such an attack. The purpose will be to destroy or at least to contain enemy planes to protect their bases, thus preventing them from participating in the fight. Since both air forces rely on planes that intercept or bomb, any plane that will be busy protecting its airfields, as was the Egyptian air force during most of the 1973 war, will not bomb ground units on the front line.

Another way to dominate the skies will be to shoot down planes in massive scale, but this tactic needs more time compared with annihilating them on the ground in their airfields, and it also requires the enemy to send its fighters to battle. Israel's air force is stronger and more modern than its Egyptian counterpart, so Egypt might be reluctant to risk its planes. Yet the Egyptian air force can be forced to do that, just like the crossing of the Suez Canal by the IDF in the 1973 war pushed the Egyptian air force to try to destroy the Israeli bridgehead, an effort that cost Egypt dozens of planes. In a future war this could happen again, for example, if the IDF tries to seize a vital spot such as a crossroad or the passes in Sinai, prompting Egypt to send its planes to bomb the Israeli ground units and enabling the IAF to intercept them. The IDF could therefore contain the battlefield into a certain sector, hoping to drag the Egyptian air force to fight there.

Air-ground attacks could be crucial, particularly in an open area like Sinai, as was proved in the 1967 showdown. In a future war it will be a major tool, particularly to Israel, since it will be a way to avoid sending its ground units to combat, which might be costly. Due to Israel's high sensitivity to casualties, the IDF might try to contain its military actions to air bombardments. It will be important even if the IAF gains air superiority, but not air supremacy, since its Egyptian counterpart might still launch some air strikes here and there. The IAF might not be able to confine every Egyptian aircraft to their base. It is enough that a few Egyptian planes such as F-16 surprise an Israeli ground unit to inflict a heavy blow. Israeli troops might not be ready to absorb air attacks, since their training focuses on hybrid enemies, which do not have air power.

The complexity and risks of close air support might push both sides to rely more on bombing the land units before they reach the front line. This was done by Israeli planes in the 1956 war. In addition, in a future war Israeli planes will try to contain Egyptian units to western Sinai. Egypt's weak spots will be the Suez Canal due to the need to cross it. Egypt could deal with that by using the Ahmed Hamdi tunnel, which goes below the Suez Canal, by deploying dozens of antiaircraft batteries to protect the crossing. Other aspects of air warfare will be air-sea operations, delivering supply and equipment, and maybe also strategic bombardment on the rear as Israel did in Egypt during the war of attrition in 1969–70. Israel might again contain such bombardments to certain areas, not including population centers.

In the land campaign there might be collisions between tanks and infantry with the support of artillery and combat engineers. The training of IDF's armored corps emphasizes shooting at infantry targets and less on hitting tanks, which could have an impact in Sinai. The IDF can still destroy most of the Egyptian armor by relying on the IAF and artillery for this task. In response Egypt might try to contain the battlefield to mountain and rugged terrain in Sinai, where Egyptian troops could dig in and be safer from Israel's firepower than in open areas. There might also be vertical flanking for all kinds of aims: laying down ambushes, launching raids, and capturing key posts like crossroads. All those operations could be used to contain the battlefield.

7

IDF's Buildup and Preparations for War

Israel strives to contain its rivals without going to war, yet demonstrating Israel's military might is an essential part of enforcing containment. The IDF has to be ready to face various challenges on several fronts: guerrilla and terrorist activities in the West Bank, ongoing tension with both Hamas in the Gaza Strip and Hezbollah in Lebanon, incidents on the border with Syria in the Golan Heights, and the fight in the Sinai between Egyptian forces and insurgents. A clash and even a war might occur on one or more of Israel's fronts at any time.

The Shift from High- to Hybrid and Low-Intensity Wars

Israel's national security policy, which was created following the 1948–49 war, contains several fundamental principles. A defeat in a war would have jeopardized the existence of the state. The balance of power, based on the size of the population, land, and natural resources, has been totally in favor of the Arabs. Israel also lacked strategic depth.[1] Its military doctrine was strategically based on preventive war or a preemptive strike to defeat the enemy before it took the initiative on the battlefield.[2]

Israel's military doctrine and buildup were tested in wars that occurred between 1948 and 1982, which were mostly high-intensity ones (1948–49, 1956, 1967, 1973, and 1982). That period included countless smaller clashes, as part of low-intensity wars.[3] Like the United States in Vietnam, Iraq, and Afghanistan, Israel had to continue to prepare "to run a high-intensity war while engaging in a low-intensity war."[4] The high-intensity wars took center stage until the 1980s. Since then there was sometimes a certain probability that such a confrontation might happen again, mostly between Israel and Syria, but it did not occur. Hybrid and low-intensity wars dominated the last decades, following the confrontations between Israel and the Palestinians and Hezbollah.

Since Israel was established, the Israeli military doctrine has been based on achieving a fast victory like in 1967, when the war lasted six days.[5] The 2014 war went on for fifty days, which may have been too long. However, Israel needed only a small part of its reserves, its expenses were not very high, and its economy was not badly damaged. The war did not disrupt Israel's economy to such a degree that the IDF had to gain a quick victory in order to prevent an economic meltdown. This stands in contrast to past wars like in 1967. By tolerating the continuance of the war in 2014, Israel demonstrated that it could handle it not only economically but also psychologically. The Israelis proved their willingness to hold on. Therefore Israel stood for a relatively long fight without trying to defeat the enemy as soon as possible, but instead striving to contain it.

According to IDF Strategy from 2015, the IDF has to "achieve full and clear military defeat" of the enemy or "to cause damage to the enemy in a limited and delineated manner."[6] Yet in Israel, including in the IDF, there were those who believed "that decisive victory against nonstate players would be impossible to achieve."[7] Such an approach explains why Israel preferred to contain its foes rather than try to beat them.

The IDF relied over the years on the offensive.[8] Maj. Gen. Doron Almog (Ret.) claimed in 2005 that there is a need for a "well-balanced offensive and defensive doctrine."[9] According to IDF Strategy, "the base assumption is that the enemy cannot be defeated through defense."[10] It has to do also with active defense against rockets and missiles. Israel has Iron Dome, David Sling, and Arrow systems that are aimed at intercepting surface-to-surface missiles and rockets that Iran and its proxies might launch. Yet, by relying on such an approach, it might be impossible to contain the firing at Israel, considering the number of rockets and missiles that could be launched, particularly by Hezbollah in Lebanon. Therefore the IDF must be able to conduct a massive and powerful offensive.

The IDF, as part of its offensive, intends to gather its forces in a specific sector, to break through or infiltrate Arabs' lines, and penetrate deep into their land.[11] The IDF strove to transfer the fight onto Arab territory because of Israel's lack of strategic depth. Israel's size is 22,072 km2, including the Golan Heights and East Jerusalem (without the West Bank). Since Israel is quite small and narrow, it is possible to strike deep inside it by launching a ground attack or by striking from the air or with rockets. The main danger to Israel has been in the Tel Aviv area, the center of life in Israel, where most of the population and industrial infrastructure are located. During the era of high-intensity wars, 1948–82, Arab militaries might have managed to reach the city by ground. In the last decades the city was attacked by rockets and mostly by ground assaults like suicide bombers, as part of the hybrid and low-intensity wars with the Palestinians.

The IDF has to do its best to prevent an attack against Israel and at least to respond rapidly in order to contain and stop that attack and to destroy the invading force before it causes casualties and damages. Then Israel could retaliate, aiming at punishing and deterring its foe from confronting Israel again. This concept was relevant mostly to Arab militaries, if they had invaded. Nonstate organizations were much less dangerous, yet there were periods such as in the 1970s and between 2000 and 2005, when guerilla and terrorist attacks inside Israel cost it dearly.

In the 1973 war, Lt. Gen. David Elazar, IDF's chief of staff, said about the Israeli deployment in Sinai, "We are here with Patton and Centurion: no Sherman, only the good types."[12] Although it fought on two fronts at the same time, the Syrian and the Egyptian, the IDF sent its best tanks to the Egyptian front. This dilemma did not exist in Israel's hybrid wars in 2006, 2008–9, and 2014, since the IDF had only one front, so the IDF could have easily dispatched there its high-quality units, including its tanks.

According to IDF *Strategy* from 2015, the force buildup has to maintain a "critical mass of capabilities." Although qualitative and technological advantage was vital, "the number of means that can be activated is also important. This affects the quality and flexibility of action. Mass together with flexibility is a way of dealing with uncertainty relating to future challenges on the battlefield."[13] In January 2016 IDF's five-year plan, Gideon, aimed to "bulk up cyber-protected, networked combat capabilities while cutting back on manpower and non-combat support services."[14] The IDF continues to rely on ground units from the infantry, armor, and combat engineers with the support of other corps and the two other arms, the IAF and the navy. Their troops have to be equipped and trained to face nonstate organizations like Hamas and Hezbollah.

The IDF is based on reserves in order to possess the maximum number of soldiers and by that to narrow down Arabs' superiority in numbers.[15] In 2015 the IDF had 465,000 reserve troops who were considered to be "relatively well trained."[16] The IDF emphasized the drilling of regular troops, not the reserves.[17] Although the reserves are the main part of the IDF, the regulars did most of the fighting, such as in the war of 2014. It makes sense to rely on the regulars, since they are much more available than the reserve soldiers who are usually called for active service for several weeks every year at most. However, the regular army is quite small. In the war of 2014, four of the five regular infantry brigades together with several regular armor brigades were sent into the Gaza Strip. It was enough then, yet if there was an outburst on another front, particularly in Lebanon, the IDF would have needed its reserves as well. The IDF has to be ready to fight on more than one front at the same time, which means its reserves have to be fit to fight, since the regulars cannot carry the burden by themselves.

As to Israel's foes, Iran's military doctrine was based on lessons from its war with Iraq in the 1980s, the wars in Iraq in 2003, in Lebanon in 2006, and confrontations between Israel and Palestinians. Iran's military "doctrine centers on asymmetric warfare. It emphasizes the use of geography, strategic depth, and a general willingness to accept losses in the name of jihad as ways to confront technologically advanced adversaries such as the United States and Israel."[18]

Near the end of the 1973 war, on October 23, Secretary of State Henry Kissinger claimed, "I think it is safe to say that the Arabs have learned more from the war in '67 than the Israelis did." He added that "the Israelis continue to adopt their tactics of '67. The Arabs developed tactics to thwart the tactics of '67."[19] It was claimed in 2015 that "Israel's hybrid adversaries have managed to develop a relatively effective strategy to neutralize Israeli air- and ground-maneuver capabilities."[20] Arab hybrid outfits, like Arab militaries in 1973, managed to learn their lessons from former clashes with the IDF.

Exercises

On March 22, 2015, the IDF ran a surprise exercise near the Gaza Strip, the biggest drill that the IDF's Gaza division had carried out since the 2014 war, which examined all three arms: ground, air, and sea.[21] Israeli units had to be flexible and fast in their response so that they could be ready to fight on different fronts, each with its own conditions and demands. This requires proper training. Brigade exercises are very expensive, so they take place maybe twice a year. Since there are at least three fronts, Lebanon, Gaza Strip, and Syria, a brigade can't devote one drill solely to one front.[22] Yet there is a certain similarity in training against nonstate organizations because the latter relies on infantry tactics and on rockets and mortars.

In 2015 one of the IDF's problems was that each year infantry units were occupied too much in guarding the borders, which left them only three months to train. This constraint requires building more units, which will be tasked with securing the borders and allowing infantry brigades more time to train for war.[23]

In early May 2015 the IDF's 36th division ran a large exercise in the Jordan rift valley, aimed against Hezbollah. This drill received an unusual amount of ammunition to fire.[24] In early June 2015 Israel also conducted a large-scale exercise, Turning Point 15, which tested several services, including the IDF, in handling a massive rocket attack on Israel.[25] In the same month the IAF had its annual exercise in which all its units participated. The scenario of that drill referred to Israel's northern front.[26] In the first half of August 2015 the IDF ran an exercise in the Golan Heights in the division level. The drill examined how the IDF deals with an assault by dozens of gunmen who infiltrate from Syria into a settlement near the border while other settlements are under mortar fire from Syria. The IDF used in that exercise aircraft, artillery, and tanks in defense and offense.[27] In early September 2015 the IDF conducted a vast exercise aimed at testing senior officers and several corps, including the navy, during a possible war in both the Gaza Strip and in the north of Israel.[28]

In January 2016, for two weeks, the IDF conducted a major drill, aimed against Hezbollah and other radical Islamic groups. The head of Northern Command, Maj. General Aviv Kochavi, said that the IDF "simulated vast maneuvers, substantial fire power, and the attack of thousands of targets in all combat areas, with high efficiency, including residential areas exploited by the enemy."[29] Maj. Gen. Yair Golan, the IDF's deputy chief of staff, said on April 20, 2016, that since Hezbollah fighters deploy in civilian areas, the only way to attack them involves causing huge damages to Lebanese infrastructure and private houses.[30]

In April 2016 IDF's battalion commanders went through a course that was aimed specifically at training them to fight Hamas in urban areas.[31] During the war in Iraq, the United States had created "Iraqi towns," places that look like local villages there, as part of training troops. The IDF did the same by building facilities on its bases that resemble Lebanese villages or urban areas in the Gaza Strip.

In March 2016 the IAF conducted an intensive exercise that examined its units in various scenarios based on a large-scale rocket attack on Israel.[32] In early October 2016 the IDF's 35th paratrooper brigade carried out an exercise that included landing from the air and attacking enemy headquarters and stockpiles of long-range rockets.[33] In mid-November 2016 the IAF ran a major exercise in which all its units participated. The missions included bombing a lot of targets in a short time, landing troops from the air, delivering supplies, and intercepting rockets in case of a war in Lebanon.[34]

In September 2017 the IDF ran its biggest exercise in almost two decades, aimed at Hezbollah.[35] One of the fields examined was information security, in order to ensure that Israeli intelligence was not exposed to Hezbollah. There was also blocking of cyberattacks on IDF's networks and communication. Some Israeli units had to operate without their technology, simulating that it was knocked out by a cyberattack.[36] The entire scenario started with an assault by dozens of Hezbollah's fighters who infiltrated an Israeli village. The IDF responded with a counterattack, and then it carried out a large-scale offensive.

In February 2018 the IDF's Galilee division, such as its 769 territorial brigade, carried out a series of major exercises aimed against Hezbollah.[37] The IDF focused on Hezbollah and Hamas, yet the IDF also conducted exercises, in recent years, aimed at preparing its troops for a possible collision in the West Bank. An outburst there might begin as a result of a severe incident. In the worst case, it might turn into a low-intensity war as the one that occurred between 2000 and 2005. The IDF will try to avoid deterioration by using nonlethal measures. The Palestinian security forces might assist the IDF or not. Some of their men might even support or initiate attacks against Israelis.

Although in recent decades most of IDF's combat operations were against nonstate organizations, running hybrid and low-intensity wars, the language and concepts of high-intensity wars have being used. There is a need therefore to create theoretical approach and practical doctrine "to guide operations and accompanying force development processes."[38]

Tunnel Warfare

The IDF prepared for the war of 2014. However, it was not fully ready to find and destroy the underground paths that were used by Hamas for defensive and offensive purposes.[39] The IDF had to uncover tunnels, particularly those that penetrated into Israel, which was often a difficult task due to lack of equipment and combat doctrine. Israel has been dealing with the enemy's tunnels since the 1990s, but in 2014 there was yet no solution to this challenge, because of its complexity. Nevertheless, during the war of 2014, the IDF managed to contain this threat by destroying more than thirty tunnels, so the Palestinians did not succeed in turning this kind of warfare into a game changer.

Hamas continues to produce rockets and to dig tunnels, aiming to both penetrate into Israel and outflank Israeli troops inside the Gaza Strip in order to kill or capture them.[40] Between 2004 and 2015, Israel spent about $250 million in an effort to handle the tunnels.[41] In early March 2017 Israel's state comptroller published a report about the 2014 war, in which the government, mostly Prime Minister Benjamin Netanyahu and Defense Minister Moshe Ya'alon, were criticized for not properly preparing the IDF to deal with the tunnels.[42]

In January 2018 the IDF's Southern Command Training Base included "two types of Hamas tunnels. One is intensely claustrophobic, approximately five feet (1.5 meters) tall and two-and-a-half feet (0.8 meters) wide, with a domed roof. A soldier with a helmet, combat boots, backpack, and rifle could only hope to move in such a tunnel while hunched over and constantly scraping against the walls and ceiling. The other is far wider and taller, more than two meters (six feet) tall and nearly as wide. This was the type of tunnel used by Hamas during the 2014 war."[43] The IDF's goal was not "to fight in a tunnel, but to deal with it from above, to seal the tunnel, to blow it up, from aboveground." However, "there will be cases where the IDF has to go into tunnels, to gather intelligence or take out senior commanders," so the soldiers have to be ready for this task. That base also serves to train troops how to handle various IEDs and mines.[44]

Firepower and Weapon Systems

For the IDF, firepower is supposed to ensure low casualties among its troops.[45] The IDF *Strategy* from 2015 urged the IDF to rely on "a combined, immediate and simultaneous strike, using two basic components: the first—immediate maneuver and a second—extensive strategic-fire campaign."[46] The IDF therefore strives for a balance between firepower and ground maneuver, following years in which firepower was more dominant. The goal was to create together "synergic and systemic effects."[47]

Israel invested heavily in its military industry.[48] The Israeli armor corps has the Merkava Mark IV tanks with their armored shield protective-active, which detects and destroys antitank projectiles before they strike the tank. This protection and also the tank's 120 mm APAM-MP-T cartridges proved their effectiveness in the 2014 war. In addition, since 2017 the IDF's artillery corps have assimilated the new AccuLAR-122, a very accurate rocket, which is essential in hitting targets inside houses and by that containing collateral damage. It was all part of the effort to upgrade both the firepower and the maneuver capabilities.

In the 2014 war it seems there were sometimes "permissive rules of engagement" and overuse of firepower by the IDF.[49] However, a group of eleven former senior officers, political leaders, and officials from the United States and other nations, mostly from Europe, claimed that in the 2014 war, "Israel not only met a reasonable international standard of observance of the laws of armed conflict, but in many cases significantly exceeded that standard." In some cases this approach cost casualties among Israelis.[50] Obviously the IDF has to be careful in any use of firepower where there is an Arab population.

Israel could run a war with the weapon systems and ammunition stockpiles it already has. Yet Israel needs to refill its stockpiles and replace weapon systems that are destroyed in combat. Since the late 1960s the IAF has been depending on U.S. arsenal more than any other Israeli corps or arm. In the 1973 war the IAF lost more than one hundred aircraft, which emphasized how much Israel needed the United States to rebuild the IAF. In a hybrid war the IAF might lose a few aircraft solely, which reduces the pressure on Israel in asking the United States for more aircraft. Yet if the IDF has to spend a lot of its U.S. ammunition during a war, then the IDF will need to be resupplied. The United States can exploit that to contain Israeli actions.

In the 2006, 2008–9, and 2014 wars, both sides struck the rear of their foe. Hezbollah in 2006 and Hamas in 2008–9 and 2014 as well could not have stopped the Israeli air bombardments for lack of advanced antiaircraft missiles. Israel could not have intercepted rockets that were fired at its population until 2012, when the IDF deployed its Iron Dome. In the 2014 war this system proved itself quite well, which brought Israel to continue to produce and improve its active defense.

Following the 2014 war, Col. Nati Cohen, head of the planning department at the C4i teleprocessing branch, described that confrontation as "Israel's first full-scale network-based war. . . . Not only can various units communicate with one another directly through a common digital map, they can pass along visual intelligence, enabling each unit to see the combat arena from the perspective of other units in the air, sea and in the field." The concept is to send information "in real time."[51]

The IDF intends to assimilate new armored personal carriers (APC) instead of its old M-113, which are too vulnerable to enemy fire.[52] The IDF also tested in 2015 the possibility of turning a tank, the old Merkava Mark 2, into an APC.[53] In 2014 the IAF retired an old weapon system, the AH-1 Cobra attack helicopter.[54] In recent years other aircraft including F-16 were taken out of service while the F-35, a highly advanced fighter-bomber with stealth capabilities, was assimilated.

In the 2014 war Hamas's frogmen, who came out of the Gaza Strip, penetrated Israel. In 2015 the Israeli navy deployed dozens of sensors of "a new system named Aqua Shield that can detect and report suspicious underwater movement. The sensors were placed on the sea floor near the Gaza Strip and Lebanon's water borders with Israel."[55] In February 2016 the Israeli navy successfully tested the C-Dome system that is meant to intercept Hamas's rockets that threaten Israel's offshore gas drilling rigs in the Mediterranean Sea. The Israeli navy has also been preparing to shoot down Hezbollah's radar-guided and supersonic missiles by using the Barak 8 antimissile system. Hezbollah missiles could put in danger several targets such as Israel's ports, ships, and offshore gas drilling rigs.[56]

Conclusion

Israel, Arab states, and the United States have been conducting and experiencing various kinds of containment in recent years, as part of confronting their external and internal enemies.

The United States and Israel against Iran

The JCPOA was a milestone in U.S.-Israel relations following their long argument regarding how to contain Iran and particularly its nuclear project. Israel and the United States should not have allowed their differences about Iran to disrupt their effort to prevent Iran from producing nuclear weapons or undermining the U.S.-Israel relations. In 2015, by focusing on common ground, Israel and the United States could have turned the Iranian challenge into an opportunity both to strengthen U.S.-Israel ties and to face Iran together. Israel and the United States have to understand the constraints and advantages of their ally. As partners they should collaborate by ensuring that Iran does not try to produce nuclear weapons.

From 2013 through 2015, with others wondering whether Israel would attack Iran or not, Israel might have urged Iran to accept restrictions about its nuclear program as part of the JCPOA. However, it seems also that the United States managed to contain Israel from bombing in Iran. Israel continued with such warnings after the deal was signed in order to encourage the international community to make an effort to contain Iran.

In spite of the JCPOA, Iran has been working on other parts of its nuclear program by running missile tests, which might carry a nuclear warhead in the future. Iran assumed correctly that the Obama administration would tolerate that. Although some U.S. sanctions were imposed on Iran, after the nuclear agreement was signed, they were not enough to prevent Iran from launching its long-range missiles.

Arab states in the Gulf are more likely to collaborate with Israel against Iran than to confront Israel. The latter does have some concerns regarding military buildup of Arab Gulf states like Saudi Arabia, which buys U.S. arsenal. Yet since there is no border between Arab Gulf states and Israel, they can't clash with each other in a ground war anyway. As to other weapon systems such as vessels and ballistic missile defense, they will help Arab Gulf states to deter and contain Iran, their main enemy.

Israel hopes that the current regimes in the Gulf will not change their relatively moderate policy toward it. There might be a shift, maybe even overnight, in case of an uprising in an Arab Gulf state. However, the new regime there might not be able to operate its sophisticated weapons like aircraft because the troops who maintain and operate them might refuse to obey their new masters. Some military personal might eventually agree or be coerced to do their job. Yet they will require spare parts and technical assistance from American manufacturers. The United States will immediately cut any aid to an Arab state that will be seized by an anti-American party. As it was with Iran following the 1979 revolution, this Arab state will quickly run into difficulties in using its American arsenal, which will help to contain it.

ISIS is Israel's enemy, but Israel did not want the fight to contain this radical nonstate organization to come at the expense of containing Iran. Israel was worried about this issue, following the cooperation between the United States and Iran against ISIS. Iran managed to use the fight against ISIS to increase its influence in Iraq and by that to contain the U.S. presence in Iraq and to exploit U.S. support to contain ISIS in Iraq.

The Iranian regime neglects large parts of its population, which causes resentment. Israel, Sunni-led Arab states, and the United

States could assist the Kurds and other minorities inside Iran, including Arabs, Balouchs, Azari, and Turkmens. Outside support for minorities inside Iran will probably not undermine Iran's regime. Yet it might contain Iran by reaching a deal, even an unofficial one, in which Iran will reduce its assistance to guerrilla and terrorist groups across the Middle East in return for a similar move by other states in regard to helping insurgents in Iran. It could also help in improving the social and economic conditions of minorities in Iran.

Israel and Arab States against Iran

For several decades Israel has not faced an Arab coalition. Actually there could be an alliance between Israel and Arab states against Iran. Iran has allies, but such a pact will not be as strong as the military power that could have been mobilized against Israel in the past.

Israel and Sunni-led Arab states like those in the Persian Gulf oppose and strive to contain Iran, including its nuclear program. This could lead to military cooperation between Israel and Arab states against Iran, particularly if Iran tries to produce a nuclear weapon. Politically Arab states could not afford to join forces with Israel, but they could permit its aircraft to fly over their territory to bomb Iran.

Hezbollah has acquired up to 150,000 rockets and missiles. It is clear that Iran could strike Israel by using Hezbollah. The latter might open fire on Israel following an Israeli attack on Iran's nuclear sites. It would be the start of a war. Another scenario is that a provocation by Hezbollah such as a terrorist attack against Israel might escalate into a war, but there are fewer chances of that. Either way Iran, in order not to face Israeli air bombardments, will strive to limit the war to Lebanon and Israel. In spite of its desire to retaliate, Israel might agree to this concept, since attacking Iran might drag the United States into the war.

The War in Syria

During the Syrian civil war there were incidents along the border between Israel and Syria in the Golan Heights. Israel, which strove to contain the battles to Syria, responded to the fire from

Syria in a moderate way by destroying tiny military targets on the border, like a Syrian tank. Those small incidents in the Golan Heights might continue without causing Israel heavy casualties and damages. But if there is a major assault against Israel at the Golan Heights, its response will be accordingly. Israel might be satisfied with air strikes, but this campaign might go on and force Israel to expand its operations by using ground units. Yet even then the Israeli goal should be to contain the threat, since the alternative might be to sink into a quagmire.

Since the 1990s Israel has restrained itself when Assad has sent missiles and rockets to Hezbollah, which put Israel at risk. Israel accepted that for lack of a better choice. Yet since 2012 Israel has launched air strikes inside Syria, aimed at stopping Assad from supplying advanced weapons such as antiaircraft missiles to Hezbollah. Until 2018 Israel generally did not admit to bombing those deliveries, which has allowed both sides to contain this fragile situation by avoiding an escalation. Israel therefore has contained Hezbollah's buildup with some success. Yet Hezbollah had managed to contain the Israeli air strikes to Syria alone and to leave Lebanon out of this campaign.

Each time Israel bombed inside Syria, the Israeli population was not put on any alert. Israeli civilians knew about the air raid only after it happened. Israel did not warn its people, assuming correctly that Assad would not retaliate. It was a calculated risk. The Israeli government exposed its people to Syrian retribution in order to gain tactical surprise during the air attack and as part of denying Israel's bombardment in Syria. Israel wished to avoid a possible escalation let alone a war. If it had called its people to run for shelters, not only Syria but also Iran and Hezbollah might have assumed that Israel was about to start a war against one of them and they might have opened fire at Israel. It was one of the risks Israel took in its effort to contain Hezbollah's military buildup.

If Assad had pounded the Israeli rear with long-range missiles and rockets, some of them probably would have missed their targets. Others might have been intercepted by the Arrow and the Iron Dome. The IAF also would have tried to contain the fire by bombing launchers of missiles and rockets, although hunting them inside Syria would not have been easy.

Assad and his allies, Hezbollah and Iran, oppose Israel, but they would rather avoid a fight, since a massive Israeli offensive might jeopardize Assad's rule. Hezbollah is also too occupied helping Assad in Syria. Hezbollah's patron, Iran, does not want a clash between its protégé and Israel unless Israel bombs Iran's nuclear sites. Therefore all sides have an interest in preventing a major crisis.

Hezbollah has paid a heavy price for its intervention in Syria, but Iran has been determined to help the Assad regime to survive, with all its cost to Iran's Lebanese protégé. For Iran and Hezbollah the civil war in Syria is their campaign between the wars, that is, a confrontation between the 2006 war with Israel and the next war with it. For Iran and Hezbollah, Israel remains a sworn enemy, but containing Sunni armed groups like those that are associated with Al-Qaida or ISIS was much more important.

Iran has thousands of men in Syria, mostly its militias, including Hezbollah. Even if they are concentrated in the Golan Heights, they still will not be a force strong enough to capture any land in the Golan Heights. Actually their weapon systems will be exposed to Israeli firepower. The main threat to Israel will be from penetrations of guerilla and terrorist details, as it was there in the late 1960s. It could lead to an ongoing low-intensity war that could be contained. It will be less costly and dangerous to Israel than a full-scale offensive, as the one Syria carried out there in 1973.

Iran might not deploy its best forces in Syria, near the Golan Heights, because those troops are needed in case there is an outburst inside Iran or a war between Iran and Saudi Arabia or the United States. If Iran does send its air force and armor corps to Syria, they can't match their Israeli counterparts. Such a project will be expensive, and already there is frustration and criticism in Iran about all the money that has been poured into Syria. This opposition will grow if Iran gets entangled again in a war in Syria, this time against Israel.

Iranian forces in the Golan Heights will have to fight more than 1,000 km from their home bases while Israel's supply lines will be much shorter. It will be quite a burden for Iran to send war materials and troops all the way to the Golan Heights, particularly if the war goes on for weeks or months. Iran gained experience in delivering supplies across the region, but not in the scale of a war against a foe like Israel. Israel will intercept arms shipments from Iran, and the IDF will sink ships and bomb convoys. Israel might also bomb Iran itself, in order to contain the Iranian war effort.

The difficulties and constraints Iran will have in confronting Israel from Syria might bring Iran to contain both its presence and its activity against Israel from Syria. It does not mean that Israel has to ignore the Iranian deployment in Syria, which is a problem by itself but not to make too much of it.

Russian Involvement in Syria

Russia has been officially involved in the Syrian civil war since October 2015. Russia often acted against Israel's interest, such as by providing the s-300 to Iran. Yet Russia respected to a certain degree Israel's concerns in regard to Syria. Therefore Russia did not prevent Israel from launching dozens of air strikes, aiming at stopping the delivery of advanced weapons from Syria to Hezbollah. Russia agreed not to use Russian aircraft and antiaircraft missiles that are deployed in Syria to intercept Israeli planes, as part of the understanding that was reached between Israel and Russia. Such friction could be contained and even prevented, since basically Russia is focusing on northwestern Syria, where it has its naval and air bases, while Israel is concentrating on southwestern Syria, near the border with the Golan Heights.

Russia joined Iran and Hezbollah but seeks to prevent them from becoming too strong in Syria, let alone undermining the Russian grip in Syria. Israel prefers that Russia and not Iran be more dominant in Syria. Although Israel suspects Russia, it is obviously better for Israel to deal with Russia than with Iran and Hezbollah.

Russia will not intervene in a war between Hezbollah and Israel, particularly if the war is fought in Lebanon, where Russia is much less involved. Even if during the war Israel attacks Hezbollah inside Syria, it might not cause Russia to turn against Israel, if Israel avoids harming Russian interests, such as going after Assad. Ironically Israel could be pleased that Hezbollah's buildup was not contained but that it actually grew, thanks to Russia. The bigger Hezbollah becomes, following its cooperation with the Russian military, the easier it will be for the IDF to find and destroy Hezbollah targets.

The United States like Israel, flies its aircraft over Syria. They both must avoid a major crisis with Russia because it might deteriorate into a nuclear war. The United States, not only in the Middle East, could contain Russia, based on lessons from the Cold War, without getting dragged into a global war.

Palestinians

In the West Bank Israel does not see much hope, if any, in restarting talks with the PA. Israel therefore tries to contain both the PA and Hamas, each in a different way. Israel strives to prevent the PA from becoming a state unless it accepts Israel's terms. Hamas is more dangerous than the PA, so Israel does its best to prevent Hamas from growing stronger.

Abu Mazen tried to contain Israel in the world. Still, he is known for opposing an armed confrontation with Israel. He managed to avoid a war with Israel and kept the security cooperation with Israel. There are some mutual understandings between the security forces of both sides that are essential in containing Hamas in the West Bank. Without this cooperation, there might have been an outbreak.

The so-called one-state solution is not practical at all, since then the Jews and Palestinians will try to control and contain each other. Meanwhile, mutual distrust between Israel and the Palestinians prevents them from reaching an agreement. This is a grim situation where both sides see the other as responsible for the stalemate. They must not only understand the other side but also create internal consensus in their own camp or else there is not much chance of ending the conflict between the two nations. Until then Israel and the PA will continue to try to contain each other.

The international community, mostly the United States and the European Union, can try to convince both Israel and the PA to renew negotiations. Arab states that have leverage over Hamas or the PA should do their best to urge both organizations to reach a real reconciliation. It will be essential in a process that might end the containment of both the PA, in the West Bank, and of Hamas, in the Gaza Strip.

Hamas sticks to its hostile approach toward Israel and refuses to be part of the talks to solve the Israeli-Palestinian conflict. Therefore Israel enforces containment on the Gaza Strip such as not permitting Hamas to have free access to the Mediterranean Sea or the air space above it. This constraint causes a decline and an increasing humanitarian crisis. Israel supervises any goods and merchandise that go in and out of the Gaza Strip. If this kind of siege ends, then civilian and military supplies will pour into the Gaza Strip, including advanced rockets and missiles. In a way the containment protects Hamas's rule, since without the blockade this group would be much better armed, which would encourage it to provoke Israel. In response Israel could attack and topple Hamas. In that sense the containment of Hamas protects the group from itself.

Israel hoped that the containment would prevent war, due to its cost and since Israel did not want to be forced to seize the Gaza Strip. This approach often worked, yet there were two major rounds with Hamas in the Gaza Strip in 2008–9 and 2014. Israel maneuvered between deterring and containing Hamas on the one hand and keeping it in power on the other hand, for lack of a better alternative. Israel bombed targets and seized a tiny part of the Gaza Strip for several weeks while Hamas launched rockets and, in 2014, infiltrated Israel. Eventually the containment continued after each war.

Egypt

Egypt has to contain its deep internal troubles, mostly its economic hardships and an ongoing fight against ISIS in Sinai. Egypt must adjust and improve its military capability so it can overcome and at least contain its new security challenges by fighting a low-intensity war. This process is not easy following decades of preparations for high-intensity war against Israel.

Sinai is about 60,000 km2, although the skirmishes there are usually contained to certain sectors like the northeast. The Egyptian government tries to defeat ISIS, but a heavy-handed approach drove some of the Bedouin population in Sinai to support and even to join the insurgents. Israel helps Egypt to contain ISIS by allowing Egyptian forces to be deployed in Sinai, which violates the demilitarization of the peninsula according to the 1979 peace treaty. Israel even unofficially launched more than one hundred air strikes against ISIS in Sinai. The United States can support Egypt in containing ISIS by providing training and equipment.

In spite of the cooperation between Israel and Egypt in Sinai, Egypt fears Israel's strength and strives to contain the latter, such as its nuclear power. Israel tolerates Egypt's military buildup, although Israel rather contains this process, since it is meant for a possible war with the IDF.

Israel and other states should also assist Egypt in dealing with its huge economic problems. If not, Egypt might become a failed state or the atmosphere there might be turned into an anti-Israeli bubbling.

The IDF Prepares for War

In the era of high-intensity wars (1948–82), the IDF strove to reach a swift victory by relying on the attack, holding the initiative, and launching deep penetrations into Arab land. Since the early 1980s Israel has fought only hybrid and low-intensity wars, where the challenge is to confront not major Arab militaries but nonstate organizations, mostly Hamas and Hezbollah. Instead of facing thousands of tanks and hundreds of aircraft, the IDF has had to deal with rockets, antitank missiles, and IEDs in urban areas. Furthermore Israel has sought to contain its foes rather than try to defeat them.

In recent years the IDF has run exercises, including large-scale ones, to examine its air, land, and sea units in dealing with Hamas and Hezbollah. Learning how to handle tunnel warfare has become an important part of training, since the war of 2014. The IDF also upgraded its firepower, such as adding artillery rockets capable of hitting houses accurately, where its foe conceals its rockets, in order to reduce collateral damage.

Containment in the Middle East is expressed in many ways. The United States and Israel strive to contain Iran, including its nuclear project. However, there were disputes between the United States and Israel about how to do that, particularly with regard to the military option. It seems that the United States managed both to contain Israel so it will not bomb Iran and to contain Iran's nuclear project to a certain degree. The United States also collaborated with Iran in containing ISIS, but it meant that Iran exploited the United States to contain ISIS and at the same time Iran used ISIS to contain the U.S. presence in Iraq.

Israel has been containing Hezbollah's military buildup by bombing deliveries of advanced weapons that were sent from Syria to Lebanon. Yet Hezbollah contained Israel by forcing it to strike only in Syria and not in Lebanon.

Another kind of containment has been the effort by Arab states to control their countries. Egypt has been trying to contain both its huge economic problems and ISIS in Sinai with Israeli assistance. With strong support from Russia, Iran, and Hezbollah, Assad has contained the rebels. Israel has been containing the friction on its border with Syria in the Golan Heights following the skirmishes there. It has also been containing the PA in the West Bank while maintaining security cooperation with the PA against Hamas. In the Gaza Strip Israel continues to contain Hamas.

Containment serves several purposes. For both Israel and the PA, it has been an alternative to negotiations until the two sides can agree or force the other to restart the talks. For the United States, it was a way to avoid a war in dealing with Iran's nuclear program. Israel also has been trying to prevent a confrontation in the Gaza Strip by relying on containment, which works most of the time but not always. This approach, the result of the policy of both sides, has been causing the population in the Gaza Strip to suffer.

In other cases, containment was meant to weaken the foe without starting a war, as Israel did by bombing shipments of weapons to Hezbollah. Containment was also part of a war, like in suppressing insurgents in Egypt and Syria, which cost the population there dearly, especially in Syria. This approach was a compromise due to an inability to defeat the enemy, yet in Syria Assad eventually managed to basically win.

All in all, in the Middle East, containment has served Israel, Arab states, and the United States in many ways, but it has had its drawbacks and constraints. Sometimes containment was also used against them.

NOTES

Preface

1. U.S. Office of the Historian, https://history.state.gov/milestones/1945–1952/kennan; James L. Gelvin, *The New Middle East: What Everyone Needs to Know* (New York: Oxford University Press, 2018), 17.

2. George McGhee, *The U.S.-Turkish-NATO Middle East Connection: How the Truman Doctrine and Turkey's NATO Entry Contained the Soviets in the Middle East* (London: Palgrave Macmillan, 1990).

3. Andrew Bacevich, *America's War for the Greater Middle East: A Military History* (New York: Random House, 2016), 29.

4. Donald E. Nuechterlein, "The Reagan Doctrine in Perspective," *Perspectives on Political Science* 19, no. 1 (1990): 43–49.

5. Peter Schweizer, *Reagan's War: The Epic Story of His Forty-Year Struggle and Final Triumph over Communism* (New York: Anchor, 2003).

1. The Effort to Contain Iran

1. Dan Schueftan, "Israel's National Security," *Israel Journal of Foreign Affairs* 9, no. 1 (2015): 7–28, http://www.tandfonline.com/doi/full/10.1080/23739770.2015.1015300.

2. *Defense News*, October 28, 2015, http://www.defensenews.com/story/defense/policy-budget/leaders/2015/10/28/israeli-dm-iran-deal-done-time-look-ahead/74754218/.

3. Arnon Gutfeld, "From 'Star Wars' to 'Iron Dome,'" *Middle Eastern Studies* 53, no. 6 (July 2017): 934–48.

4. Patricia Zengerle, "Large Majority of U.S. Senate Pushes Obama to Boost Israel Aid," Reuters, April 25, 2016, http://www.reuters.com/article/us-usa-israel-defense-exclusive-iduskcn0xm14e.

5. Paul D. Miller, "Evangelicals, Israel, and U.S. Foreign Policy," *Israel Journal of Foreign Affairs* 56, no. 1 (2014): 7–26, http://www.tandfonline.com/doi/full/10.1080/00396338.2014.882149.

6. Testimony submitted to House Foreign Affairs Committee hearing, "Israel Imperiled: Threats to the Jewish State," a joint meeting held by the Subcommittee on Terror-

ism, Nonproliferation, and Trade and the Subcommittee on the Middle East and North Africa, David Makovsky, Ziegler Distinguished Fellow and Director, Project on the Middle East Peace Process, Washington Institute for Near East Policy, April 19, 2016.

7. Bacevich, *America's War for the Greater Middle East,* 12.

8. On Iran-Israel relations, see Ephraim Kam, *From Terror to Nuclear Bombs: The Significance of the Iranian Threat* (Tel Aviv: Ministry of Defense, 2004); Ronen Bergman, *Point of No Return* (Or Yehuda: Kinneret, Zmora-Bitan, Dvir 2007); Yoaz Hendel and Yaakov Katz, *Israel vs. Iran: The Shadow War* (Dulles VA: Potomac, 2012); Ehud Eilam, *Israel, the Arabs, and Iran: International Relations and Status Quo* (New York: Routledge, 2017), 73–89; Louis René Beres, *Surviving amid Chaos: Israel's Nuclear Strategy* (Lanham MD: Rowman & Littlefield: 2016). On U.S.-Iran relations, see David Crist, *The Twilight War: The Secret History of America's Thirty-Year Conflict with Iran* (New York: Penguin, 2012); Christian Emery, *U.S. Foreign Policy and the Iranian Revolution: The Cold War Dynamics of Engagement and Strategic Alliance* (New York: Palgrave Macmillan, 2013); James Bill, *The Eagle and the Lion: The Tragedy of American-Iranian Relations* (New Haven CT: Yale University Press, 1988).

9. Kenneth Katzman, "Iran: Internal Politics," Congressional Research Service (CRS), March 30, 2016, http://fas.org/sgp/crs/mideast/RL32048.pdf.

10. *Washington Post,* September 18, 2014, http://www.washingtonpost.com/opinions /2014/09/18/f786fd1c-3f56–11e4–9587–5dafd96295f0_story.html.

11. Kenneth Katzman, "Iran's Foreign and Defense Policies," Council on Foreign Relations (CFR), April 6, 2017, http://www.fas.org/sgp/crs/mideast/R44017.pdf.

12. Ben Hubbard, Isabel Kershner, and Anne Barnard, "Iran, Deeply Embedded in Syria, Expands 'Axis of Resistance,'" *New York Times,* February 19, 2018, https://www .nytimes.com/2018/02/19/world/middleeast/iran-syria-israel.html.

13. Chuck Freilich, "But Is It Good for the Jews?" *Jerusalem Post,* November 26, 2014, http://www.jpost.com/Opinion/But-is-it-good-for-the-Jews-382924.

14. "The Revolution Is Over," *Economist,* November 1, 2014, http://www.economist .com/news/special-report/21628597-after-decades-messianic-fervour-iran-becoming -more-mature-and-modern-country?frsc=dg%7ca.

15. Jay Solomo, *The Iran Wars: Spy Games, Bank Battles, and the Secret Deals That Reshaped the Middle East* (New York: Random House, 2016), 9.

16. *Washington Post,* October 30, 2014, http://www.washingtonpost.com/opinions /david-ignatius-ali-shamkhani-is-a-rising-figure-in-iranian-nuclear-talks/2014/10/30 /b6ea1238–606e-11e4–9f3a-7e28799e0549_story.html.

17. Charles D. Freilich, "National Security Decision-Making in Israel: Processes, Pathologies, and Strengths," *Middle East Journal* 60, no. 4 (2006): 635–63, http://belfercenter .ksg.harvard.edu/files/freilich_mej_autumn_2006.pdf.

18. On the Israeli nuclear option, see Abner Yaniv, *Politics and Strategy in Israel* (Tel Aviv: Sifriat Poalim, 1994), 150; Frank Barnaby, "Capping Israel's Nuclear Volcano," in *Between War and Peace: Dilemmas of Israeli Security,* ed. Efraim Karsh (London: Frank Cass, 1996), 106.

19. Michael Herzog, "Israel Views Extension of Iran Talks as Lesser of Two Evils,"

Al-Monitor, November 25, 2014, http://www.al-monitor.com/pulse/originals/2014/11
/iran-nuclear-talks-agreement-israel-influence-attack.html.

20. AFP, "Iran: Saudi Arabia Aligned with 'Zionists,'" *Times of Israel*, January 6, 2016,
http://www.timesofisrael.com/iran-calls-on-saudi-arabia-to-stop-confounding-its
-diplomacy/.

21. Full interview with Iranian foreign minister Mohammad Javad Zarif, NBC News,
March 4, 2015, http://www.nbcnews.com/news/world/full-interview-iranian-foreign
-minister-mohammad-javad-zarif-n317516.

22. Agence France-Presse, "Iran Leader Urges Defensive Preparedness," *Defense News*,
April 19, 2015, http://www.defensenews.com/story/defense/international/mideast-africa
/2015/04/19/iran-leader-urges-military-increase-preparedness/26033157/.

23. Michael Crowley, "Plan B for Iran," *Politico*, June 24, 2015, http://www.politico
.com/magazine/story/2015/06/plan-b-for-iran-119344.html#.VYsxbOnbKpo.

24. Tovah Lazaroff and Reuters, "Russia Won't Supply S-300 Missile to Iran Soon,
Minister Says," *Jerusalem Post*, April 23, 2015, http://www.jpost.com/International/Report
-Russia-says-it-wont-supply-S-300-missile-to-Iran-soon-399000.

25. Zachary Roth, "Obama Warns Iran on Aiding Yemeni Rebels," MSNBC, April 21,
2015, http://www.msnbc.com/msnbc/obama-warns-iran-aiding-yemeni-rebels.

26. Clint Hinote, "Russia's Sale of the S-300 to Iran Will Shift Military Balance,"
Newsweek, April 23, 2015, http://www.newsweek.com/russias-sale-S-300-iran-will-shift
-military-balance-324341.

27. TOI Staff, "Air Force Chief Can 'Get Job Done' If Order Comes to Hit Iran," *Times
of Israel*, April 23, 2015, http://www.timesofisrael.com/israels-air-force-chief-can-get-job
-done-if-order-comes-to-strike-iran/.

28. *Washington Post*, May 10, 2016, https://www.washingtonpost.com/world/iran
-announces-delivery-of-russian-s-300-missile-defense-system/2016/05/10/944afa2e
-16ae-11e6-971a-dadf9ab18869_story.html.

29. Haviv Rettig Gur, "Zionist Union's Soft-Spoken Nuclear Bombardier," *Times of
Israel*, March 15, 2015, http://www.timesofisrael.com/zionist-unions-soft-spoken-nuclear
-bombardier/.

30. Yossi Kuperwasser, "Israel's Role in the Struggle over the Iranian Nuclear Project,"
Besa Center, *Mideast Security and Policy Studies*, no. 114 (June 2015): 34.

31. Raphael Ahren, "Obama: If Congress Kills Iran Deal, Rockets Will Fall on Tel
Aviv," *Times of Israel*, August 5, 2015, http://www.timesofisrael.com/obama-if-congress
-kills-iran-deal-rockets-will-rain-on-tel-aviv/.

32. "Remarks by the President on the Iran Nuclear Deal," White House Press Office,
August 5, 2015, https://www.whitehouse.gov/the-press-office/2015/08/05/remarks
-president-iran-nuclear-deal.

33. Thom Shanker and David E. Sanger, "No Bunker-Buster Bomb in Israel's Weapons Deal with U.S.," http://www.nytimes.com/2013/04/23/world/middleeast/israel
-hagel-iran.html?_r=1.

34. United Nations Security Council, Resolution 2231 (2015), http://www.un.org
/en/sc/2231/.

35. J. Matthew McInnis, "Did the Supreme Leader Cut Rouhani Down to Size?" American Enterprise Institute (AEI), September 10, 2015, https://www.aei.org/publication /did-the-supreme-leader-cut-rouhani-down-to-size/.

36. *Washington Post*, August 6, 2015, https://www.washingtonpost.com/opinions/the -iran-deal-is-a-big-bet-on-a-revolutionary-outlier/2015/08/06/13d213f8–3a10–11e5 -b3ac-8a79bc44e5e2_story.html.

37. *Washington Post*, September 9, 2015, https://www.washingtonpost.com/world /middle_east/iranian-leader-no-wider-talks-with-washington-after-nuclear-deal/2015 /09/09/4e98e8ea-56da-11e5–8bb1-b488d231bba2_story.html.

38. Simon Chin and Valerie Lincy, "In Shadow of Nuclear Deal, State and Commerce Sanction Iran Proliferators," *Iran Watch*, September 15, 2015, http://www.iranwatch.org /our-publications/nuclear-iran-weekly/shadow-nuclear-deal-state-commerce-sanction -iran-proliferators.

39. Jennifer Agiesta, "Poll: Americans Skeptical," CNN, September 13, 2015, http:// www.cnn.com/2015/09/13/politics/iran-nuclear-deal-poll/index.html.

40. White House, "Remarks by President Obama to the United Nations General Assembly," September 28, 2015, https://www.whitehouse.gov/the-press-office/2015/09 /28/remarks-president-obama-united-nations-general-assembly.

41. Adam Kredo, "Iran on Israel: 'We Are Going to Destroy Them,'" *Free Beacon*, September 23, 2015, http://freebeacon.com/national-security/iran-on-israel-we-are-going -to-destroy-them/.

42. TOI Staff, "Ahead of Europe Trip, Rouhani Won't Disavow Desire to Destroy Israel," *Times of Israel*, November 12, 2015, http://www.timesofisrael.com/ahead-of-europe-trip -rouhani-wont-disavow-desire-to-destroy-israel/.

43. Tamar Pileggi, "New Mossad Chief," *Times of Israel*, January 6, 2016, https://www .timesofisrael.com/new-mossad-chief-iran-deal-significantly-increases-threat-to-israel/.

44. On Clapper, see Statement for the Record, Worldwide Threat Assessment of the U.S. Intelligence Community, Senate Armed Services Committee, James R. Clapper, Director of National Intelligence, February 9, 2016, http://www.armed-services.senate .gov/imo/media/doc/Clapper_02–09–16.pdf.

45. "PM, President Turn Out to Welcome Israel's Newest Submarine," *Times of Israel*, January 12, 2016, http://www.timesofisrael.com/pm-president-turn-out-to-welcome -israels-newest-submarine/.

46. Matthew Kroenig, "How to Unwind the Iran Nuclear Deal," *American Interest*, February 11, 2016, http://www.the-american-interest.com/2016/02/11/how-to-unwind -the-iran-nuclear-deal/.

47. Louis Charbonneau, "Exclusive: Iran Missile Tests Were 'in Defiance of' U.N. Resolution-U.S., Allies," Reuters, March 30, 2016, http://www.reuters.com/article/us -iran-missiles-idUSKCN0WV2HE.

48. "S.Res.65," U.S. Congress (official site), May 22, 2013, https://www.congress.gov /bill/113th-congress/senate-resolution/65/text.

49. Judah Ari Gross, "Army Tests Patriot Missile System as Israel-US Drill Ends,"

Times of Israel, March 7, 2016. http://www.timesofisrael.com/army-tests-patriot-missile-system-as-israel-us-drill-ends/.

50. Barbara Opall-Rome, "More than 2,500 U.S. Troops Wrapping Up Juniper Cobra in Israel," *Army Times*, March 15, 2018, https://www.armytimes.com/news/your-army/2018/03/14/more-than-2500-us-troops-wrapping-up-juniper-cobra-in-israel/.

51. "A Conversation with Javad Zarif," Council on Foreign Relations (CFR), September 23, 2016, http://www.cfr.org/iran/conversation-javad-zarif/p38314.

52. Heinz-Peter Bader, "U.N. Atomic Agency Chief Says Iran Sticking to Nuclear Deal," Reuters, October 1, 2016, http://www.reuters.com/article/us-iran-nuclear-iduskcn1213dx.

53. AP and TOI Staff, "Trump Administration Says Iran Complying with Nuclear Deal," *Times of Israel*, April 19, 2017, http://www.timesofisrael.com/trump-administration-says-iran-complying-with-nuclear-deal/.

54. Rowan Scarborough, "Iran Violating U.S. Deal with Secret Nukes Research, Opposition Group Says," *Washington Times*, April 21, 2017, http://www.washingtontimes.com/news/2017/apr/21/iran-cheat-deal-nuclear-research-opposition-group/.

55. Institute for Science and International Security, May 30, 2017, http://isis-online.org/uploads/isis-reports/documents/Mass_Production_of_Centrifuges_30may2017_Final.pdf.

56. Stephen Dinan, "Senate Voters for New Iran Sanctions over Nuclear Program," *Washington Times*, June 15, 2017, http://www.washingtontimes.com/news/2017/jun/15/iran-sanctions-backed-in-bipartisan-senate-vote.

57. Michelle Nichols, "At U.N., Western Powers Warn Iran Rocket Test a 'Threatening Step,'" Reuters, August 2, 2017, http://www.reuters.com/article/us-iran-satellite-un-iduskbn1ai1uh.

58. The White House, May 23, 2017, https://www.whitehouse.gov/the-press-office/2017/05/23/readout-meeting-between-president-donald-j-trump-and-israeli-prime.

59. TOI Staff, "Report: U.S., Israel Sign Secret Pact," *Times of Israel*, December 28, 2017, https://www.timesofisrael.com/report-us-israel-sign-secret-pact-to-tackle-iran-nuclear-and-missile-threat/.

60. Brookings, August 6, 2014, http://www.brookings.edu/blogs/iran-at-saban/posts/2014/08/06-rouhani-report-card-domestic-politics-islamic-republic.

61. "The Revolution Is Over."

62. Daniel L. Byman, "Iran's Foreign Policy Weaknesses, and Opportunities to Exploit Them," Brookings, January 3, 2018, https://www.brookings.edu/blog/markaz/2018/01/03/irans-foreign-policy-weaknesses-and-opportunities-to-exploit-them/.

63. AFP, "Iran Currency Hits Record Low, Crashing through 50,000 Rial to the U.S. Dollar," *Times of Israel*, March 26, 2018, https://www.timesofisrael.com/iran-currency-hits-record-low-crashing-through-50000-rial-to-the-us-dollar/.

64. On what the United States should do, see Michael Eisenstadt, "Regional Pushback, Nuclear Rollback," Washington Institute for Near East Policy, *Policy Notes*, 2018, http://www.washingtoninstitute.org/uploads/Documents/pubs/PolicyNote44-Eisenstadt.pdf.

65. Karim Sadjadpour, "Cold War Lessons for Iran Strategy," Hoover Institute, December 12, 2017, https://www.hoover.org/research/cold-war-lessons-iran-strategy.

66. Andrea Shalal and Sabine Siebold, "U.S. Calls for Action to Halt Iran's Growing 'Network of Proxies,'" Reuters, February 17, 2018, https://www.reuters.com/article/us-germany-security-usa-iran/u-s-calls-for-action-to-halt-irans-growing-network-of-proxies-iduskcn1g10id.

67. Josef Federman, "Mossad Chief '100 Percent Certain' Iran Still Seeks Nuclear Bomb," *Times of Israel*, April 4, 2018, https://www.timesofisrael.com/mossad-chief-100-percent-certain-iran-still-seeks-nuclear-bomb/.

68. Heshmat Alavi, "Analysis: Are Syria Strikes a Wake-Up Call for Iran?" *Al-Arabiya*, April 16, 2018, https://english.alarabiya.net/en/perspective/features/2018/04/16/analysis-Are-Syria-strikes-a-wake-up-call-for-Iran-.html.

69. Monitor's Editorial Board, "Why Trump Cannot Merely Contain Iran," *Christian Science Monitor*, May 9, 2018, https://www.csmonitor.com/Commentary/the-monitors-view/2018/0509/Why-Trump-cannot-merely-contain-Iran.

70. Jonathan Ernst, "U.S. Preparing to Impose New Sanctions on Iran: White House," Reuters, May 9, 2018, https://www.reuters.com/article/us-iran-nuclear-usa-sanctions/u-s-preparing-to-impose-new-sanctions-on-iran-white-house-iduskbn1ia37t.

71. *Washington Post*, May 21, 2018, https://www.washingtonpost.com/opinions/contain-iran-trump-should-copy-reagan/2018/05/15/42a7ede2–587b-11e8–8836-a4a123c359ab_story.html?noredirect=on&utm_term=.b5b567a88ff5.

72. Seyed Yasser Jebraily, "How Will the U.S. Nuclear Deal Pullout Affect Iran's Economy?" Aljazeera, May 29, 2018, https://www.aljazeera.com/indepth/opinion/nuclear-deal-pullout-affect-iran-economy-180528104638815.html.

73. Press TV, "Iran Putting into Service New Long-Range Radar System," Iran Project, mid-September 2015, http://theiranproject.com/blog/2015/09/14/iran-putting-into-service-new-long-range-radar-system/.

74. On the Iranian "stealth" plane, see Alexander Abad-Santos, "Iran's New 'Super' Stealth Fighter Jet Is Totally Fake," *Atlantic*, February 4, 2013, https://www.theatlantic.com/international/archive/2013/02/iran-new-stealth-fighter-jet-fake/318714/.

75. The State Comptroller and Ombudsman of Israel, September 9, 2015, http://www.mevaker.gov.il/he/Reports/Report_347/75f5a4c9–3af4–48bc-87ca-332df7a53731/007–002-oref.pdf.

76. Pride, May 2015, http://pride.org/download/pb202_Iran_in_the_Middle_East.pdf.

77. White House, "Annex to U.S.-Gulf Cooperation Council Camp David Joint Statement," May 14, 2015, https://www.whitehouse.gov/the-press-office/2015/05/14/annex-us-gulf-cooperation-council-camp-david-joint-statement.

78. Christopher Phillips, *The Battle for Syria: International Rivalry in the New Middle East* (New Haven: Yale University Press, 2016), 234.

79. Alexandra Zavis, "Saudi Arabia Signals a More Muscular Foreign Policy Less Reliant on U.S.," *LA Times*, April 20, 2015, http://www.latimes.com/world/middleeast/la-fg-saudi-foreign-policy-20150420-story.html#page=2.

80. Kenneth M. Pollack, "Why the Iran Deal's Second Anniversary May Be Even More Important than the First," Brookings, July 14, 2016, http://www.brookings.edu/blogs/markaz/posts/2016/07/14-iran-deal-anniversary-pollack.

81. Anthony H. Cordesman, "Saudi Arabia and the United States," Center for Strategic International Studies (CSIS), March 10, 2016, http://csis.org/files/publication/160310 _cordesman_saudi_arabia.pdf.

82. Carolyn Barnett, "Egypt in the Region," In *Rocky Harbors*, ed. Jon B. Alterman, Center for Strategic International Studies (CSIS), 2015. http://csis.org/files/publication /150311_rocky_harbors_chapter8.pdf.

83. Zalmay Khalilzad, "The Neoconservative Case for Negotiating with Iran," *Politico*, March 28, 2016, http://www.politico.com/magazine/story/2016/03/iran-negotiation -foreign-policy-middle-east-213772#ixzz44m1wbliq.

84. Nawaf Obaid, "Saudi Arabia Is Preparing Itself in Case Iran Develops Nuclear Weapons," *Telegraph*, June 29, 2015, http://www.telegraph.co.uk/news/general-election -2015/politics-blog/11705381/Nawaf-Obaid-Saudi-Arabia-is-preparing-itself-in-case -Iran-develops-nuclear-weapons.html.

85. "Saudi Crown Prince," CBS News, March 15, 2018, https://www.cbsnews.com /news/saudi-crown-prince-mohammed-bin-salman-iran-nuclear-bomb-saudi-arabia/.

86. Bruce Riedel, "Iran and the Bomb," Brookings Institute, December 1, 2016, https:// www.brookings.edu/blog/markaz/2016/12/01/iran-and-the-bomb-what-would-saudi -arabia-do/.

87. Aaron Mehta and Awad Mustafa, "State: $33 Billion in GCC Weapon Sales in 11 Months," *Defense News*, March 25, 2016, http://www.defensenews.com/story/defense /policy-budget/budget/2016/03/25/state-33-billion-gcc-weapon-sales-11-months /82255660/.

88. Efraim Inbar, "U.S. Mideast Retreat a Boon for Moscow and Tehran," *Middle East Quarterly*, Summer 2016, http://www.meforum.org/6042/us-mideast-retreat.

89. "Supporting Saudi Arabia's Defense Needs," U.S. Department of State, May 20, 2017, https://www.state.gov/r/pa/prs/ps/2017/05/270999.htm.

90. Tamar Pileggi and AFP, "After Saudi Arms Deal, Ministers Fret about Israel's Military Edge," *Times of Israel*, May 21, 2017, http://www.timesofisrael.com/after-saudi-arms -deal-ministers-fret-about-israels-military-edge/.

91. AFP, "Liberman Expresses Unease over Massive Saudi Arms Deal," *Times of Israel*, May 25, 2017, http://www.timesofisrael.com/liberman-expresses-unease-over-massive -saudi-arms-deal/.

92. On that deal, see Nicholas Laham, *Selling AWACS to Saudi Arabia: The Reagan Administration and the Balancing of America's Competing Interests in the Middle East* (Westport CT: Praeger, 2002).

93. "Supporting Saudi Arabia's Defense Needs," U.S. Department of State, May 20, 2017, https://www.state.gov/r/pa/prs/ps/2017/05/270999.htm.

94. On selling the Iron Dome, see Benjamin Weinthal, "Report: Saudi Arabia Sought to Buy Israel's Iron Dome System," *Jerusalem Post*, January 8, 2018, http:// www.jpost.com/Middle-East/Report-Saudi-Arabia-sought-to-buy-Israels-Iron-Dome -system-533185.

95. Martin Indyk, *Innocent Abroad: An Intimate Account of American Peace Diplomacy in the Middle East* (New York: Simon and Schuster, 2009).

96. *Washington Post*, September 18, 2014, http://www.washingtonpost.com/opinions /2014/09/18/f786fd1c-3f56–11e4–9587–5dafd96295f0_story.html.

97. Toby Dodge, "Can Iraq Be Saved?" *Survival* 56, no. 5 (October-November 2014): 7–20.

98. Raphael Ahren, "Israel Acknowledges It Is Helping Syrian Rebel Fighters," *Times of Israel*, June 29, 2015, http://www.timesofisrael.com/yaalon-syrian-rebels-keeping-druze -safe-in-exchange-for-israeli-aid/.

99. Tim Arango, "Iran Dominated in Iraq after U.S. 'Handed the Country Over,'" *New York Times*, July 25, 2017, https://www.nytimes.com/2017/07/15/world/middleeast/iran -iraq-iranian-power.html.

100. Michael Eisenstadt, "Iran and Iraq," Washington Institute for Near East Policy, September 13, 2015, http://www.washingtoninstitute.org/policy-analysis/view/iran-and-iraq.

101. Sergei Karpukhin, "Iran and Iraq Sign Accord to Boost Military Cooperation," Reuters, July 23, 2017, http://www.reuters.com/article/us-iran-iraq-military-iduskbn1a80hj.

102. Tim Arango, "Iran Dominated."

103. Ahmed Rasheed and Sylvia Westall, "With a Wary Eye on Iran, Saudi and Iraqi Leaders Draw Closer," Reuters, August 16, 2017, http://www.reuters.com/article/us-mideast -crisis-saudi-iraq-iduskcn1aw1la.

104. Arango, "Iran Dominated."

105. Arango, "Iran Dominated."

106. Karim Sadjadpour, "Cold War Lessons for Iran Strategy," Hoover Institute, December 12, 2017, https://www.hoover.org/research/cold-war-lessons-iran-strategy.

107. Daniel L. Byman, "Is Hezbollah Less Dangerous to the United States?" Brookings Institute, October 18, 2016, https://www.brookings.edu/blog/markaz/2016/10/18 /is-hezbollah-less-dangerous-to-the-united-states/.

108. Eric Cortellessa, "U.S. Offers Millions for Two of Hezbollah's Top Operatives," *Times of Israel*, October 10, 2017, https://www.timesofisrael.com/us-offers-millions-for -two-of-hezbollahs-top-operatives/.

109. Ron Prosor, "There's Still Time to Avert War in Lebanon," *Wall Street Journal*, May 29, 2017, https://www.wsj.com/articles/theres-still-time-to-avert-war-in-lebanon -1496095992.

110. TOI Staff and Agencies, "Israel Envoy Hails 'Victory' as UN Expands Lebanon Peacekeeping Role," *Times of Israel*, August 31, 2017, https://www.timesofisrael.com/israel -envoy-hails-victory-as-un-expands-lebanon-peacekeeping/.

111. Emanuele Ottolenghi, "Hezbollah in Latin America Is a Threat the U.S. Cannot Ignore," *Hill*, June 11, 2017, http://thehill.com/blogs/pundits-blog/homeland-security /337299-hezbollah-in-latin-america-is-a-security-threat-the-us.

112. Jonathan Ernst, "Attorney General Sessions Sets Up Hezbollah Investigation Team," Reuters, January 11, 2018, https://www.reuters.com/article/us-usa-hezbollah/attorney -general-sessions-sets-up-hezbollah-investigation-team-iduskbn1f01v3.

113. Charles D. Freilich, "Has Israel Grown Too Dependent on the United States?" *Mosaic*, February 5, 2018,

114. John Waterbury, Alan Richards, Melani Cammett, and Ishac Diwan, *A Political Economy of the Middle East* (New York: Routledge, 2018).

115. David Schenker, "Twenty Years of Israeli-Jordanian Peace," Washington Institute for Near East Policy, October 23, 2014, http://www.washingtoninstitute.org/policy-analysis/view/twenty-years-of-israeli-jordanian-peace-a-brief-assessment.

116. Congressional Research Service (CRS), November 14, 2017, https://fas.org/sgp/crs/mideast/rl33546.pdf.

117. Hardin Lang, William Wechsler, and Alia Awadallah, "The Future of U.S.-Jordanian Counterterrorism Cooperation," Center for American Progress, November, 30, 2017, https://www.americanprogress.org/issues/security/reports/2017/11/30/443272/future-u-s-jordanian-counterterrorism-cooperation/.

118. "Growing Stress on Jordan," CFR, March 2016, http://www.cfr.org/jordan/growing-stress-jordan/p37635.

119. Jacob Olidort, "Terrorists and Territory," *Lawfare*, July 7, 2017, https://www.lawfareblog.com/terrorists-and-territory-what-jordan-can-teach-us-about-managing-jihadists.

120. Anna Ahronheim, "Israel to Be Key Player in the Next Chapter of Syria's War," *Jerusalem Post*, February 1, 2018, http://www.jpost.com/Arab-Israeli-Conflict/Israel-to-be-key-player-in-the-next-chapter-of-Syrias-war-542326.

121. Marc Lynch, *The New Arab Wars: Uprisings and Anarchy in the Middle East* (New York: Public Affairs, 2016), 38.

122. Bruce Riedel, "In Yemen, Iran Outsmarts Saudi Arabia Again," Brookings, December 16, 2017, https://www.brookings.edu/blog/markaz/2017/12/06/in-yemen-iran-outsmarts-saudi-arabia-again/.

123. Lynch, *The New Arab Wars*, 2.

124. Riedel, "In Yemen, Iran Outsmarts Saudi Arabia Again,"

125. James F. Jeffrey, "Contain Iran? Fine, but Answer These Questions First," Washington Institute for Near East Policy, June 1, 2017, http://www.washingtoninstitute.org/policy-analysis/view/contain-iran-fine-but-answer-these-questions-first.

126. Ray Takeyh, "It's Time to Prepare for Iran's Political Collapse," *Washington Post*, July 5, 2017, https://www.washingtonpost.com/news/global-opinions/wp/2017/07/05/its-time-to-prepare-for-irans-political-collapse/?utm_term=.0927b5734294.

127. Galip Dalay, "Why Iranian Kurds Have Been Resistant to the Regional Turmoil So Far," *Middle East Eye*, September 14, 2017, http://www.middleeasteye.net/essays/are-iranian-kurds-impervious-regional-turmoil-674728237.

128. Arash Saleh, "Iranian Kurds, a Key Partner in 'Containment of Iran,'" *Jerusalem Post*, March 1, 2017, http://www.jpost.com/Opinion/Iranian-Kurds-a-key-partner-in-containment-of-Iran-482950.

129. "Return to Arms," Aljazeera, September 26, 2017, http://www.aljazeera.com/programmes/aljazeeraworld/2017/04/return-arms-hadaka-170424172311654.html.

130. Saleh, "Iranian Kurds."

131. Shahin Gobadi, "Growing Understanding of the Viability of Regime Change in Iran," *Al-Arabiya*, June 28, 2017, https://english.alarabiya.net/en/views/2017/06/28/Growing-understanding-of-the-viability-of-regime-change-in-Iran.html.

132. Saleh, "Iranian Kurds."

2. The Iranian-Israeli-Arab Triangle

1. David Ben Gurion, *Uniqueness and Destiny* (Tel Aviv: Ministry of Defense, 1972); Yaniv, *Politics and Strategy in Israel*; Israel Tal, *National Security* (Tel Aviv: Dvir, 1996); Michael L. Handel, *Israel's Political-Military Doctrine* (Cambridge: Harvard University Press, 1973); Avi Shlaim, *The Iron Wall* (Tel Aviv: Ydiot Ahronot, 2005); Ehud Eilam, *Israel's Way of War: A Strategic and Operational Analysis, 1948–2014* (Jefferson NC: McFarland, 2016); Charles D. Freilich, *Israeli National Security* (New York: Oxford University Press, 2018).

2. "Final Communiqué of the Extraordinary Islamic Summit Conference," Member States of the Organization of Islamic Cooperation (OIC), December 13, 2017, https://www.oic-oci.org/docdown/?docid=1699&refid=1073.

3. Avi Primor, "'No Permanent Allies, No Permanent Enemies, Only Permanent Interests': Israeli-Iranian Relations," *Israel Journal of Foreign Affairs* 8, no.1 (January 2014): 36.

4. Luke Baker and Dan Williams, "As Iran Deal Takes Shape, Israel Plays Up Regional Common Ground," Reuters, June 18, 2015, http://www.reuters.com/article/2015/06/18/us-nuclear-iran-israel-idUSKBN0OX1TI20150618.

5. Yoel Guzansky, "Israel and the Arab Gulf States," *Israel Affairs* 21, no. 1 (2015): 131–47.

6. Adam Entous, "Donald Trump's New World Order," *New Yorker*, June 18, 2018, https://www.newyorker.com/magazine/2018/06/18/donald-trumps-new-world-order.

7. IDF, November 23, 2015, https://www.idfblog.com/blog/2015/11/23/idf-strategy/.

8. JTA, "Israel's Foreign Ministry Chief," *Times of Israel*, July 30, 2015, http://www.timesofisrael.com/foreign-ministry-sunni-arab-nations-are-allies/.

9. TOI Staff, "Some in Saudi Media Criticize Anti-Semitism, Warm Up to Israel," *Times of Israel*, August 12, 2016, http://www.timesofisrael.com/saudi-media-battles-anti-semitism-warms-up-to-israel/.

10. "The Misconceptions of Israeli-Gulf Cooperation," Middle East Institute, July 26, 2016, http://www.mei.edu/content/article/misconceptions-israeli-gulf-cooperation.

11. Anthony H. Cordesman, "Iran and the Gulf Military Balance," Center for Strategic International Studies (CSIS), October 4, 2016, https://www.csis.org/analysis/iran-and-gulf-military-balance-1.

12. TOI Staff, "11 Arab Countries Accuse Iran of Sponsoring Middle East Terror," *Times of Israel*, November 14, 2016, http://www.timesofisrael.com/11-arab-countries-accuse-iran-of-sponsoring-middle-east-terror/.

13. Simon Henderson, "Oil and Islam," Washington Institute for Near East Policy, July 15, 2016, http://www.washingtoninstitute.org/policy-analysis/view/oil-and-islam-saudi-policy-post-jcpoa.

14. Dr. Theodore Karasik, "Is the Time Up for Iran's Forays in the Middle East?" *Al Arabiya*, May 30, 2017, https://english.alarabiya.net/en/views/2017/05/30/Is-the-time-up-for-Iran-s-forays-in-the-Middle-East-.html.

15. On the 2006 war, see Amos Harel and Avi Issacharoff, *34 Days: Israel, Hezbollah, and the War in Lebanon* (New York: Palgrave Macmillan, 2008); Amir Rapaport, *Friendly Fire* (Tel Aviv: Ma'ariv, 2007); Shmuel Gordon, *The Second Lebanon War: Strategic Decisions and Their Consequences* (Ben-Shemen, Israel: Modan, 2012).

16. Lynch, *The New Arab Wars*, 16.

17. Dennis Ross, "The Next Mideast Explosion," Washington Institute for Near East Policy, May 20, 2018, http://www.washingtoninstitute.org/policy-analysis/view/the -next-mideast-explosion.

18. About the 150,000 rockets, see the testimony submitted to House Foreign Affairs Committee hearing, "Israel Imperiled: Threats to the Jewish State," a joint meeting held by the Subcommittee on Terrorism, Nonproliferation, and Trade and the Subcommittee on the Middle East and North Africa, David Makovsky, Ziegler Distinguished Fellow and Director, Project on the Middle East Peace Process, Washington Institute for Near East Policy, April 19, 2016.

19. Israel's Changing Threat Environment: Testimony before the House Foreign Affairs Committee, Joint Hearing of the Subcommittee on Terrorism, Nonproliferation, and Trade and the Subcommittee on the Middle East and North Africa, Tamara Cofman Wittes, Senior Fellow and Director, Center for Middle East Policy, Brookings Institution, April 19, 2016.

20. Daniel Sobelman, "Deterrence Has Kept Hezbollah and Israel at Bay for 10 Years," *National Interest*, July 14, 2016, http://nationalinterest.org/feature/deterrence-has-kept -hezbollah-israel-bay-10-years-16970?page=2.

21. Yaakov Lappin, "The Low-Profile War between Israel and Hezbollah," BESA, *Mideast Security and Policy Studies*, no. 138 (August 2017): 12.

22. Byman, "Is Hezbollah Less Dangerous to the United States?."

23. Anna Ahronheim, "Hezbollah Spread Too Thin to Start a War with Israel," *Jerusalem Post*, September 5, 2017, http://www.jpost.com/Arab-Israeli-Conflict/Hezbollah -spread-too-thin-to-start-a-war-with-Israel-504234.

24. Dmitry Adamsky, "Russia and the Next Lebanon War," *Foreign Affairs*, October 6, 2017.

25. Anna Ahronheim, "Liberman Tells Hezbollah's Nasrallah to 'Stay in His Bunker,'" *Jerusalem Post*, February 21, 2017, http://www.jpost.com/Arab-Israeli-Conflict/Liberman -tells-Hezbollahs-Nasrallah-to-stay-in-his-bunker-482165.

26. Mark Dubowitz and Mike Gallagher, "Averting a Third Lebanon War," *Wall Street Journal*, August 1, 2017, https://www.wsj.com/articles/averting-a-third-lebanon-war -1501615194.

27. Bethan McKernan, "Israel Holds Largest Military Drill in 20 Years, 'Simulating War' with Hezbollah," *Independent*, September 5, 2017, http://www.independent.co.uk /news/world/middle-east/israel-hezbollah-military-drill-lebanon-idf-defence-force -war-simulation-syria-iran-a7930461.html.

28. Sulome Anderson, "Hezbollah's New Strength Leaves Israeli Border Tense," NBC News, September 16, 2017, https://www.nbcnews.com/news/world/hezbollah-s-new -strength-leaves-israeli-border-tense-n801596.

29. On Hezbollah's activities, see Matthew Levitt, *Hezbollah: The Global Footprint of Lebanon's Party of God* (Washington DC: Georgetown University Press, 2013).

30. Ori Lewis, "Hezbollah Using U.S. Weaponry in Syria," Reuters, December 21, 2016, http://www.reuters.com/article/us-mideast-crisis-israel-hezbollah-iduskbn14a19w.

31. Byman, "Is Hezbollah Less Dangerous to the United States?"

32. Hanin Ghaddar, "A War with Hizbollah Would Essentially Mean War with Iran This Time Around," Washington Institute for Near East Policy, September 4, 2017, http://www .washingtoninstitute.org/policy-analysis/view/a-war-with-hizbollah-would-essentially -mean-war-with-iran-this-time-around.

33. Ali Al-Amin, "Hezbollah's Hegemony Will Fail in Lebanon," *Al Arabiya*, August 16, 2017, https://english.alarabiya.net/en/views/2017/08/16/Hezbollah-s-hegemony -will-fail-in-Lebanon.html.

34. Joseph Daher, *Hezbollah: The Political Economy of Lebanon's Party of God* (London: Pluto, 2016).

35. Jonathan Spyer, "Israel and Hezbollah," *Jerusalem Post*, July 22, 2017, http://www .jpost.com/International/Israel-and-Hezbollah-The-battle-before-the-battle-499654.

36. Katzman, "Iran's Foreign and Defense Policies."

37. Marissa Newman, "Iranian Supreme Leader Calls for Israel's 'Annihilation,'" *Times of Israel*, November 9, 2014, http://www.timesofisrael.com/iranian-supreme-leader-calls -for-israels-annihilation/.

38. Raphael Ahren, "Arab World Won't Go for Israeli Diplomatic Blitz, and Netanyahu Knows It," *Times of Israel*, July 29, 2016, http://www.timesofisrael.com/arab-world-wont -go-for-israeli-diplomatic-blitz-and-netanyahu-knows-it/.

39. Lally Weymouth, "King Abdullah," *Washington Post*, April 6, 2017, https://www .washingtonpost.com/opinions/king-abdullah-compromise-with-russia-on-crimea-to -get-its-help-in-syria/2017/04/06/b985b894–1a61–11e7-bcc2–7d1a0973e7b2_story .html?utm_term=.c0830488f1f5.

40. "Saudi Arabia and Egypt Sign 'Cairo Declaration,'" Aljazeera, July 30, 2015, http://www.aljazeera.com/news/2015/07/saudi-arabia-egypt-sign-cairo-declaration -150731005229377.html.

41. Khaled Dawoud, "Egypt and Saudi Make a Public Show of Support," Atlantic Council, August 11, 2015, http://www.atlanticcouncil.org/blogs/egyptsource/egypt -and-saudi-make-a-public-show-of-support.

42. Weber and Craig, "Cooperating Not Condoning."

43. "Sisi Approves Cooperation Agreement on Peaceful Use of Nuclear Energy with Saudi Arabia," *Ahram*, September 28, 2017, http://english.ahram.org.eg/NewsContent/1 /64/277929/Egypt/Politics-/Sisi-approves-cooperation-agreement-on-peaceful-us.aspx.

44. Ahmend Eleiba, "Egyptian, Saudi Air Forces Start 'Faisal 11' Joint Military Drill," *Ahram*, September 14, 2017, http://english.ahram.org.eg/NewsContent/1/64/277122 /Egypt/Politics-/Egyptian,-Saudi-air-forces-start-Faisal—joint-mil.aspx.

45. Ron Ben-Yishai, "The PBC Has Its Own Rules," *Ynet*, March 19, 2014, http://www .ynet.co.il/articles/0,7340,l-4500826,00.html.

46. IDF, November 23, 2015, https://www.idfblog.com/blog/2015/11/23/idf-strategy/.

47. IDF, November 23, 2015, https://www.idfblog.com/blog/2015/11/23/idf-strategy/.

48. "The United Nations," On the UN, see *Ynet*, June 28, 2014, http://www.ynet.co.il /articles/0,7340,l-4535381,00.html.

49. Nana 10, February 25, 2014, http://news.nana10.co.il/Article/?Articleid=1040412.

3. The War in Syria

1. Avner Yaniv, Mohse Ma'oz, and Avi Kober, eds., *Syria and Israel's National Security* (Tel Aviv: Ministry of Defense, 1991); Mohse Ma'oz, *Syria and Israel: From War to Peace-Making* (Tel Aviv: Ma'ariv, 1996); Itamar Rabinovich, *The Lingering Conflict: Israel, the Arabs, and the Middle East* (Washington: Brookings Institute, 2012).

2. Phillips, *The Battle for Syria*, 11–12.

3. Jonathan Spyer, "Assad's Hollow Crown," Rubin Center, May 9, 2017, http://www.rubincenter.org/2017/05/assads-hollow-crown/.

4. "Syria Regional Refugee Response," UNCHR, May 31, 2018, https://data2.unhcr.org/en/situations/syria.

5. Megan Specia, "How Syria's Death Toll Is Lost in the Fog of War," *New York Times*, April 13, 2018, https://www.nytimes.com/2018/04/13/world/middleeast/syria-death-toll.html.

6. TOI Staff, full text of Netanyahu 2015 address to the UN General Assembly, *Times of Israel*, October 1, 2015, http://www.timesofisrael.com/full-text-of-netanyahu-2015-address-to-the-un-general-assembly/.

7. Rory Jones, Noam Raydan, and Suha Ma'ayeh, "Israel Gives Secret Aid to Syrian Rebels," *Wall Street Journal*, June 18, 2017, https://www.wsj.com/articles/israel-gives-secret-aid-to-syrian-rebels-1497813430.

8. On the number of rockets in 2006, see Bruce Riedel, "Israel's Dilemma: If It Attacks Iran, Will It Also Have to Hit Hezbollah?," Brookings, February 9, 2012, http://www.brookings.edu/research/opinions/2012/02/09-iran-israel-riedel. For 2013, see Dan Williams, 'Israel Says David's Sling Missile Interceptor Passes New Test," Reuters, November 20, 2013, http://www.reuters.com/article/2013/11/20/us-arms-israel-interceptor-idusbre9aj0bc20131120. About the 150,000 rockets, see the testimony submitted to House Foreign Affairs Committee hearing, "Israel Imperiled," a joint meeting held by the Subcommittee on Terrorism, Nonproliferation, and Trade and the Subcommittee on the Middle East and North Africa. David Makovsky, Ziegler Distinguished Fellow and Director, Project on the Middle East Peace Process, Washington Institute for Near East Policy, April 19, 2016.

9. Jean-Loup Samaan, "From War to Deterrence? Israel-Hezbollah Conflict since 2006," Strategic Studies Institute and U.S. Army War College Press, 2014, 45. https://ssi.armywarcollege.edu/pdffiles/PUB1198.pdf.

10. Anna Ahronheim and jpost.com Staff, "Liberman: Israel Strikes Aimed at Thwarting WMD Transfers to Hezbollah," *Jerusalem Post*, December 7, 2016, http://www.jpost.com/Arab-Israeli-Conflict/Liberman-Israel-is-working-to-thwart-Hezbollah-weapon-transfers-474710.

11. Tamar Pileggi, "IDF Chief Says Lebanon Responsible for Next Conflict with Hezbollah," *Times of Israel*, March 20, 2017, http://www.timesofisrael.com/idf-chief-says-lebanon-responsible-for-next-conflict-with-hezbollah/.

12. Suleiman Al-Khalidi and Angus McDowall, "Israel Strikes Arms Depot near Damascus Airport," Reuters, April 27, 2017, http://www.reuters.com/article/us-mideast-crisis-syria-air-strike-idUSKBN17T0GU.

13. AP and TOI Staff, "Israel Said to Have Hit Hezbollah Convoys Dozens of Times," *Times of Israel*, August 18, 2017, http://www.timesofisrael.com/israel-said-to-have-hit-hezbollah-convoys-dozens-of-times/.

14. Luke Baker and Laila Bassam, "Israeli Strikes Raise Stakes in Face-off with Hezbollah," Reuters, May 2, 2017, http://www.reuters.com/article/us-mideast-crisis-israel-hezbollah-analy-idUSKBN17Y20O.

15. Lappin, "The Low-Profile War between Israel and Hezbollah."

16. Amos Yadlin, "How to Understand Israel's Strike on Syria," *New York Times*, September 8, 2017, https://www.nytimes.com/2017/09/08/opinion/how-to-understand-israels-strike-on-syria.html?smid=fb-share.

17. Ahronheim, "Israel to Be Key Player in the Next Chapter of Syria's War."

18. "Israel Strikes Iranian Targets in Syria in Response to Rocket Fire," BBC, May 10, 2018, http://www.bbc.com/news/world-middle-east-44063022.

19. Anna Ahronheim, "Senior Official: Iran Still Has Long-Range Capabilities to Strike Israel," *Jerusalem Post*, May 10, 2018, https://www.jpost.com/Arab-Israeli-Conflict/Senior-official-Iran-still-has-long-range-capabilities-to-strike-Israel-556108; Anna Ahronheim, "Israel Strikes Dozens of Iranian Targets in Syria," https://www.jpost.com/Middle-East/Israel-strikes-dozens-of-Iranian-targets-in-Syria-556034.

20. "Israel Says It Hit Iranian Military Targets in Syria," Aljazeera, May 10, 2018, https://www.aljazeera.com/news/2018/05/israel-hit-iranian-targets-syria-180510045201451.html.

21. TOI Staff, "House Scraps Proposal for U.S. Recognition of Israeli Sovereignty in Golan Heights," *Times of Israel*, May 26, 2018, https://www.timesofisrael.com/house-scraps-proposal-for-us-recognition-of-israeli-sovereignty-in-golan-heights/.

22. Jubin M. Goodarzi, "Syria and Iran: Alliance Cooperation in a Changing Regional Environment," *Middle East Studies* 4, no. 2 (2013): 31–59.

23. Joseph Olmert, "Israel and Alawite Syria: The Odd Couple of the Middle East?" *Israel Journal of Foreign Affairs* 7, no. 1 (January 2013): 24–25.

24. Amir Taheri, "Why Iran's Plan in Syria Will Fail," *Al Arabiya*, September 16, 2017, https://english.alarabiya.net/en/views/2017/09/16/Why-Iran-s-plan-in-Syria-will-fail.html.

25. Phillips, *The Battle for Syria*, 234.

26. "Tehran: 2,100 Iranian Soldiers Killed in Syria and Iraq," *Middle East Monitor*, March 7, 2018, https://www.middleeastmonitor.com/20180307-tehran-2100-iranian-soldiers-killed-in-syria-and-iraq/.

27. Nicole Gaouette, "Israel Claims 82,000 Fighters Are under Iranian Control in Syria," CNN, January 25, 2018, https://www.cnn.com/2018/01/25/politics/danon-israel-iran-syria-un/index.html.

28. Farzin Nadimi, "Iran's Air Force Overshadowed by the IRGC," Washington Institute for Near East Policy, May 27, 2016, http://www.washingtoninstitute.org/policy-analysis/view/irans-air-force-overshadowed-by-the-irgc.

29. "Israel, Hizbollah, and Iran," Crisis Group, February 7, 2018, https://www.crisisgrouorg/middle-east-north-africa/eastern-mediterranean/syria/182-israel-hizbollah-and-iran-preventing-another-war-syria.

30. David W. Lesch, "Iran Is Taking Over Syria. Can Anyone Stop It?" *New York Times*, August 29, 2017, https://www.nytimes.com/2017/08/29/opinion/iran-syria.html?ref=opinion&_r=0.

31. Tom Perry and Laila Bassam, "Hezbollah: We Don't Want War," Reuters, January 30, 2015, http://www.reuters.com/article/us-mideast-crisis-hezbollah-israel-idUSKBN0L31QE20150130?irpc=932.

4. Russian Involvement in Syria

1. Phillips, *The Battle for Syria*, 30.

2. Dave Majumdar, "Not So Scary," *National Interest*, October 20, 2015, http://nationalinterest.org/blog/the-buzz/not-so-scary-why-russias-military-paper-tiger-14136?page=2.

3. Alexander Shein, "Russian Ambassador Defends Country's 'Anti-Terror' Syria Ops in JPOST Op-ed," *Jerusalem Post*, September 26, 2017, http://www.jpost.com/Opinion/Two-years-of-our-fight-against-terrorism-in-Syria-506057.

4. Julian Borger and Kareem Shaheen, "Russia Accused of War Crimes in Syria at UN Security Council Session," *Guardian*, September 26, 2016, https://www.theguardian.com/world/2016/sep/25/russia-accused-war-crimes-syria-un-security-council-aleppo.

5. Yosef Govrin, *Israeli-Soviet Relations, 1953–1967* (London: Routledge, 1998).

6. Edward C. Keefer, gen. ed., *Arab-Israeli Crisis and War 1973* (Washington DC: Government Printing Office, 2011), 693.

7. Efraim Karsh, *The Soviet Union and Syria: The Asad Years* (New York: Routledge, 1988).

8. L. Todd Wood, "Jordanian King Says Israel and Jordan Confronted Russian Aircraft near Syria's Border," *Washington Times*, March 26, 2016, http://www.washingtontimes.com/news/2016/mar/26/king-abdullah-of-jordan-says-israel-and-jordan-con/print/.

9. Barbara Opall-Rome, "Top Israeli Commander Endorses Obama Doctrine; Gives Kudos to Moscow," *Defense News*, March 17, 2016, http://www.defensenews.com/story/defense/international/mideast-africa/2016/03/17/top-israeli-commander-endorses-obama-doctrine-gives-kudos-moscow/81938066/.

10. Ben Caspit, "Who Sent Mystery Drone into Israeli Airspace?" *Al-Monitor*, July 25, 2016, http://www.al-monitor.com/pulse/en/originals/2016/07/israeli-air-force-idf-drone-russia-jets-cooperation.html.

11. Avi Issacharoff, "In Syrian Skies, Israel Flies a Tricky Path," *Times of Israel*, December 7, 2016, http://www.timesofisrael.com/in-syrian-skies-israel-flies-a-tricky-path/.

12. Ben Caspit, "Israel Wary of Russian Comeback to the Region," *Al-Monitor*, October 24, 2016, http://www.al-monitor.com/pulse/originals/2016/10/israel-russia-syria-hezbollah-fighter-jets-idf-radar.html.

13. Ahronheim, "Senior Official: Iran Still Has Long-Range Capabilities to Strike Israel"; Ahronheim, "Israel Strikes Dozens of Iranian Targets in Syria."

14. Ross, "The Next Mideast Explosion."

15. "Israel on the Outer in Syria's Civil War," Middle East Institute, July 19, 2016, http://www.mei.edu/content/article/israel-outer-syria-s-civil-war.

16. Ashish Kumar Sen, "Are Israel and Iran Headed to War?" Atlantic Council, May 4, 2018, http://www.atlanticcouncil.org/blogs/new-atlanticist/are-israel-and-iran-headed-to-war.

17. Caspit, "Israel Wary of Russian Comeback to the Region."

18. Josef Federman, "Israeli Defense Officials: Assad Has Up to 3 Tons of Chemical Weapons," *Times of Israel*, April 20, 2017, http://www.timesofisrael.com/israeli-defense-officials-assad-still-has-chemical-weapons/; Amir Bouhbut, "Senior Officer: 'Assad Has About Three Tons of Chemical Weapons Left,'" http://news.walla.co.il/item/3058108.

19. Molly O'Toole, "Defense Secretary Ash Carter: U.S. Won't Be Clearing Syria's Skies for Russia," *Defense One*, September 30, 2015, http://www.defenseone.com/news/2015/09/defense-secretary-ash-carter-us-wont-be-clearing-syrias-skies-russia/122430/.

20. Remarks by President Obama to the United Nations General Assembly, White House, September 28, 2015, https://www.whitehouse.gov/the-press-office/2015/09/28/remarks-president-obama-united-nations-general-assembly.

21. Readout of meeting between President Donald J. Trump and Israeli prime minister Benjamin Netanyahu, White House, May 23, 2017, https://www.whitehouse.gov/briefings-statements/readout-meeting-president-donald-j-trump-israeli-prime-minister-benjamin-netanyahu/.

22. Itamar Rabinovich, "The Syrian Crisis," Brookings, September 12, 2017, https://www.brookings.edu/blog/markaz/2017/09/12/the-syrian-crisis-a-reckoning-and-a-road-map/.

23. Jeffrey, "Contain Iran?"

24. Steven A. Cook, "Russia Is in the Middle East to Stay," Council on Foreign Relations (CFR), March 26, 2018, https://www.cfr.org/blog/russia-middle-east-stay.

25. Assad Hanna and Jacob Wirtschafter, "To Undercut Iran, Russians Pressure Assad to Cut Syria's Longtime Ties to Hezbollah," *Washington Times*, July 17, 2017, http://www.washingtontimes.com/news/2017/jul/17/russia-pressures-bashar-assad-to-cut-syrias-hezbol/.

26. "Israel Constrained by New Realities in Syria," MEI, August 31, 2017, https://www.mei.edu/content/article/israel-constrained-new-realities-syria.

27. Sue Surkes, "Hamas, Hezbollah 'Not Terrorists,' Russian Envoy to Israel Says," *Times of Israel*, June 14, 2017, http://www.timesofisrael.com/hamas-hezbollah-not-terrorists-russian-envoy-to-israel-says/.

28. Adamsky, "Russia and the Next Lebanon War."

29. Alexandra N. Gutowski, "Israel Completes Largest Exercise in 20 Years, Setting Sights on Hezbollah," Federation for Defense of Democracies (FDD), September 19, 2017, http://www.defenddemocracy.org/media-hit/israel-completes-largest-exercise-in-20-years-setting-sights-on-hezbollah/.

5. Israel, Hamas, and the PA

1. Michael Gasper, "The Making of the Modern Middle East," in *The Middle East*, ed. Ellen M. Lust (London: Sage, 2017), 38.

2. Benny Morris, *Israel's Border Wars, 1949–1956* (Tel Aviv: Am Oved, 1996), 17.

3. Martin Van Creveld, *The Sword and the Olive: A Critical History of the Israeli Defense Force* (New York: Public Affairs, 1998), 170.

4. On the 2000–2005 war, see Amos Harel and Avi Isacharoff, *The Seventh War* (Tel Aviv: Miskal-Yedioth Ahronoth Books and Chemed Books, 2004); Daniel Byman, *A High Price: The Triumphs and Failures of Israeli Counterterrorism* (New York: Oxford University Press, 2011); Uri Ben-Eliezer, *Old Conflict, New War: Israel's Politics toward the Palestinians* (New York: Palgrave Macmillan, 2012).

5. Raphael S. Cohen, David E. Johnson, David E. Thaler, Brenna Allen, Elizabeth M. Bartels, James Cahill, and Shira Efron, *From Cast Lead to Protective Edge Lessons from Israel's Wars in Gaza* (Santa Monica CA: RAND, 2017). https://www.rand.org/pubs /research_reports/RR1888.html.

6. Bernard Gwertzman, "Tensions and Stalemate in Israel," Council on Foreign Relations (CFR), November 5, 2014, http://www.cfr.org/israel/tensions-stalemate-israel/p33742.

7. Fares Akram, "Israel, Hamas in Unspoken Alliance against Gaza Jihadists," *Times of Israel*, June 22, 2015, http://www.timesofisrael.com/israel-hamas-in-unspoken-alliance -against-gaza-jihadists/.

8. "French FM: Israel, Palestinian Stalemate Will Set Conflict 'Ablaze,'" *Ynet*, June 20, 2015, http://www.ynetnews.com/articles/0,7340,L-4670598,00.html.

9. Anthony H. Cordesman, "Israel and the Palestinians," Center for Strategic International Studies (CSIS), November 10, 2015, http://csis.org/publication/israel-and -palestinians-issues-obama-netanyahu-meeting-failed-address.

10. "Israel's Changing Threat Environment: Testimony before the House Foreign Affairs Committee Joint Hearing of the Subcommittee on Terrorism, Nonproliferation, and Trade and the Subcommittee on the Middle East and North Africa," Tamara Cofman Wittes, Senior Fellow and Director, Center for Middle East Policy, Brookings Institution, April 19, 2016.

11. Jeffrey Heller, "Egypt's Foreign Minister Talks Up Mideast Peace in Rare Visit to Israel," Reuters, July 10, 2016, http://www.reuters.com/article/us-egypt-israel-peace -idUSKCN0ZQ09.

12. AFP, "Egypt's Sisi Wants to 'Break Deadlock' in Peace Process," *Daily Mail*, July 21, 2016, http://www.dailymail.co.uk/wires/afp/article-3701701/Egypts-Sisi-wants-break -deadlock-peace-process.html.

13. Jonathan Schanzer, "International Community Must Focus on Palestinian Unity, Not Israel, to Kick-Start Peace," *Newsweek*, September 20, 2016, http://www.defenddemocracy .org/media-hit/schanzer-jonathan-international-community-must-focus-on-palestinian -unity-not-israel-to-kick/#sthash.Unhyt1oH.dpuf.

14. Jeffrey Heller, "Jews, Arabs Nearing Population Parity in Holy Land," Reuters, March 26, 2018, https://www.reuters.com/article/us-israel-palestinians-population /jews-arabs-nearing-population-parity-in-holy-land-israeli-officials-idUSKBN1H222T.

15. On the number 789, see Israeli Security Agency, http://www.shabak.gov.il/English /EnTerrorData/Reviews/Pages/terror-victims.aspx.

16. Max Abrahms, "Why Terrorism Does Not Work," *International Security* 31, no. 2 (Fall 2006): 72.

17. Yossi Mekelberg, "An Israeli Government That Alienates the Rest of the World," *Al Arabiya*, November 5, 2014, http://english.alarabiya.net/en/views/news/middle-east/2014/11/05/An-Israeli-government-that-alienates-the-rest-of-the-world.html.

18. Harriet Sherwood, "Population of Jewish Settlements in West Bank Up 15,000 in a Year," CNN, July 26, 2012, http://www.theguardian.com/world/2012/jul/26/jewish-population-west-bank-u.

19. Oren Liebermann, "What You Need to Know about the Israeli Settlements," CNN, February 1, 2017, https://www.cnn.com/2017/02/01/middleeast/settlements-explainer/index.html.

20. TOI Staff, full text of "UNSC Resolution 2334, Demanding Israel Stop All Settlement Activity," *Times of Israel*, December 23, 2016, http://www.timesofisrael.com/full-text-of-unsc-resolution-approved-dec-23-demanding-israel-stop-all-settlement-activity/.

21. Somini Sengupta and Rick Gladstone, "Rebuffing Israel, U.S. Allows Censure over Settlements," *New York Times*, December 23, 2016, http://www.nytimes.com/2016/12/23/world/middleeast/israel-settlements-un-vote.html?_r=0.

22. Marissa Newman, "Ya'alon: Palestinians Will Have Autonomy, Not Statehood," *Times of Israel*, October 15, 2014, http://www.timesofisrael.com/yaalon-palestinians-will-have-autonomy-not-statehood/.

23. Ben Caspit, "Israel's New Defense Minister Draws Up Plan to Topple Hamas," *Al-Monitor*, July 13, 2016, http://www.al-monitor.com/pulse/originals/2016/07/avigdor-liberman-hamas-idf-gaza-strip-mahmoud-abbas.html#ixzz4EOOISTEI.

24. TOI Staff, "Liberman to Palestinian Paper: Israel Would 'Completely Destroy' Hamas in Next War," *Times of Israel*, October 24, 2016, http://www.timesofisrael.com/liberman-israel-would-completely-destroy-hamas-in-future-war/.

25. TOI Staff, "'Let's Talk,' Says Defense Minister, in Overture to Gaza Residents," *Times of Israel*, February 17, 2017, http://www.timesofisrael.com/lets-talk-says-defense-minister-in-overture-to-gaza-residents/.

26. TOI Staff, "Liberman: Israel Has No Interest in Conquering Gaza in Next War,'" *Times of Israel*, June 11, 2017, http://www.timesofisrael.com/liberman-israel-has-no-interest-in-conquering-gaza-in-next-war/.

27. Raphael Ahren and Alexander Fulbright, "Netanyahu Slams Iran Deal in Fiery UN Speech, Urges World to 'Fix It or Nix It,'" *Times of Israel*, September 19, 2017, https://www.timesofisrael.com/netanyahu-blasts-iran-deal-at-un-speech-urges-world-to-fix-it-or-nix-it/.

28. Tal Shalev, "While Barak Is Examining the Area," *Walla*, September 6, 2016, http://news.walla.co.il/item/2994815.

29. Luke Baker and Arshad Mohammed, "Plenty of Diplomacy but Slim Hope for New Middle East Peace Push," *Al Arabiya*, October 24, 2015, http://english.alarabiya.net/en/perspective/analysis/2015/10/24/Plenty-of-diplomacy-but-slim-hope-for-new-Middle-East-peace-push.html.

30. AFP and TOI Staff, "Two-Thirds of Israelis Think Peace Deal Won't Ever Be Reached—Poll," *Times of Israel*, October 2, 2016, http://www.timesofisrael.com/two-thirds-of-israelis-think-peace-deal-wont-ever-be-reached-poll/.

31. Adam Rasgon, "Under 50% of Palestinians, Israeli Jews Support Two State Solu-

tion," *Jerusalem Post*, January 25, 2018, http://www.jpost.com/Arab-Israeli-Conflict/Poll -Under-50-percent-of-Palestinians-Israeli-Jews-support-two-state-solution-539780.

32. Michael Martinez, Oren Liebermann, and Richard Roth, "Mahmoud Abbas: Palestinians 'Cannot Continue to Be Bound' by Oslo Accords," CNN, September 30, 2015, http:// www.cnn.com/2015/09/30/world/palestinian-president-abbas-oslo-accords-israel/.

33. Khaled Abu Toameh and Herb Keinon, "PA to Ask Security Council for Resolution on 67 Lines in Coming Weeks, Official Says," *Jerusalem Post*, October 16, 2014, http:// www.jpost.com/Arab-Israeli-Conflict/PA-to-ask-UN-Security-Council-for-resolution -on-67-lines-in-coming-weeks-official-says-379007; Ghassan Shabaneh and Ibrahim Fraihat, "Keeping the Keys: The Rise of Palestinian Diplomatic Intifada," Brookings, December 18, 2014, http://www.brookings.edu/research/opinions/2014/12/18-rise -of-palestinian-diplomatic-intifada-sharqieh-shabaneh.

34. Natan Sachs, "Dilemmas of the Israeli-Palestinian Impasse," Brookings, September 17, 2015, http://www.brookings.edu/blogs/markaz/posts/2015/09/17-israeli -palestinian-impasse-dilemmas-sachs.

35. Tamar Pileggi, "Shin Bet Head Warns of Possible Fresh Outbreak of West Bank Violence," *Times of Israel*, July 12, 2016, http://www.timesofisrael.com/shin-bet-head -warns-of-fresh-outbreak-of-west-bank-violence/.

36. Adam Kredo, "Hamas Refuses to Stop Killing Jews," *Free Beacon*, May 16, 2014, http://freebeacon.com/national-security/hamas-refuses-to-stop-killing-jews/.

37. Shai Feldman, "The 2014 Israel-Hamas War," *National Interest*, September 8, 2014, http://nationalinterest.org/feature/the-2014-israel-hamas-war-preliminary-net-assessment -11222?page=2.

38. Tom Rayner, "Hamas Leader Says 'Stripping Palestinians of Hope' Will Lead to Chaos," *Sky News*, December 4, 2014, https://medium.com/@RaynerSkyNews/hamas -leader-warns-against-stripping-palestinians-of-hope-20c3aab595c5.

39. Tareq Baconi, *Hamas Contained: The Rise and Pacification of Palestinian Resistance* (Stanford: Stanford University Press, 2018).

40. Nidal al-Mughrabi and Tom Finn, "Hamas Softens Stance on Israel, Drops Muslim Brotherhoods Link," Reuters, May 2, 2017, http://www.reuters.com/article/us-palestinians -hamas-document-idUSKBN17X1N8.

41. Fahad Suleiman Shoqiran, "Hamas and an 'Eternity of Conflict,'" *Al Arabiya*, May 13, 2017, https://english.alarabiya.net/en/views/2017/05/13/Hamas-and-an-eternity -of-conflict-.html.

42. Daoud Kuttab, "To Make Peace in Middle East, Start from the End," Aljazeera, June 7, 2017, http://www.aljazeera.com/indepth/opinion/2017/05/peace-middle-east -start-170529110334031.html.

43. David Pollock, "Palestinian Public Are Tactical Moderates, but Strategic Militants," Washington Institute for Near East Policy, June 2017, http://www.washingtoninstitute .org/fikraforum/view/palestinian-public-are-tactical-moderates-but-strategic-militants -where-doe.

44. Rasgon, "Poll: Under 50%."

45. Adnan Abu Amer, "Why Is Hamas Refusing to Lay Down Arms?" Aljazeera,

June 10, 2017, http://www.aljazeera.com/indepth/opinion/2017/06/hamas-refusing-lay-arms-170611104206177.html.

46. On the war, see Cohen et al., *From Cast Lead to Protective Edge Lessons from Israel's Wars in Gaza*.

47. "Key Preliminary Findings of the High Level International Military Group on the Gaza Conflict," *UNwatch*, June 12, 2015, http://blog.unwatch.org/index.php/2015/06/12/key-findings-of-the-high-level-international-military-group-on-the-gaza-conflict/.

48. Uzi Rabi and Harel Chorev, "To Deter Hamas," *World Post*, August 12, 2014.

49. Ron Knutkin, "The End of 50 Days of Fighting?" *Ynet*, August 27, 2014, http://www.ynet.co.il/articles/0,7340,L-4564529,00.html.

50. Rayner, "Hamas Leader Says 'Stripping Palestinians of Hope' Will Lead to Chaos."

51. "Key Preliminary Findings of the High Level International Military Group on the Gaza Conflict."

52. Anthony H. Cordesman, "The Real Revolution in Military Affairs," *CSIS*, August 5, 2014, http://csis.org/publication/real-revolution-military-affairs.

53. "Key Preliminary Findings of the High Level International Military Group on the Gaza Conflict."

54. Rabi and Chorev, "To Deter Hamas."

55. Report of the Detailed Findings of the Independent Commission of Inquiry Established Pursuant to Human Rights Council Resolution s-21/1, June 22, 2015, 181–83, https://www.ohchr.org/en/hrbodies/hrc/coigazaconflict/pages/commissionofinquiry.aspx.

56. Ehud Yaari, "Hamas Searches for a New Strategy," Washington Institute for Near East Policy, *Policy Notes* 19 (October 2014), http://www.washingtoninstitute.org/uploads/PolicyNote19_Yaari4.pdf.

57. Amost Yadlin, "Dealing with Hamas' Military Force Reconstruction," Institute for National Security Studies (INSS), September 11, 2014, http://www.inss.org.il/index.aspx?id=4538&articleid=7651.

58. Dr. Max Singer, "A Middle Way for the Gaza Fight," Besa Center, August 11, 2014, http://besacenter.org/perspectives-papers/middle-way-gaza-fight/.

59. Azzam Al-Kassir, "Formalizing Regime Control over Syrian Religious Affairs," Carnegie, September 25, 2014. http://carnegieendowment.org/sada/2014/09/25/hamas-after-ceasefire/hpzd.

60. Lally Weymouth, "An Interview with Israeli Defense Minister Moshe Yaalon," *Washington Post*, October 24, 2014, www.washingtonpost.com/opinions/an-interview-with-israeli-defense-minister-moshe-yaalon/2014/10/24/4b44a218-5aca-11e4-8264-deed989ae9a2_story.html?utm_term=.42ae92bf2c0f

61. Khaled Elgindy, "Welcome to the Third Intifada," *Foreign Affairs*, July 28, 2014, http://www.foreignaffairs.com/articles/141662/gypts-elgindy/welcome-to-the-third-intifada.

62. Nidal al-Mughrabi, "Lack of Stability in Gaza Risks Return to War, Says U.N.," Reuters, November 4, 2014, http://www.reuters.com/article/2014/11/04/us-mideast-palestinians-un-idUSKBN0IO1J020141104.

63. Rayner, "Hamas Leader Says 'Stripping Palestinians of Hope' Will Lead to Chaos."

64. Uri Savir, "Rejectionist Israeli Government Becomes Palestinian Asset," *Al-Monitor*, May 3, 2015, http://www.al-monitor.com/pulse/en/originals/2015/05/gypts-new-government-pa-strategy-international-community.html#.

65. Nidal al-Mughrabi and Luke Baker, "Hamas-Fatah Face-off Leaves Hard Road Ahead for Palestinians," Reuters, May 6, 2015, http://www.reuters.com/article/2015/05/06/us-palestinians-reconciliation-idUSKBN0NR0YX20150506.

66. "Gaza Economy on the Verge of Collapse, Youth Unemployment Highest in the Region at 60 Percent," World Bank, May 21, 2015, http://www.worldbank.org/en/news/press-release/2015/05/21/gaza-economy-on-the-verge-of-collapse.

67. UN News Centre, September 1, 2015, http://www.un.org/apps/news/story.asp?NewsID=51770#.VzjQ9PkrJD8.

68. "Press Release: IMF Staff Concludes Visit," International Monetary Fund, February 11, 2016, https://www.imf.org/en/News/Articles/2015/09/14/01/49/pr1657.

69. Shane Harris, "Israel Warns: Another Gaza War Is Coming," Daily Beast, June 2, 2016, http://www.thedailybeast.com/articles/2016/06/02/gypts-warns-another-gaza-war-is-coming.html.

70. Lior Akerman, "There's No Existential Threat against Israel," *Jerusalem Post*, July 9, 2015, http://www.jpost.com/Opinion/Theres-no-existential-threat-against-Israel-408547.

71. Elhanan Miller, "Hamas Could Be Removed in Next Conflict with Israel, General Says," *Times of Israel*, September 17, 2015, http://www.timesofisrael.com/hamas-could-be-removed-in-next-conflict-with-israel-general-says/.

72. TOI Staff, "IDF Intel Chief Warns Despair in Gaza Could Explode toward Israel," *Times of Israel*, February 24, 2016, http://www.timesofisrael.com/idf-intel-chief-warns-despair-in-gaza-could-explode-towards-israel/.

73. United Nations Country Team in the Occupied Palestinian Territory, July 2017, https://unsco.unmissions.org/sites/default/files/gaza_10_years_later_-_11_july_2017.pdf.

74. "Gaza-Israel Violence," BBC, March 30, 2018, http://www.bbc.com/news/world-middle-east-43603199.

75. Moni Chorev, "Deterrence Campaigns: Lessons from IDF Operations in Gaza," Besa Center, March 2016.

76. Chorev, "Deterrence Campaigns."

77. Judah Ari Gross, "IDF: Next Conflict with Hamas Will Take Place on Israeli Terms," *Times of Israel*, April 14, 2016, https://www.timesofisrael.com/idf-next-conflict-with-hamas-will-take-place-on-israels-terms/.

78. Yaakov Lappin, "'Our Intelligence on Hamas Has Improved Significantly,' Senior Security Source Says," *Jerusalem Post*, April 14, 2016, http://www.jpost.com/Israel-News/Our-intelligence-on-Hamas-has-improved-significantly-senior-security-source-says-451262.

79. Chorev, "Deterrence Campaigns."

80. Chorev, "Deterrence Campaigns."

81. Pileggi, "Shin Bet Head Warns of Possible Fresh Outbreak of West Bank Violence."

82. Gross, "IDF: Next Conflict with Hamas."

83. Adnan Abu Amer, "Why Is Hamas Refusing to Lay Down Arms?"

84. Tamar Pileggi, "Hamas Military Capabilities Said Restored to Pre-2014 War Strength," *Times of Israel*, January 31, 2017, http://www.timesofisrael.com/hamas-military-capabilities-said-restored-to-pre-2014-war-strength/.

85. Judah Ari Gross, "Hamas Said to Acquire Highly Explosive Short-Range Rockets," *Times of Israel*, March 28, 2017, http://www.timesofisrael.com/hamas-reported-to-acquire-highly-explosive-short-range-rockets/.

86. Ian Deitch, "Israel Plans Mass Evacuations If War Erupts Again," *Times of Israel*, March 21, 2017, http://www.timesofisrael.com/gypts-plans-mass-evacuation-if-war-erupts-again/.

87. Barbara Opall-Rome, "In Israel, Race to Safeguard Borders from Multi-Dimensional Threats," *Defense News*, November 28, 2016, http://www.defensenews.com/articles/in-israel-race-to-safeguard-borders-from-multi-dimensional-threats.

88. Yaakov Lappin, "IDF Uncovers Hamas Tunnel Stretching from Gaza into Israel," *Jerusalem Post*, April 18, 2016, http://www.jpost.com/Arab-Israeli-Conflict/IDF-uncovers-Hamas-tunnel-stretching-from-Gaza-into-Israel-451556.

89. Anna Ahronheim, "IDF Completes Large-Scale Gaza Drill Simulating Hamas Infiltration," *Jerusalem Post*, February 4, 2017, http://www.jpost.com/Israel-News/IDF-completes-large-scale-Gaza-drill-simulating-Hamas-infiltration-480538.

90. TOI Staff, "Liberman: Hamas Has 'Far Fewer than 15 Tunnels into Israel,'" *Times of Israel*, March 26, 2017, http://www.timesofisrael.com/liberman-hamas-has-far-fewer-than-15-tunnels-into-israel/.

91. Judah Ari Gross, "Army Believes Hamas Focusing Tunnels More on Defense than Attack," *Times of Israel*, September 27, 2017, https://www.timesofisrael.com/army-believes-hamas-focusing-tunnels-more-on-defense-than-attack/.

92. Kobi Michael, "The Weight of the Demographic Factor in Israel's Strategic Considerations on the Palestinian Issue," INSS, October 2014, http://www.inss.org.il/uploadImages/systemFiles/adkan17_3ENG%20(3)_Michael.pdf.

93. Opall-Rome, "In Israel, Race to Safeguard Borders from Multi-Dimensional Threats."

94. Lally Weymouth, "An Interview with Israeli Defense Minister Moshe Yaalon."

95. Ehud Yaari, "Hamas Searches for a New Strategy."

96. Daniel L. Byman, "Hamas or the Palestinian Authority," Brookings, September 21, 2015, http://www.brookings.edu/blogs/markaz/posts/2015/09/21-hamas-palestinian-authority-failure.

97. AP, "Abbas Would Win in West Bank, Hamas in Gaza, If Palestinians Voted Today," *Times of Israel*, June 9, 2015, http://www.timesofisrael.com/gyptsiya-unhappy-with-hamas-but-back-rocket-fire-poll/.

98. Daniel Byman, "Israel's Gaza Withdrawal 10 Years Later," *War on the Rocks*, August 13, 2015, http://warontherocks.com/2015/08/israels-gaza-withdrawal-more-successful-than-you-think/.

99. Ali Sawafta, "Most Palestinians No Longer Support Two-State Solution," Reuters, September 21, 2015, http://www.reuters.com/article/2015/09/21/us-palestinians-israel-survey-idUSKCN0RL1DF20150921.

100. "Wave of Terror 2015–2018," Israel Ministry of Foreign Affairs, February 13, 2018,

http://mfa.gov.il/MFA/ForeignPolicy/Terrorism/Palestinian/Pages/Wave-of-terror-October-2015.aspx.

101. Ilan Goldenberg, "A Security System for the Two-State Solution," Center for a New American Security (CNAS), May 31, 2016, https://www.cnas.org/publications/reports/advancing-the-dialogue-a-security-system-for-the-two-state-solution.

102. Ben Caspit, "Why Israelis Flock to Small Tomb in Nablus at Night," Al-Monitor, October 19, 2016, http://www.al-monitor.com/pulse/en/originals/2016/10/gypts-joseph-tomb-jews-night-idf-forces-intifada.html.

103. Pileggi, "Shin Bet Head Warns of Possible Fresh Outbreak of West Bank Violence."

104. "The Staggering Economic Cost of Occupation," UNCTAD, September 6, 2016, http://unctad.org/en/pages/newsdetails.aspx?OriginalVersionID=1317.

105. Marwan Muasher, "Reimagining Palestine," Project Syndicate, June 26, 2017, https://www.project-syndicate.org/commentary/civil-liberties-before-palestinian-statehood-by-marwan-muasher-2017-06?barrier=accesspaylog/.

106. "Israel, Palestinian Authority Reach Water-Sharing Deal," Aljazeera, July 12, 2017, http://www.aljazeera.com/news/2017/07/gypts-palestinian-authority-reach-water-sharing-deal-170713165223323.html.

107. Martin S. Indyk and David Rothkopf, "The U.S.-Israel Relationship Arrives at a Moment of Reckoning," Brookings Institute, August 26, 2014, http://www.brookings.edu/research/interviews/2014/08/26-us-israel-relationship-indyk-rothkopf.

108. Elhanan Miller, "Can the Palestinian Authority Survive without the IDF?" Times of Israel, October 24, 2014, http://www.timesofisrael.com/can-the-palestinian-authority-survive-without-the-idf/.

109. Ben Caspit, "Israeli Security Defends Abbas," Al-Monitor, November 20, 2014, http://www.al-monitor.com/pulse/originals/2014/11/abbas-israel-security-apparatus-netanyahu-bennett-yaalon.html.

110. Ron Ben Yishai, "The Nightmare of the IDF," Ynet, November 22, 2014, http://www.ynet.co.il/articles/0,7340,L-4594463,00.html.

111. Shlomi Eldar, "Despite Netanyahu, PA Continues Security Cooperation with Israel," Al-Monitor, November 26, 2014, www.al-monitor.com/pulse/originals/2014/11/adnan-al-damiri-interview-pa-security-cooperation-israel.html.

112. Akerman, "There's No Existential Threat against Israel."

113. Geoffrey Aronson, "Palestinian Security Forces: Living on Borrowed Time," Middle East Institute, October 16, 2015, www.mei.edu/content/article/gyptsiya-security-forces-living-borrowed-time.

114. Mazal Mualem, "Former Defense Minister Condemns Bibi's 'Divisive' Message," Al-Monitor, January 8, 2016, www.al-monitor.com/pulse/en/originals/2016/01/gypts-mofaz-interview-violence-intifada-diplomatic-plan.html#.

115. Judah Ari Gross, "Army Chief Hints at Hidden Efforts to Counter Gazan Tunnels," Times of Israel, February 9, 2016, www.timesofisrael.com/army-chief-hints-at-hidden-efforts-to-counter-gazan-tunnels/.

116. Judah Ari Gross, "While Hebron Gets the Press, Jenin and Tulkarem Are the Sleeping Giants Israel Should Be Worried About," Times of Israel, October 4, 2016, www

.timesofisrael.com/while-hebron-gets-the-press-jenin-and-tulkarem-are-the-sleeping
-giants-israel-should-be-worried-about/.

117. "Palestinian Prime Minister Says Israel Prevented a Third Intifada in 2015," 124
news, June 5, 2017, www.i24news.tv/en/news/gypts/147105–170605-palestinian-prime
-minister-says-israel-prevented-a-third-intifada-in-2015.

118. Judah Ari Gross, "IDF Chief Says Iranian Missiles Overhyped, but Sent a Message," *Times of Israel*, June 20, 2017, www.timesofisrael.com/idf-chief-says-iranian-missile
-overhyped-but-sent-a-message/.

119. Shimon Arad, "Why Israel Can't Afford to Destroy Hamas," *National Interest*,
June 6, 2017, http://nationalinterest.org/feature/why-israel-cant-afford-destroy-hamas
-21033?page=2.

120. U.S. Department of State Publication Bureau of Counterterrorism, Country
Reports on Terrorism 2016, July 2017, 188.

121. TOI Staff, "Israel, Palestinians Said Back to Full West Bank Security Cooperation," *Times of Israel*, October 27, 2017, www.timesofisrael.com/gypts-palestinians-said
-back-to-full-west-bank-security-cooperation/.

122. Neri Zilber and Ghaith al-Omari, "State with No Army, Army with No State," Washington Institute for Near East Policy, *Policy Focus* 154, March 2018, www.washingtoninstitute
.org/uploads/Documents/pubs/PolicyFocus154-ZilberOmari.pdf.

123. Gwertzman, "Tensions and Stalemate in Israel."

124. "Kerry Says Status Quo between Israel, Palestinians 'Unsustainable,'" Reuters,
October 22, 2014, http://www.reuters.com/article/2014/10/22/us-mideast-israel-kerry
-idUSKCN0IB11X20141022.

125. White House, "Annex to U.S.-Gulf Cooperation Council Camp David Joint
Statement."

126. Jim Zanotti, "U.S. Foreign Aid to the Palestinians," Congressional Research
Service (CRS), March 18, 2016, http://wwwwww.fas.org/sgp/crs/gypts/RS22967.pdf.

127. U.S. Department of State, Country Reports on Terrorism 2016, 191.

128. Lydia Saad, "Americans' Views toward Israel Remain Firmly Positive," Gallup,
February 29, 2016, http://www.gallucom/poll/189626/americans-views-toward-israel
-remain-firmly-positive.aspx.

129. Khaled Elgindy, "Obama's Record on Israeli-Palestinian Peace," *Foreign Affairs*,
October 5, 2016, https://www.foreignaffairs.com/articles/gypts/2016–10–05/obamas
-record-israeli-palestinian-peace.

130. Country Reports on Terrorism 2016, 190.

131. "EU Says It Has No Plans for Sanctions on Israel," Reuters, November 17, 2014,
https://www.reuters.com/article/us-mideast-israel-eu/eu-says-it-has-no-plans-for
-sanctions-on-israel-idUSKCN0J123K20141117.

132. Robin Emmott, "After Iran Deal, EU Bids to Restart Israel-Palestinian Talks,"
Reuters, September 4, 2015, http://www.reuters.com/article/2015/09/04/us-israel
-palestinians-eu-idUSKCN0R41YB20150904.

133. "Remarks by High Representative/Vice-President Federica Mogherini at the
Joint Press Point Ahead of the 2018 Spring Session of the Ad Hoc Liaison Committee,"

European Union External Action, March 20, 2018, https://eeas.europa.eu/headquarters /headquarters-Homepage/41709/remarks-high-representativevice-president-federica -mogherini-joint-press-point-ahead-2018_en.

134. Elie Podeh, "Israel and the Arab Peace Initiative, 2002–2014," *Middle East Journal* 68, no. 4 (Autumn 2014): 584–603.

135. Dovid Efune, "Kissinger: Israel Should Not Seek Final Peace Deal," *Algemeiner*, November 12, 2014, http://www.algemeiner.com/2014/11/12/gyptsiy-israel-should-not -seek-final-peace-deal-with-palestinians-until-mideast-chaos-subsides/.

136. AFP and TOI Staff, "Jordan's King Warns Israel against Jerusalem 'Provocation,'" *Times of Israel*, September 14, 2015, http://www.timesofisrael.com/jordans-king-warns -israel-against-jerusalem-provocation/.

137. Marissa Newman, "West Bank Violence, Fueled by Hamas, in Decline, Defense Chief Says," *Times of Israel*, December 9, 2014, www.timesofisrael.com/west-bank-violence -fueled-by-hamas-in-decline-defense-chief-says/.

138. Amos Harel, "Turkey Sends Message to Local Hamas Operatives to Cut Back on Anti-Israel Terror," *Haaretz*, August 22, 2016, www.haaretz.com/news/diplomacy -defense/.premium-1.660431.

139. AFP, "Sisi: Egypt Could Send Forces to Stabilize Future Palestinian State," *Al Arabiya*, November 23, 2014, http://english.alarabiya.net/en/News/middle-east/2014/11 /23/Sisi-Egypt-could-send-forces-to-stabilize-future-Palestinian-state.html.

140. Efraim Inbar, "The Six-Day War," *Middle East Quarterly*, Summer 2017, http:// www.meforum.org/6727/gypts-costs-vs-its-benefits#_ftn4.

6. Egypt's Security Problems

1. Mohannad Sabry, *Sinai: Egypt's Linchpin, Gaza's Lifeline, Israel's Nightmare* (Cairo: American University in Cairo Press, 2015); Steven Simon, "Egypt's Security Challenge," Middle East Institute, February 19, 2015, www.mei.edu/content/at/gypts-security-challenge -isis-sinai-and-libyan-border.

2. Avi Issacharoff, "Thus, Israel Can Help Sisi Defeat Terrorism in Sinai," *Walla News*, October 26, 2014, http://news.walla.co.il/item/2795878.

3. "Rafah Residents Forced to Leave Their Homes," *Al-Monitor*, November 2, 2014, http://www.al-monitor.com/pulse/originals/2014/11/rafah-egypt-government -evacuation-palestinians.html; Merrit Kennedy and Fares Akram, "Egypt Crackdown Angers People in Sinai Border Town," *Times of Israel*, November 7, 2014, http://www .timesofisrael.com/egypt-crackdown-angers-people-in-sinai-border-town/.

4. Vin Weber and Gregory B. Craig, "Cooperating Not Condoning," Washington Institute for Near East Policy, November 2015, www.washingtoninstitute.org/uploads /Documents/pubs/WebCraig2015; Jeremy M. Sharp, "Egypt: Background and U.S. Relations," *Congressional Research Service* , June 7, 2018.

5. Shadi Hamid, "Sisi's Regime Is a Gift to the Islamic State," *Foreign Policy*, August 6, 2015, http://foreignpolicy.com/2015/08/06/sisi-is-the-best-gift-the-islamic-state-ever-got/.

6. David Schenker, "Back to the Bad Old Days," *American Interest*, June 23, 2015, http:// www.the-american-interest.com/2015/06/23/back-to-the-bad-old-days/.

7. "Egypt's Conventional Military Thinking," *Stratfor*, June 12, 2015, https://www.stratfor.com/analysis/egypts-conventional-military-thinking.

8. "Egypt: Two Years after Morsi," Council on Foreign Relations (CFR), December 16, 2015, http://www.cfr.org/egypt/egypt-two-years-after-morsi/p37380.

9. "Egypt's War on Terror," Middle East Institute, November 6, 2014, http://www.mei.edu/publications/egypts-war-terror-isis-president-sisi-and-us-led-coalition.

10. Khalid Hassan, "Egyptian Islamic Jihad Founder," *Al-Monitor*, April 7, 2016, http://www.al-monitor.com/pulse/originals/2016/04/egypt-islamic-jihad-founder-nabil-naeem-sinai-terrorism.html#ixzz45uqDutsb.

11. Avi Issacharoff, "In Sinai, a Local Tribe Fights to Push Back the Islamic State," *Times of Israel*, June 5, 2017, http://www.timesofisrael.com/islamic-states-two-pronged-war-in-sinai/.

12. Schenker, "Back to the Bad Old Days."

13. Agencies, "Egypt Says Sinai Fighting Kills 12 Security Forces," *Times of Israel*, March 23, 2017, http://www.timesofisrael.com/egypt-says-sinai-fighting-kills-12-security-forces/.

14. "At Least 23 Egyptian Soldiers Killed in Deadliest Sinai Attack in Years," Reuters, July 7, 2017, https://www.reuters.com/article/us-egypt-security-iduskbn19s13g.

15. "21 Egyptian Soldiers Killed in Rocket Attack in Al-Wadi Al Gedid," *Ahram* online, July 20, 2014, http://english.ahram.org.eg/NewsContent/1/64/106626/Egypt/Politics-/breaking—Egyptian-soldiers-killed-in-AlWadi-AlGed.aspx; Erica Wenig, "Egypt's Security and the Libyan Civil War," Washington Institute for Near East Policy, April 17, 2016, http://www.washingtoninstitute.org/policy-analysis/view/egypts-security-and-the-libyan-civil-war.

16. "Egypt Says Air Strikes Destroy Militant Camps after Attack on Christians," Reuters, May 27, 2017, http://www.reuters.com/article/us-egypt-security-iduskbn18n0d1.

17. Ali Abdelaty, "Egypt's Sisi Calls on Military Chief to Secure Sinai in Three Months," Reuters, November 29, 2017, https://www.reuters.com/article/us-egypt-security/egypts-sisi-calls-on-military-chief-to-secure-sinai-in-three-months-iduskbn1dt13e.

18. "How Israel Spies on Sinai," *Al-Monitor*, September 23, 2014, http://www.al-monitor.com/pulse/originals/2014/09/egypt-sinai-israel-mossad-shin-bet-spies-smugglers.html.

19. TOI Staff, "Egyptian Army in Sinai Peninsula Doubles in a Year, with Israel's Blessing," *Times of Israel*, February 28, 2018, https://www.timesofisrael.com/egyptian-army-in-sinai-peninsula-doubles-in-a-year-with-israels-blessing/.

20. On building the posts, see "Smuggling and Firing," *Ynet*, October 23, 2014, http://www.ynet.co.il/articles/0,7340,l-4583331,00.html.

21. On armed groups that are against Israel and Egypt, see "Israel's Balancing Act in Sinai," *Daily Beast*, August 16, 2013, http://www.thedailybeast.com/articles/2013/08/16/israel-s-balancing-act-in-sinai.html.

22. Daniel Byman and Khaled Elgindy, "The Deepening Chaos in Sinai," *National Interest*, September-October 2013, http://nationalinterest.org/article/the-deepening-chaos-sinai-8957.

23. Geoffrey Aronson, "Improved Egypt-Israel Relations through Sinai Crisis," Middle East Institute, July 24, 2015, http://education.mei.edu/content/article/improved-egypt-israel-relations-through-sinai-crisis-will-they-last.

24. David D. Kirkpatrick, "Secret Alliance," *New York Times*, February 3, 2018, https://www.nytimes.com/2018/02/03/world/middleeast/israel-airstrikes-sinai-egypt.html?rref=collection%2fsectioncollection%2fmiddleeast&action=click&contentCollection=middleeast&region=stream&module=stream_unit&version=latest&contentPlacement=1&pgtype=sectionfront.

25. Judah Ari Gross, "IDF Prepares for Possible Islamic State Attacks across Southern Border on Foot, in Cars," *Times of Israel*, April 2, 2017, http://www.timesofisrael.com/idf-prepares-for-islamic-state-to-attack-on-foot-in-cars/.

26. Melanie Lidman, "In 'Restive' Sinai, Israelis Once Again Finding a Restful Paradise," *Times of Israel*, September 2, 2016, http://www.timesofisrael.com/in-restive-sinai-israelis-once-again-finding-a-restful-paradise/.

27. Weber and Craig, "Cooperating Not Condoning."

28. Nathan J. Brown and Yasser El-Shimy, "Did Sisi Save Egypt?" *Carnegie*, January 25, 2016. http://carnegieendowment.org/2016/01/25/did-sisi-save-egypt/ita5.

29. Khaled Dawoud, "Running Egypt as an Army Commander," *Atlantic Council*, June 16, 2015, http://www.atlanticcouncil.org/blogs/egyptsource/running-egypt-as-an-army-commander.

30. Dawoud, "Running Egypt as an Army Commander." On the popularity of the Egyptian regime at the time, see also Lynch, *The New Arab Wars*, 36.

31. Eric Trager, "Egypt's Durable Misery," Washington Institute for Near East Policy, July 21, 2015, http://www.washingtoninstitute.org/policy-analysis/view/egypts-durable-misery-why-sisis-regime-is-stable.

32. Steven A. Cook, "Egypt: Two Years after Morsi," CFR, December 16, 2015, http://www.cfr.org/egypt/egypt-two-years-after-morsi/p37380.

33. Eric Trager, *Arab Fall: How the Muslim Brotherhood Won and Lost Egypt in 891 Days* (Washington DC: Georgetown University Press, 2016).

34. Sudarsan Raghavan, "In New Egyptian Textbooks, 'It's Like the Revolution Didn't Happen,'" *Washington Post*, April 23, 2016, https://www.washingtonpost.com/world/middle_east/in-new-egyptian-textbooks-its-like-the-revolution-didnt-happen/2016/04/23/846ab2f0-f82e-11e5-958d-d038dac6e718_story.html.

35. Marc Lynch, "Is the Muslim Brotherhood a Terrorist Organization or a Firewall against Violent Extremism?" *Washington Post*, March 7, 2016, https://www.washingtonpost.com/news/monkey-cage/wp/2016/03/07/is-the-muslim-brotherhood-a-terrorist-organization-or-a-firewall-against-violent-extremism/.

36. Weber and Craig, "Cooperating Not Condoning."

37. Jon B. Alterman, "Middle East Notes and Comment," Center for Strategic International Studies (CSIS), February 11, 2016, http://csis.org/publication/middle-east-notes-and-comment-egypt-five-years.

38. Andrew Exum, "Egypt and America Are Destined to Disappoint Each Other," *Defense One*, April 3, 2017, http://www.defenseone.com/ideas/2017/04/egypt-and-america-are-destined-disappoint-each-other/136671/.

39. Patrick Markey and Nadine Awadalla, "Middle-Class Egypt Adapts to Survive

as Austerity Bites," Reuters, December 15, 2017, https://www.reuters.com/article/us-egypt-politics/middle-class-egypt-adapts-to-survive-as-austerity-bites-iduskbn1e90zy.

40. Michele Dunne interviewed by Zachary Laub, "Washington's Egypt Dilemma," CFR, June 23, 2015, http://www.cfr.org/egypt/washingtons-egypt-dilemma/p36720.

41. Steven A. Cook, "Egypt: Two Years after Morsi," CFR, December 16, 2015, http://www.cfr.org/egypt/egypt-two-years-after-morsi/p37380.

42. Eric Trager, "Egypt's Costly Nuclear Project," Washington Institute for Near East Policy, June 16, 2016, http://www.washingtoninstitute.org/policy-analysis/view/egypts-costly-nuclear-project.

43. Project on Middle East Democracy, October 2016, http://pomed.org/pomed-publications/new-report-rethinking-u-s-economic-aid-to-egypt/.

44. Christopher Cavas, "CNO Greenert Reconnects with Egyptian Navy," *Defense News*, July 12, 2015, http://www.defensenews.com/story/defense/naval/navy/2015/07/12/navy-chief-of-naval-operations-greenert-osama-mounir-rabie-egypt-egyptian-navy-frigates-perry-class-knox-fast-missile-craft-suez-canal-central-command/30053399/.

45. "Israel's Changing Threat Environment: Testimony before the House Foreign Affairs Committee Joint Hearing of the Subcommittee on Terrorism, Nonproliferation and Trade and the Subcommittee on the Middle East and North Africa," by Tamara Cofman Wittes, Senior Fellow and Director, Center for Middle East Policy, Brookings Institution, April 19, 2016.

46. Lesley Wroughton and Lara Jakes, "In Egypt, Kerry Presses Sisi to Adopt Moderate Policies," *Haaretz*, June 22, 2014, http://www.haaretz.com/news/middle-east/1.600355.

47. Oscar Nkala, "As US-Egypt Tensions Thaw, M1A1 Abrams Tank Co-Production to Resume," *Defense News*, November 1, 2015, http://www.defensenews.com/story/defense/2015/11/01/us-egypt-tensions-thaw-m1a1-abrams-tank-co-production-resume/74861412/.

48. AP, "Egypt Says West Hasn't Helped in War on Terror," *Times of Israel*, November 7, 2015, http://www.timesofisrael.com/egypt-says-west-hasnt-helped-in-war-on-terror/.

49. Author interview with Robert Springborg, March 25, 2016.

50. Staff Sgt. Michael Battles, "U.S., Egypt Kick Off Exercise Bright Star 2017," CENTCOM, September 13, 2017, http://www.centcom.mil/media/news-articles/News-Article-View/Article/1308877/us-egypt-kick-off-exercise-bright-star-2017/.

51. Bradley Klapper and Julie Pace, "U.S. May Pull Out Sinai Force that Helps Keep Israel-Egypt Peace," *Times of Israel*, August 19, 2015, http://www.timesofisrael.com/us-may-pull-out-sinai-force-that-helps-keep-israel-egypt-peace/.

52. *Military Times*, September 10, 2015, http://www.militarytimes.com/story/military/pentagon/2015/09/10/new-troops—sinai/72018008/.

53. W. J. Hennigan, "U.S. Shifts Troops in the Sinai Peninsula after Attacks by Militants," *LA Times*, April 23, 2016, http://www.latimes.com/world/middleeast/la-fg-us-sinai-20160423-story.html.

54. Egypt, "EU Ratify Partnership Priorities for 2017–2020," *Ahram* online, July 25 2017, http://english.ahram.org.eg/NewsContent/1/64/274208/Egypt/Politics-/Egypt,-eu-ratify-partnership-priorities-for-.aspx.

55. On the poll in 2015, see Roi Case, "Israel Number 1," *Ynet*, September 30, 2015, http://www.ynet.co.il/articles/0,7340,l-4705516,00.html.

56. David Schenker, "America's Least-Known Mideast Military Force," *Politico*, November 1, 2015, http://www.politico.com/magazine/story/2015/11/sinai-crash-americas-least-known-mideast-military-force-213314#ixzz3qOfcdpdu.

57. Bruce Maddy-Weitzman, "Between Alliance and Rivalry," Rubin Center, February 16, 2016, http://www.rubincenter.org/2016/02/between-alliance-and-rivalry-egyptian-israeli-relations-remain-solid-if-not-particularly-warm/.

58. Haisam Hassanein, "The Future of Egyptian-Israeli Relations," *Jerusalem Post*, February 18, 2017, http://www.jpost.com/Opinion/The-future-of-Egyptian-Israeli-relations-Cairo-more-committed-to-peace-than-normalization-481938.

59. Maddy-Weitzman, "Between Alliance and Rivalry."

60. Haisam Hassanein, "How a Soap Opera Explains Egyptian-Israeli Relations," Washington Institute for Near East Policy, June 29, 2017, http://www.washingtoninstitute.org/policy-analysis/view/how-a-soap-opera-explains-egyptian-israeli-relations.

61. Hassanein, "The Future of Egyptian-Israeli Relations."

62. "Egypt's Importance in a Time of Troubles," Middle East Institute, June 16, 2016, http://www.mei.edu/content/article/egypts-importance-time-troubles.

63. "Israel in the Room? Egypt Quits Nuke Talks over 'Inefficiency' in Middle East," RT, May 2, 2013, http://rt.com/news/egypt-israel-nuclear-weapons-604/.

64. AP and TOI Staff, "U.S. Blocks Nuclear Disarmament Move over Israel Concerns," *Times of Israel*, May 23, 2015, http://www.timesofisrael.com/us-rejects-nuclear-disarmament-document-over-israel-concerns/.

65. Trager, "Egypt's Costly Nuclear Project."

66. Raghavan, "In New Egyptian Textbooks."

67. Josef Olmert, "Israel and the Middle East after the Arab Spring: Challenges and Opportunities," in *The Middle East: New Order or Disorder?*, ed. Mohammed A. Aman and Mary Jo Aman and MLIS (Washington DC: Westphalia, 2016), 178.

68. Shadi Hamid and Tamara Cofman Wittes, "Camp David Peace Treaty Collapse," Brookings Institute, January 17, 2013, http://www.brookings.edu/research/papers/2013/01/camp-david-peace-treaty-collapse.

69. Steven A. Cook, "Egypt: Two Years after Morsi," CFR, December 16, 2015, http://www.cfr.org/egypt/egypt-two-years-after-morsi/p37380.

70. Andrew Exum, "Egypt and America Are Destined to Disappoint Each Other."

71. Hamza Hendawi, "Food Cart Shut Down? Ask Egypt's President," *Times of Israel*, May 20, 2017, http://www.timesofisrael.com/food-cart-shut-down-ask-egypts-president/.

72. On Nasser and el-Sisi, see Robert Springborg, "The Nasser Playbook," *Foreign Affairs*, November 5, 2013, http://www.foreignaffairs.com/articles/140242/robert-springborg/the-nasser-playbook.

73. AP and TOI Staff, "Sisi Claims Egypt Has Completed Transition to Democratic Rule," *Times of Israel*, February 13, 2016, http://www.timesofisrael.com/sissi-claims-egypt-has-completed-transition-to-democratic-rule/.

74. Raoul Wootliff and Agencies, "Egypt Sees 'Real Opportunity' for Israel-Palestinian

Deal," *Times of Israel*, May 17, 2016, http://www.timesofisrael.com/egypt-president-backs-french-proposal-for-mideast-talks/.

75. Heller, "Egypt's Foreign Minister Talks Up Mideast Peace in Rare Visit to Israel."

76. AFP, "Egypt's Sisi Wants to 'Break Deadlock' in Peace Process."

77. "Egypt's Sisi Discusses Israel-Palestine Issue with Netanyahu in New York," *Ahram* online, September 19, 2017, http://english.ahram.org.eg/NewsContent/1/64/277365/Egypt/Politics-/Egypts-Sisi-discusses-IsraelPalestine-issue-with-N.aspx.

78. Zvi Bar'el, "Israel Should Take Advantage of Anti-Hamas Regional Alliance," *Haaretz*, August 19, 2016, http://www.haaretz.com/news/diplomacy-defense/.premium-1.608335; Matthew S. Cohen, "Israel's Big Decision," *National Interest*, July 30, 2014, http://nationalinterest.org/feature/israels-big-decision-time-take-hamas-out-10975.

79. "Egypt and Hamas—Cooperation in the Works?" Middle East Institute, June 16, 2016, http://www.mei.edu/content/article/egypt-and-hamas-cooperation-works.

80. "Egypt's Conventional Military Thinking," *Stratfor,* June 12, 2015.

81. Jon B. Alterman, "Making Choices," Center for Strategic International Studies, August 2016, https://csis-prod.s3.amazonaws.com/s3fs-public/publication/160802_Alterman_MakingChoices_Web.pdf.

82. Prepared statement by Elliott Abrams before the Senate Committee on Appropriations, Subcommittee on State, Foreign Operations, and Related Programs, April 25, 2017, https://www.cfr.org/sites/default/files/pdf/2017/04/Abrams%20testimony%204.25.17.pdf.

83. Jamey Keaten, "French Official: Egypt to Buy 24 Rafale Jet Fighters," *U.S. News*, February 12, 2015, http://www.usnews.com/news/business/articles/2015/02/12/official-egypt-1st-foreign-buyer-of-french-rafale-fighters; *Walla News*, March 5, 2015, http://news.walla.co.il/item/2835362.

84. Ben Caspit, "Israeli Air Force Debates Purchase of F-35 Fighter Planes," *Al-Monitor*, February 17, 2016, http://www.al-monitor.com/pulse/en/originals/2016/02/f-35-fighter-jets-israeli-air-force-mig-syrian-skies.html#.

85. Ehud Eilam, *The Next War between Israel and Egypt* (Edgware, UK: Vallentine Mitchell, 2014).

7. IDF's Buildup for War

1. Ben Gurion, *Uniqueness and Destiny*; Yaniv, *Politics and Strategy in Israel*; Tal, *National Security*; Freilich, *Israeli National Security*; Handel, *Israel's Political-Military Doctrine*; Shlaim, *The Iron Wall*; Eilam, *Israel's Way of War*; Yossi Alpher, *Periphery: Israel's Search for Middle East Allies* (Lanham MD: Rowman & Littlefield, 2015); Kenneth M. Pollack, *Arabs at War* (Lincoln: University of Nebraska Press, 2004). On the nuclear issue, see Beres, *Surviving amid Chaos*.

2. Avi Kober, *Military Decision in the Arab-Israeli Wars, 1948–1982* (Tel Aviv: Ministry of Defense, 1995); Van Creveld, *The Sword and the Olive*; Arial Levite, *Offense and Defense* (Tel Aviv: Hakibbutz Hameuchad, 1988); IDF Archives, file no. 261/488/55; Edward Luttwak and Dan Horowitz, *The Israeli Army* (New York: Harper and Row, 1975).

3. On this period, see Benny Morris, *Righteous Victims: A History of the Zionist-Arab Conflict, 1881–2001* (Tel Aviv: Am Oved, 2003); Van Creveld, *The Sword and the Olive*.

4. "Addressing the Fog of COG: Perspectives on the Center of Gravity in U.S. Military Doctrine," December 2012, https://www.coursehero.com/file/37611928/Addressing-the-Fog-of-COGpdf/.

5. *IDF Strategy*, IDF blog, November 23, 2015, https://www.idf.il/%D7%9E%D7%90%D7%9E%D7%A8%D7%99%D7%9D/%D7%90%D7%95%D7%93%D7%95%D7%AA-%D7%A6%D7%94%D7%9C/%D7%90%D7%A1%D7%98%D7%A8%D7%98%D7%92%D7%99%D7%99%D7%AA-%D7%A6%D7%94%D7%9C/; IDF Archives, file no. 96/854/52; Ghani Abdel Mohamed El Gamasy, *The October War* (Cairo: American University in Cairo, 1993), 136.

6. *IDF Strategy*, November 23, 2015.

7. Avi Kober, *Practical Soldiers: Israel's Military Thought and Its Formative Factors* (Brill: Boston, 2015), 144.

8. IDF Archives, file no. 66/292/85; Levite, *Offense and Defense*, 38; El Gamasy, *The October War*, 136.

9. Maj. Gen. Doron Almog (Ret.), "Cumulative Deterrence and the War on Terrorism," *Parameters*, Winter 2004–5, 13–14.

10. *IDF Strategy*, November 23, 2015.

11. IDF Archives, file no. 17/161/59; IDF Archives, file no. 85/292/66.

12. "The Investigation Committee of the Yom Kippur War: The Agranet Report," IDF Archives, 1995, 372.

13. *IDF Strategy*, November 23, 2015.

14. Barbara Opall-Rome, "Israel's 5-Year Plan Bulks Up Combat Capabilities; Cuts Manpower," *Defense News*, January 7, 2016, http://www.defensenews.com/story/defense/policy-budget/policy/2016/01/07/israels-5-year-plan-bulks-up-combat-capabilities-cuts-manpower/78421050/.

15. IDF Archives, file no. 1/174/62; diary of David Ben Gurion, IDF Archives, August 26, 1953.

16. Aram Nerguizian, "The Military Balance in a Shattered Levant," Center for Strategic International Studies (CSIS), June 15, 2015, http://csis.org/files/publication/150615_Nerguizian_Levant_Mil_Bal_Report_w_cover_v2.pdf.

17. Yaakov Lappin, "IDF Place Training for War Back at Top of Priorities," *Jerusalem Post*, March 24, 2015, http://www.jpost.com/Israel-News/IDF-places-training-for-war-back-at-top-of-priorities-394935.

18. Firas Elias, "Iranian Military Doctrine," Washington Institute for Near East Policy, November 15, 2017, http://www.washingtoninstitute.org/fikraforum/view/iranian-military-doctrine.

19. Keefer, *Arab-Israeli Crisis and War 1973*, 691.

20. Alon Paz, "Transforming Israel's Security Establishment," Washington Institute for Near East Policy, October 2015, http://www.washingtoninstitute.org/uploads/Documents/pubs/PF_140_Paz.pdf.

21. Yoav Zeiton, "A Surprise IDF Exercise Against the Gaza Strip," *Ynet*, March 22, 2015, http://www.ynet.co.il/articles/0,7340,L-4639493,00.html.

22. Judah Ari Gross, "One IDF Officer's Quest to Teach His Tanks How to Turn on a

Dime," *Times of Israel*, November 1, 2015, http://www.timesofisrael.com/one-idf-officers
-quest-to-teach-his-tanks-how-to-turn-on-a-dime/.

23. Alon Ben David, "A Confrontation around the Corner," *Marriv*, May 17, 2015,
http://www.maariv.co.il/journalists/journalists/Article-477301.

24. Yoav Zeiton, "The IDF's New Rocket," *Ynet*, May 12, 2015, http://www.ynet.co.il
/articles/0,7340,L-4656223,00.html.

25. TOI Staff, "Rocket Siren Sounds across Country in Ongoing Drill," *Times of Israel*,
June 2, 2015, http://www.timesofisrael.com/rocket-sirens-sound-across-country-in-civil
-defense-drill/.

26. On the IAF, see Israel Defense Forces, July 16, 2015, http://www.idf.il/1133–22293
-he/Dover.aspx.

27. Yoav Zeiton, "Preparing for Attacks from Syria," *Ynet*, August 16, 2015, http://www
.ynet.co.il/articles/0,7340,l-4691341,00.html.

28. IAF, September 10, 2015, http://www.iaf.org.il/4425–45429-he/IAF.aspx.

29. TOI Staff, "IDF Holds Multi-Front War Games on Northern Border," *Times of
Israel*, January 20, 2016, http://www.timesofisrael.com/idf-holds-multi-front-war-games
-on-northern-border/.

30. AP and TOI Staff, "Top IDF General: Israel-Egypt Have Unprecedented Cooperation," *Times of Israel*, April 20, 2016, http://www.timesofisrael.com/top-idf-general
-israel-egypt-have-unprecedented-intel-cooperation/.

31. Lappin, "'Our Intelligence on Hamas Has Improved Significantly."

32. IAF, March 16, 2016, http://www.iaf.org.il/4445–46279-he/IAF.aspx.

33. Yoav Zeiton "Paratroopers in Training," *Ynet*, October 21, 2016, http://www.ynet
.co.il/articles/0,7340,L-4865626,00.html.

34. IAF, November 17, 2016, http://www.iaf.org.il/4453–47969-he/IAF.aspx.

35. McKernan, "Israel Holds Largest Military Drill in 20 Years."

36. Judah Ari Gross, "Simulating War with Hezbollah, IDF Looks to Avoid Past Mistakes," *Times of Israel*, September 12, 2017, https://www.timesofisrael.com/in-mock-war
-with-hezbollah-idf-looks-to-avoid-past-mistakes/.

37. Judah Ari Gross, "IDF Simulates War in Lebanon, amid Tensions with Iran, Hezbollah," *Times of Israel*, February 22, 2018, https://www.timesofisrael.com/idf-simulates
-war-in-lebanon-amid-tensions-with-iran-hezbollah/.

38. Chorev, "Deterrence Campaigns."

39. On the issue of the tunnels during the 2014 war, see Udi Dekel and Shlomo
Brom, "The Second Stage of Operation Protective Edge: A Limited Ground Maneu-
ver," Institute for National Security Studies, July 21, 2014; Yiftah S. Shapir and Gal
Perel, "Subterranean Warfare: A New-Old Challenge," Institute for National Secu-
rity Studies, July 2014; Janine Zacharia, "Tunnel Mapping Could Have Neutralized
Hamas Threat without Fatalities," *Washington Post*, August 11, 2014; "2014 Gaza War
Assessment: The New Face of Conflict," a report by the JINSA-commissioned Gaza
conflict task force, March 2015.

40. Chorev, "Deterrence Campaigns."

41. TOI Staff and Judah Ari Gross, "Israel Said to Have Spent $250M Trying to Thwart

Hamas Tunnels," *Times of Israel*, February 12, 2016, http://www.timesofisrael.com/israel-said-to-have-spent-250m-trying-to-thwart-hamas-tunnels/.

42. Judah Ari Gross, "Blistering Gaza War Report Scorches Netanyahu, Ya'alon, and Gantz over Tunnel Failures," *Times of Israel*, February 28, 2017, http://www.timesofisrael.com/blistering-gaza-war-report-scorches-netanyahu-yaalon-and-gantz-over-tunnel-failures/.

43. Judah Ari Gross, "Need to Fight in a Tunnel or Find Hidden IEDs? Ask Lt. Col. Liron Aroch How," *Times of Israel*, January 30, 2018, https://www.timesofisrael.com/want-to-learn-to-fight-in-a-tunnel-or-find-hidden-ieds-ask-lt-col-liron-aroch/.

44. Gross, "Need to Fight in a Tunnel or Find Hidden IEDs?"

45. Kober, *Practical Soldiers*, 84.

46. *IDF Strategy*, November 23, 2015.

47. Michael Herzog, "New IDF Strategy Goes Public," Washington Institute for Near East Policy, August 28, 2015, http://www.washingtoninstitute.org/policy-analysis/view/new-idf-strategy-goes-public.

48. Yaakov Katz and Amir Bohbot, *The Weapon Wizards* (New York: St. Martin's, 2017).

49. *Washington Post*, May 4, 2015, http://www.washingtonpost.com/world/middle_east/israeli-veterans-say-permissive-rules-of-engagement-fueled-gaza-carnage/2015/05/04/ab698d16-f020–11e4–8050–839e9234b303_story.html.

50. "Key Preliminary Findings of the High Level International Military Group on the Gaza Conflict," UNwatch, June 12, 2015, http://blog.unwatch.org/index.php/2015/06/12/key-findings-of-the-high-level-international-military-group-on-the-gaza-conflict/.

51. Yaakov Lappin, "Security and Defense," *Jerusalem Post*, September 20, 2014, http://www.jpost.com/Israel-News/New-Tech/Security-and-Defense-Israels-first-network-centric-war-375789.

52. On the M-113, see Amir Bouhbut, "Following Criticism, the IDF Will Replace Old Armored Vehicles," *Walla News*, May 19, 2015, http://news.walla.co.il/item/2855741.

53. Yoav Zeiton, "The IDF's New Armored Vehicle," *Ynet*, October 27, 2015, http://www.ynet.co.il/articles/0,7340,L-4662606,00.html.

54. "The End of the Cobra Era," *Israel Defense*, August 29, 2014, http://www.israeldefense.co.il/en/content/end-cobra-era.

55. Anna Ahronheim, "The Changing Face of the Israel Navy," *Jerusalem Post*, August 17, 2017, http://www.jpost.com/jpost2016/SitePage.aspx?articleid=502657&sitepageid=205.

56. Yaakov Lappin, "Israel Navy Preparing for Hamas, Hezbollah Rocket and Missile Threats," *Jerusalem Post*, May 18, 2016, http://www.jpost.com/Israel-News/Israel-Navy-preparing-for-Hamas-Hezbollah-rocket-and-missile-threats-454297.

INDEX

Abdullah, king of Jordan, 44

Abrahms, Max, 89

Adamsky, Dmitry, 39

Agarman, Nadav, 94, 109

Ahmadinejad, Mahmoud, 27

Akerman, Lior, 105

Albright, David: on Iran's nuclear capability, 11

Allahdadi, Ali Mohammad, 68

Almog, Doron, 148

Alterman, Jon, 132

Arab Gulf States: join Israel against Iran, 32–35; relations with the U.S., 14–19

Aronson, Geoffrey, 130

Assad, Bashar Al: role in the Israeli–Iranian conflict, 62; and war in Syria, 52

Assad, Hafez Al, 51

Bab-el-Mandeb Strait, 18

Banna, Hasan al-, 137

Barak, Ehud, 91

Brandenburg, Rachel, 75

Byman, Daniel L., 40, 112–13, 130

Carter, Ashton: considers attack on Iran, 4; in talks with Iran, 1; on the U.S. in Syria, 78

chemical weapons: in Syria, 77

Chorev, Harel, 102

CIA: in Syria, 81

Clapper, James: on Iran as threat to U.S interests, 8

Cohen, Yossi: on Iranian threat to Israel, 8; on Iran's desire for nuclear weapon, 13

Cook, Steven, 81, 140

Cordesman, Anthony, 88; on change in modern warfare, 101

Danin, Robert M., 88

Dore, Gold, 33

Duenwald, Christoph, 104

Dunne, Michele, 133

Egypt: assistance from Israel to, 129–31; economic problems of, 131–33; fighting ISIS, 125–28; relations with the U.S., 133–36

Eiland, Giora, 40

Eisenkot, Gadi, 56, 117

Eisenstadt, Michael, 21

Elgindy, Khaled, 103, 130

Erdogan, Tayyip Recep, 122

Eshel, Amir: sends S–300 to Iran, 4

Etzion, Eran, 74

European Union: relations with PA, 121; relations with Egypt, 136

Fabius, Laurent: on Israel and Palestinians, 88

Freilich, Charles: on Iran's nuclear threat, 2

Gaddafi, Muammar, 77

Gaza Strip: 2014 war in, 98–104; humanitarian crisis in, 104–7

Golan, Yair, 74, 152

Golan Heights: as base against Israel, 64–65; strategic importance of, 53–55

Goldenberg, Ilan, 114

Greenert, Jon, 134

Gulf Arab states, 14–18

Halevi, Herzl, 106

Hamas: during 2014 war, 98–104; approach toward Israel, 95–98; and humanitarian crisis in Gaza Strip, 104–7; preparations for war by, 107–11

Hamdallah, Rami, 117

Hebron, 116

Heinonen, Olli: on Iran's nuclear capability, 11

Herzog, Michael: on Iran's attempts at nuclear weapons, 3

Hezbollah: approach toward U.S., 23–24; conflict with Israel, 35–42; relations with Russia, 82–85; in Syria, 67–68

Hussein, Saddam, 77

"IDF Strategy," 37, 47, 148, 150

Inbar, Efraim, 123

Indyk, Martin, 116

International Atomic Energy Agency (IAEA), 10

Iran: economy of, 12; minorities in, 29–30; and presence in Syria, 60–63; raid on nuclear sites in, 13; regime change in, 27–29; and threat to Israel from Syria, 63–67

Iraq, U.S. presence in, 19–23

Islamic Revolutionary Guard Corps (IRGC), 37; firing on Israel, 59; troops in Syria, 61

Israel: during 2014 war, 98–104; air strikes in Syria by, 55–60; with Arabs against Iran, 32–35; and assistance to Egypt in Sinai, 129–31; policy on Palestinians, 89–93; relations with U.S. vis-à-vis Iran, 4–13; state comptroller in, 14; and U.S.-ISIS conflict, 20–21

JCPOA: deal with Iran in 2015, 1; implications for Israel, 5

Jeffrey, James F., 27

Jordan: stability in, 24–26

Juniper Cobra (U.S.-Israeli exercise), 10

Kamel al-Sayed, Mostafa, 131

Katz, Israel, 56

Khalilzad, Zalmay, 15

Khamenei, Ali: calls for arming Palestinians, 44; ends talks with the U.S., 7; against Israel and the U.S., 3;

Khatami, Mohammad, 27

Kissinger, Henry, 71, 121, 151

Klos-C (ship), 48

Kochavi, Aviv, 152

Kroenig, Matthew: on dismantling Iran's nuclear sites, 9

Kuperwasser, Yossi: on Israeli policy about Iran, 5

Kurds: in Iraq, 22–23; in Iran, 29–30

Lavrov, Sergei: on delivering s–300 to Iran, 4

Lieberman, Avigdor: against Iranian presence in Syria, 61; on policy over Palestinians, 90–91; and U.S.-Saudi arms deal, 17

Lynch, Marc, 27

Maddy-Weitzman, Bruce, 136

Makovsky, David: on the U.S. in the Middle East, 2

Marzouk, Mousa Abu, 95

Mazen, Abu, 94–95, 112–13

McMaster, H. R: and Iran's proxies, 13

Mendes, Uri, 88

Meshaal, Khalid, 96; on firing on military targets, 101

Mofaz, Shaol, 117

Mogherini, Federica, 121

Morsi, Mohamed, 135, 140

Muasher, Marwan, 115

Mubarak, Hosni, 139–40

Multinational Force and Observers (MFO), 136

Nablus, 114

Naeem, Nabil, 127

Nasrallah, Hassan, 40

Nasser, Gamal Abdel, 140

Netanyahu, Benjamin: on attacks in Syria, 54; and dispute with Obama, 4; against Iranian presence in Syria, 61; on Israel's strike capability, 9; policy on the Palestinians, 91

Obama, Barack: against Assad, 78; and policy in Syria, 77; promises military aid to Israel, 7; sets sanctions on Iran, 7–8; in talks with Iran, 1; against war with Iran, 4

Olmert, Joseph, 60

Organization of Islamic Cooperation (OIC), 32

Palestine Liberation Organization (PLO), 87

Palestinian Authority (PA): relations with Israel, 94–8, 111–16; and security cooperation, 116–19

the Pentagon: reveals bunker buster bomb, 3

Peres, Simon, 91

Pollack, Kenneth M., 14

Pompeo, Mike: and speech about Iran, 13

Qawasme, Osama al-, 96

Rabi, Uzi, 102

Rouhani, Hassan: Iran's economy, 12; on Israel's illegitimacy as a state, 8

Russia: intervention in Syria by, 69–70; and relations with Hezbollah, 82–85; and relations with Israel, 70–76, 80; and relations with the U.S., 77–82

Sadat, Anwar, 139–40

Sadjadpour, Karim, 12

Salehi, Ataollah: on Iran's desire to destroy Israel, 8

Salem, Paul, 138

Salman, Bin Mohammed, 15

Saudi Arabia: arms deal with the U.S., 16–19

Shein, Alexander, 83

Shoqiran, Fahad, 96

Shoukry, Sameh, 88, 135

Sisi, Abdel Fattah el-, 46, 88, 122, 140

Sistani, Ali al-, 22

Syria: civil war, 51–52

Takeyh, Ray: on Iran's policy, 7

Timothy, Ray, 10

Trump, Donald: about the PA, 120; policy on Iran of, 11–13; on Syria, 81

Turgeman, Sami, 106

Turkey: shoots down Russian plane, 79

UNIFIL, 23–24

United Nations Conference on Trade and Development (UNCTAD), 104, 115

United States: in Iraq, 19–23; relations with Israel in regard to Iran, 4–13; relations with the PA, 119–21

Wittes Cofman, Tamara, 38, 88, 134

Ya'alon, Moshe: about Iran, 20; on Israel's relations with the U.S., 1; on the PA, 90, 103; on terror activity in the West Bank, 122

Yadlin, Amos: on dispute between Israel and the U.S. over Iran, 4–5

Yemen, war in, 26–27

Zarif Javad, Mohammad: on Iran's goals, 10; in talks with Iran on nuclear weapon, 3